EU-Turkey relations have a long historic trajectory. Turkey is in future likely to remain, despite political tensions, an important country for the EU in economic, political and geostrategic terms. On the one hand, recent developments affecting the EU have motivated the Heads of State or Government to rediscover Turkey's relevance as ‚key strategic partner'. On the other hand, prospects of Turkey's accession to the EU have reached an all-time low in the light of Turkey distancing itself from the political accession criterion as well as the multiple internal crises the EU has been confronted with. This renders EU-Turkey relations a highly topical issue for academic research.

The Centre for Turkey and European Union Studies (CETEUS) aims at providing a framework for publications dealing with Turkey, the European Union as well as EU/German-Turkish relations regarding multiple thematic dimensions as well as geographic contexts including the neighbourhood and the global scene.

Turkey and European Union Studies

edited by

Funda Tekin
Ebru Turhan
Wolfgang Wessels

Volume 3

Beken Saatçioğlu | Funda Tekin [eds.]

Turkey and the European Union

Key Dynamics and Future Scenarios

Nomos

This edited volume is one of the final outputs of the Research and Innovation Action "The Future of EU-Turkey Relations: Mapping Dynamics and Testing Scenarios" (FEUTURE) summarizing its key research findings. This project has received funding from the *European Union's Horizon 2020 research and innovation programme* under grant agreement No 692976.

The finalisation of the present edited volume beyond the project's lifetime was supported by Institut für Europäische Politik, Berlin.

This publication reflects the views only of the authors, and the Commission cannot be held responsible for any use which may be made of the information contained therein.

The Deutsche Nationalbibliothek lists this publication in the Deutsche Nationalbibliografie; detailed bibliographic data are available on the Internet at http://dnb.d-nb.de

ISBN   978-3-8487-5939-2 (Print)
         978-3-7489-0069-6 (ePDF)

British Library Cataloguing-in-Publication Data
A catalogue record for this book is available from the British Library.

ISBN   978-3-8487-5939-2 (Print)
         978-3-7489-0069-6 (ePDF)

Library of Congress Cataloging-in-Publication Data
Saatçioğlu, Beken / Tekin, Funda
Turkey and the European Union
Key Dynamics and Future Scenarios
Beken Saatçioğlu / Funda Tekin (eds.)
218 pp.
Includes bibliographic references and index.

ISBN   978-3-8487-5939-2 (Print)
         978-3-7489-0069-6 (ePDF)

Onlineversion
Nomos eLibrary

1st Edition 2021
© Nomos Verlagsgesellschaft, Baden-Baden, Germany 2021. Overall responsibility for manufacturing (printing and production) lies with Nomos Verlagsgesellschaft mbH & Co. KG.

Table of Contents

Table of Contents

List of Abbreviations

AKP	Justice and Development Party
BPTF	Bilateral Preferential Trade Frame
BREXIT	Withdrawal of the United Kingdom from the European Union
CAATSA	Countering America's Adversaries Through Sanctions Act
CAQDAS	Computer-Assisted Qualitative Data Analysis Software
CBRN	Chemical, biological, radiological and nuclear
CBRT BOP Statistics	Balance of payments statistics of the Central Bank of the Republic of Turkey
COP21	United Nations Climate Change Conference
COVID-19	Coronavirus SARS-CoV-2
CSDP	Common Security and Defence Policy
CU	Customs Union
DCFTA	Deep and Comprehensive Free Trade Agreement
DGMM	Directorate General of Migration Management
ECHR	European Convention on Human Rights
ECtHR	European Court of Human Rights
EEA	European Economic Area
EFTA	European Free Trade Association
EIB	European Investment Bank
ENTSO-E	European Network of Transmission System Operator for Electricity
ENTSO- G	European Network of Transmission System Operator for Gas
EP	European Parliament
EPP	European People's Party
ERA	European Research Area
EU	European Union
EUCS	European Union Communication Strategy
EUGS	European Union Global Strategy
EURA	EU-Turkey Readmission Agreement
EUROPOL	European Police Agency
EUROSAM	European manufacturer of air defence systems
FAC	EU Foreign Affairs Council
FDI	Foreign Direct Investments
FETO	Fethullahist Terrorist Organisation
FEUTURE	Horizon 2020 research project: "The Future of EU-Turkey Relations: Mapping Dynamics and Testing Scenarios"
FP	Framework Programme
FRONTEX	European Border and Coast Guard Agency

FTA	Free Trade Agreement
GDP	Gross Domestic product
GNA	Government of National Accord
G20	Group of Twenty
HR/VP	High Representative of the Union for Foreign Affairs and Security Policy/ Vice president of the European Commission
H2020	Horizon 2020
IKV	Economic Development Foundation
IS	International Society
ISIL	Islamic State of Iraq and the Levant
ISIS	Islamic State in Iraq and Syria
JCPOA	Joint Comprehensive Plan of Action
KRG	Kurdistan Regional Government
LEA	Greek Law Enforcement Agency
LFIP	Law on Foreigners and International Protection
LNG	Liquefied natural gas
LT	long-term
MENA	Middle East and North Africa
NATO	North Atlantic Treaty Organization
NUTS	Nomenclature of Territorial Units for Statistics
PESCO	Permanent Structured Cooperation
PKK	Kurdistan Workers' Party
PYD	Democratic Union Party
RES	Renewable Energy Services
SAIPEM	Società Anonima Italiana Perforazioni E Montaggi
SCO	Shanghai Cooperation Organization
SMEs	Small and Medium sized Enterprises
ST	short-term
S&D	Group of the Progressive Alliance of Socialists and Democrats in the European Parliament
TEKPOL	Science and Technology Policy Research Centre
TEU	Treaty on European Union
TR	Turkey
TTIP	Transatlantic Trade and Investment Partnership
UK	United Kingdom
UN	United Nations
UNIFIL	United Nations Interim Force in Lebanon
US/USA	United States/ United States of America
WMD	Weapons of mass destruction
WWII	World War II
YPG	People's Protection Units
9/11	11 September 2001 attacks on the United States

Introduction

The Future of EU-Turkey Relations: Exploring the Dynamics and Relevant Scenarios

Funda Tekin

1. A Glimpse into the Future of EU-Turkey Relations

Relations between the European Union (EU) and Turkey have seen better days than they did during the second decade of the 21st century. As of 2020, the relationship is at an all-time low for various reasons[1] ranging from the process of de-democratisation in Turkey, and rising nationalism and populism on both sides to bilateral conflicts between Turkey and individual EU member states such as Germany and the Netherlands in 2017 and recently Greece, Cyprus and France in the Eastern Mediterranean region.[2] Nevertheless, EU-Turkey relations have historically proven resilient in the face of conflict and tensions. They have persisted following critical episodes of ups and downs representing anything but a linear trend, which was rather reminiscent of a rollercoaster ride.[3] Additionally, they exhibit a multifaceted character which consists of various dimensions and mutual interdependencies. This means that conflictual dynamics in certain dimensions such as politics and security go hand in hand with demands and interests for cooperation in others such as the economy, trade, migration and energy. This contrasting and simultaneous mix of conflict and cooperation

---

1 For a detailed account of the state of relations see European Commission. Turkey 2020 Report. Commission Staff Working Document, SWD(2020) 355 final. Brussels, 6.10.2020.

2 See Marcou, Jean. The conundrum of the great gas game and the ensuing strategic realignment in the eastern Mediterranean. European issues, Foundation Robert Schuman. No. 571, 22.09.2020.

3 Tekin, Funda/ Wessels, Wolfgang. German-Turkish Relations: Think Ahead. In: Turhan, Ebru (ed). German-Turkish Relations Revisited. The European Dimension, Domestic and Foreign Politics and Transnational Dynamics. Baden-Baden, 2019, pp. 269-279.

which could also be viewed as a "mutual love-hate relationship"[4], has always characterised EU-Turkey relations.[5]

Thus, despite Turkey's current move "further away from the EU"[6] and the high tensions in the relationship that have culminated in the EU's considerations on targeted measures including sanctions against Turkey in October 2019,[7] an absolute rupture of the relationship seems unlikely. In fact, this has also been confirmed by the European Council that "agreed to launch a positive political agenda for EU-Turkey relations [...] provided constructive efforts to stop illegal activities vis-à-vis Greece and Cyprus are sustained" by Turkey.[8]

Yet, the EU-Turkey relationship will continue to face challenges and obstacles originating from the EU and Turkey as well as the troubled neighbourhood and the global order that is witnessing a "major power diffusion away from the West, with the rise of new actors leading to the formation of a multipolar system".[9] The open question of what form the relations will evolve into in the future is complicating the relations further as both existing and potential institutional frameworks get diluted or even blocked.[10] EU-Turkey membership negotiations stagnated soon after their

---

4   Yabancı, Bilge. The future of EU-Turkey relations: between mutual distrust and interdependency. FEUTURE Online Paper No. 1, November 2016, p. 5.
5   See also Tocci, Nathalie/ Aydın-Düzgit, Senem. Turkey and the European Union. London, New York, 2015.
6   See European Commission. Turkey 2020 Report, p. 115; European Commission. Turkey 2019 Report. Commission Staff Working Document, SWD(2019) 220 final. Brussels, 29.5.2019, p. 105; European Commission. Turkey 2018 Report. Commission Staff Working Document, SWD(2018) 153 final. Strasbourg, 17.4.2018, p. 3.
7   Council of the European Union. Outcome of the Council Meeting. Foreign Affairs. 3720th Council meeting, 13066/19. Luxembourg 14.10.2019; European Council. European Council conclusions on external relations. 01 October 2020. Press release, https://www.consilium.europa.eu/en/press/press-releases/2020/10/01/european-council-conclusions-on-external-relations-1-october-2020/ [03.10.20].
8   Euorpean Council. Conclusions. Special meeting of the European Council, 1 and 2 October 2020, EUCO 13/20. Brussels, 2.10.2020, p. 8.
9   Eralp, Atila. Multilateralism matters: Towards a rules-based Turkey-EU relationship. IPC-Mercator Policy Brief, Istanbul, May 2019.
10 For a detailed overview on the different paths of EU-Turkey relations see also Schröder, Mirja/ Tekin, Funda. Institutional Triangle EU-Turkey-Germany: Change and Continuity. In: Turhan, Ebru (ed.): German-Turkish Relations Revisited. The European Dimension, Domestic and Foreign Politics and Transnational Dynamics. Baden-Baden, 2019, pp. 31-58; Müftüler-Baç, Meltem. Divergent Pathways: Turkey and the European Union. Re-Thinking the Dynamics of Turkish-European Union Relations. Opladen, 2016.

launch in 2005 and have effectively come to a standstill, with only one chapter ("Science and Research") having been provisionally closed among the 16 that have been opened (out of a total of 35 chapters) and no further chapters being considered for opening or closing for the time being.[11] Institutional engagement on the basis of the 1963 Association Agreement is also in suspense since the July 2019 European Council decision to abstain from convening the EU-Turkey Association Council. Additionally, the modernisation of the EU-Turkey Customs Union that the European Commission proposed in December 2016 has been blocked for political reasons since June 2018 and considerations have only been taken up by the positive political agenda outlined by the European Council in October 2020.

Amidst these uncertainties, migration has emerged as the only dimension that initially promised some momentum to the relations. The EU-Turkey Statements on migration of 29 November 2015 and 18 March 2016 promised a full package for revitalising EU-Turkey relations including, among other things, facilitation of visa liberalisation for Turkish citizens traveling to Europe, frequent EU-Turkey high-level dialogues exploring the relations' vast potential in the areas of energy, the economy, foreign and security policy (i.e., counterterrorism) as well as regular EU-Turkey Summits to be held twice a year.[12] Yet, after Turkey's July 2016 failed coup attempt and the subsequent period of state of emergency (2016-2018) in Turkey, almost all the paths of the relationship slowed down or were cancelled altogether.[13] EU-Turkey cooperation over migration management has also been far from smooth. In particular, the full implementation of the Facility for Refugees equipped with 6 billion euros to help Turkey host the refugees has been a major point of contention between the two sides. Turkey is hosting the largest refugee community in the world – almost 4 million refugees of which 3.6 million are Syrian – and has pressured the EU to provide sufficient and promised financial support in order to continue to assume its refugee burden. Additionally, this transactional approach of paying Turkey for holding the refugees for Europe has been widely criticised for turning the EU-Turkey relationship into a zero-sum

---

11 Council of the European Union. Council conclusions on enlargement and stabilisation and association process. Press release, 18.06.2019, https://www.consilium.europa.eu/en/press/press-releases/2019/06/18/council-conclusions-on-enlargement-and-stabilisation-and-association-process/ [07.10.20].

12 European Council. Meeting of heads of state or government with Turkey. EU-Turkey statement, 29.11.2015, https://www.consilium.europa.eu/en/press/press-releases/2015/11/29/eu-turkey-meeting-statement/ [08.10.20].

13 See Schröder/ Tekin, Institutional Triangle EU-Turkey-Germany.

game.[14] The negative implications of this transactionalism materialised particularly in February 2020 when the Turkish President Recep Tayyip Erdoğan authorised the opening of the Turkish-Greek land border in order to maximise political pressure on the EU and boost his governing Justice and Development Party (AKP)'s domestic popularity within its nationalist vote base. In any event, the developments of February 2020 demonstrated that the March 2016 EU-Turkey Statement on migration is in need of a make-over. This pending challenge is further complemented by the other "landmines" of EU-Turkey relations that include, inter alia, territorial disputes and problematic relations in the EU's neighbourhood, Turkey's Kurdish issue, the war in Syria and problems arising from the damaged Western alliance and irritations between NATO and Turkey.[15]

Against this background, the key question motivating this volume is what the future holds for EU-Turkey relations. Given the existing multiple challenges and the fact that the various frameworks of the relationship are in disarray, the answer is crucial but neither simple nor straightforward. Above all, it necessitates a comprehensive analysis of what binds the EU and Turkey together and what drives them apart in the relevant thematic dimensions of the relationship. This volume seeks to achieve this critical analytical task by building and expanding upon the findings of the Horizon 2020 research project FEUTURE ("The Future of EU-Turkey Relations: Mapping Dynamics and Testing Scenarios").[16] Between 2016 and

---

14 See among others Tocci, Nathalie. Beyond blackmail at the Turkish-Greek border. The EU needs to work with Ankara to rebuild a mutually beneficial relationship. Politico, 03.10.2020, https://www.politico.eu/article/beyond-blackmail-at-the-greek-turkish-border-european-commission-josep-borrell-asylum-seekers-recep-tayyip-erdogan/ [08.10.20]; Şenyuva, Özgehan/ Üstün, Çiğdem. A Deal to End "the" Deal: Why the Refugee Agreement is a Threat to Turkey-EU Relations. The German Marshall Fund of Foreign Relations, July 2016; Saatçioğlu, Beken. Turkey and the EU: Strategic Rapprochement in the Shadow of the Refugee Crisis. E-International Relations. 21.01.2016.

15 Soler i Lecha, Eduard. EU-Turkey Relations. Mapping landmines and exploring alternative pathways. FEPS Policy Paper, September 2019; Ergun, Doruk/ Ülgen, Sinan. EU-Turkey security relations: Key drivers and future scenarios. In this volume, pp. 103-120.

16 Between April 2016 and March 2019 this project was coordinated by Wolfgang Wessels and Funda Tekin at Centre for European Union and Turkey Studies at the University of Cologne and Nathalie Tocci at Istituto Affari Internazionali in Rome. It gathered a consortium of 15 research institutes from the EU, Turkey and the neighbourhood and received funding from the European Union's Horizon 2020 research and innovation programme under the grant agreement No 692976. More information can be found here: www.feuture.eu.

2019, FEUTURE explored the possible future scenarios for EU-Turkey relations in a mid-term perspective in addition to discussing the challenges and opportunities associated with Turkey's further integration into the EU.

Two main assumptions guide the analysis of the volume. First, Turkey has always been an integral part of Europe's history. As argued by FEUTURE scientific coordinator Nathalie Tocci in the FEUTURE background paper: "Turkey is and will remain one of the most significant countries for the EU, standing almost on a par with Russia in the neighbourhood, and just one step down from the United States of America (USA) and China on the global scene".[17] Second, the density of the EU-Turkey relationship is considered as an asset underpinning its multifaceted nature rather than an impediment for future progress.

2. Seeking the State of the Art in Research on EU-Turkey Relations: Contributions to the Literature

EU-Turkey relations are a key subject of both academically-oriented and policy-relevant research. Indeed, this growing body of literature is just as multifaceted as the EU-Turkey relationship itself. For analytical purposes, it is possible to discuss and differentiate these works by using three different perspectives via which the relations can be assessed: (1) Turkey as an enlargement country, (2) Turkey as an EU neighbour and/or a strategic EU partner, (3) Turkey as a global partner.[18]

Analyses dealing with Turkey's EU accession process (i.e., Turkey as an enlargement country) focus on trends of Europeanisation[19] and de-Europeanisation[20] in Turkey, member state preferences including public opinion and the so-called *enlargement fatigue* in the EU[21] as well as the EU's in-

---

17 Tocci, Nathalie. Turkey and the European Union: Scenarios for 2023. FEUTURE Background Paper. September 2016.

18 See Tocci/ Aydın-Düzgit. Turkey and the European Union.

19 See Nas, Çiğdem/ Özer, Yonca. Turkey and the European Union. Processes of Europeanisation. Routledge, 2012.

20 See Adyın-Düzgit, Senem/ Kaliber, Alper. Encounters with Europe in an Era of Domestic and International Turmoil: Is Turkey a De-Europeanising Candidate Country?. In: South European Society and Politics. 2016, Vol. 21(1), pp. 1-14.

21 E.g. Icoz, Gulay/ Martin, Natalie. Opportunities missed: Turkey-EU accession since 2005. In: Journal of Contemporary European Studies. 2016, Vol. 24(4), pp. 442-445; Turhan, Ebru. Turkey's EU accession process: Do member states matter?. In: Journal of Contemporary European Studies. 2016 Vol. 24(4), pp. 463-477.

tegration capacity.[22] Only recently studies have sought to "think out of the accession box"[23] in order to assess, inter alia, "rising functionalism in EU-Turkey relations"[24] and the explanatory value of external differentiated integration in the EU.[25] The United Kingdom (UK)'s decision to exit the EU has drawn further attention to this question, guided by the assumption that the future UK-EU relations could represent some sort of blueprint for the relationship between the EU and Turkey.[26]

Identity-oriented research debates the question of whether Turkey is genuinely perceived as an EU candidate country in the enlargement process or rather, as an outsider or a neighbour. A related issue that is discussed is whether Turkey's accession process has transformed European identity.[27] More generally, this strand of research traces the reconstruction and negotiation processes of European and Turkish identities from a his-

---

22 See Schimmelfennig, Frank et.al. Enlargement and the inegration capacity of the EU. Interim Scientific Results. Maximizing the Integration Capacity of the European Union, No. 1, May 2015.

23 Turhan, Ebru. Thinking Out of the Accession Box: The Potential and Limitations of Internal and External Differentiated Integration Between Turkey and the EU. CIFE Policy Paper No. 58. 2017, Nice, https://www.cife.eu/Ressources/FCK/files/publications/policy%20paper/CIFE_Policy_Paper_58_Thinking_out_of_The_Accession_Box_EU_Turkey_Ebru_Turhan_2017_1.pdf [08.10.20].

24 See Saatçioğlu, Beken. The European Union's refugee crisis and rising functionalism in EU-Turkey relations. In: Turkish Studies, 2020 Vol. 21(2), pp. 169-187.

25 See among others Karakaş, Cemal. EU-Turkey: Integration without Full Membership or Membership without Full Integration? A Conceptual Framework for Accession Alternatives. In: Journal of Common Market Studies. 2013, Vol. 51(6), pp. 1057-1073; Müftüler-Baç, Meltem. Turkey's future with the European Union: an alternative model of differentiated integration. In: Turkish Studies. 2017, Vol. 18(3), pp. 416-438; Tekin, Funda. Differentiated Integration: An Alternative Conceptualization of EU-Turkey Relations. In: Reiners, Wulf/ Turhan, Ebru (eds): EU-Turkey Relations – Theories, Institutions and Policies. Palgrave Macmillan, 2021, forthcoming.

26 E.g. Esen, Erol/ Şekeroğlu, Duygu (eds). Opportunities and Threats in EU Integration and EU-Turkey Relations after Brexit. Peter Lang, 2016; Ülgen, Sinan. Negotiating Brexit. The Prospect of a UK-Turkey Partnership. Turkey Project Policy Paper. No. 11. Center on the United States and Europe in Brookings. March 2017.

27 Kylstad, Ingrid. Turkey and the EU: A 'new' European identity in the making?. LSE 'Europe in Question' Discussion Paper Series. LEQS Paper No. 27/2010; Selçen, Öner. Turkey and the European Union. The question of European identity. Lanham, 2011.

torical perspective.[28] Parallel literature studying the geostrategic aspects of EU-Turkey ties investigates the question of Turkey's EU accession [29] while bringing to the fore its complementary role as an EU neighbour and global partner. Policy issues like trade, migration, security and energy often guide this research based on the understanding that the EU and Turkey are mutually indispensable geopolitical actors.[30]

This volume contributes to the relevant literature by offering a comprehensive and future-oriented assessment of EU-Turkey relations unfolding at multiple levels. This means that developments in the EU and Turkey are as relevant as developments in the neighbourhood and at the global scene. Hence, the present analysis is conducted at three levels for the purpose of adopting a holistic approach. The first is the national/domestic level where relevant policy developments, institutions and processes are discussed both in Turkey and the EU. Regarding Turkey, the emphasis is on reflecting on the implications of rising deterioration in the political/democratic and economic domains, following the "golden years of Europeanisation" of the early 2000s.[31] As far as the EU is concerned, recent crises of European integration are particularly considered as relevant since they represent instances of public disenchantment with the EU and evidence of Euroscepticism across Europe, both of which closely impact the relations with Turkey. This is coupled with a focus on the growing rule of law crises in individual member states such as Poland and Hungary. Last but not least, the economic problems and the Eurozone crisis following the 2008 global financial crisis, the 2015 Syrian refugee crisis, Brexit and more recently, the COVID-19 pandemic are taken into account as factors that have aggravated

---

28 See Aydın-Düzgit, Senem. Constructions of European Identity. Debates and Discourses on Turkey and the EU. Palgrave Macmillan UK, 2012; Rumelili, Bahar. Negotiating Europe: EU-Turkey Relations from an Identity Perspective. In: Insight Turkey. 2008, Vol. 10(1), pp. 97-11.

29 E.g. Kardaş, Şaban. Geo-strategic position as leverage in EU accession: the case of Turkish–EU negotiations on the Nabucco pipeline. In: Southeast European and Black Sea Studies. 2011, Vol. 11(1), pp. 35-52; Martin, Natalie. Security and the Turkey-EU accession process. Norms, Reforms and the Cyprus Issue. Palgrave Macmillan UK, 2015.

30 Martin, Security and the Turkey-EU accession process; Aydın-Düzgit, Senem et.al. (eds): Global Turkey in Europe. Political, Economic, and Foreign Policy Dimensions of Turkey's Evolving Relationship with the EU. IAI Research Papers. Rome, 2013.

31 Deniz, Yesil/ Tekin, Funda: Tracing Ebbs and Flows in Political and Legislative Reforms in Turkey in View of EU-Turkey Relations. FEUTURE Online Paper No. 30, March 2019; Soler i Lecha, EU-Turkey Relations.

the EU's problems and shaken the European project at its core. These challenges have accentuated the push for (both internal and external) differentiation in the EU as a structural feature of European integration. In turn, this trend towards further differentiation is relevant for the future of EU-Turkey relations since it may inspire and/or necessitate the creation of new frameworks for institutionalising the EU-Turkey relationship.[32]

The second level of analysis is the neighbourhood. The EU-Turkey relationship has undoubtedly unfolded within an unravelling neighbourhood affected by critical developments such as the conflict over the Ukraine, conflicts in the Middle East (e.g., Syria, Libya) and tensions in the Eastern Mediterranean.

Finally, the global level is incorporated into the analysis as an angle that is often overlooked and yet, that significantly weighs on EU-Turkey relations. The international system has been undergoing a profound power shift towards emerging countries in the non-West along with a power diffusion away from the nation-state. Additionally, the traditional transatlantic alliance is deeply shaken under the presidency of Donald Trump in the USA. In this changing global context, how the transatlantic triangle (Turkey, the EU, the US) chooses to engage the issues between the EU and Turkey is particularly relevant for the future of EU-Turkey relations.

In terms of realising its future-oriented analysis, the present volume is unique in simultaneously tackling three specific challenges weighing on EU-Turkey relations. The first is the problem of the fast pace of time and/or volatility for rightly capturing the evolution of the relationship. Specifically, EU-Turkey relations represent a moving target that is far from immune from fast and unexpected developments as well as changes. A striking example is the fact that only twelve months lie between the November 2015 EU-Turkey Statement's promise to revitalise the accession negotiations[33] and the European Parliament's November 2016 demand to freeze them as long as the emergency rule imposed by the Turkish government following the July 2016 failed coup attempt was in place.[34] This

---

32 See Soler i Lecha, Eduard et.al. Politics are taking EU-Turkey Relations Hostage. In this volume, pp. 77-102.

33 European Council. Meeting of heads of state or government with Turkey - EU-Turkey statement. Press release. 29.11.2015, https://www.consilium.europa.eu/en/press/press-releases/2015/11/29/eu-turkey-meeting-statement/ [12.10.20].

34 European Parliament. Freeze EU accession talks with Turkey until it halts repression, urge MEPs. Press release. 24.11.2016, https://www.europarl.europa.eu/news/en/press-room/20161117IPR51549/freeze-eu-accession-talks-with-turkey-until-it-halts-repression-urge-meps [12.10.20].

volatility makes it extra difficult to investigate EU-Turkey relations with a view towards outlining the future of the relationship. Hence, an intertemporal approach linking the past and present developments with the foreseeable future was adopted by the volume's contributors. The second challenge arises from the multi-dimensional and complex character of the EU-Turkey relationship. This was addressed by studying the key dynamics within the principal thematic areas (namely, identity, politics, security, the economy, energy and migration) along with their cross-cutting effects on the overall EU-Turkey relationship. Last but not least was the need to rightly capture the narratives on EU-Turkey relations (arising from both Europe and Turkey) for a precise understanding of the strategies and plots employed by both sides throughout their mutual engagement over time.[35]

3. Assessing the Future of EU-Turkey Relations

The main aim of this volume is to evaluate the future of EU-Turkey relations with as much precision as possible while remaining cognisant of the limitations of an exact prediction. For this purpose, it first identifies and unpacks the main narratives and the so-called *drivers* underpinning the EU-Turkey relationship. In turn, this facilitates the formulation of expectations about the future, which is structured by the three ideal-type scenarios of conflict, cooperation and convergence.

The volume begins with an analysis of the narratives where post-World War II EU-Turkey relations are discussed with a view towards identifying the most salient narratives shaping the EU, Turkey and the EU-Turkey relationship. This historical analysis underpins and informs the forward-looking scenario assessment along with the discussion of the challenges and opportunities – associated with each scenario – that arise for Turkey, the EU the neighbourhood and the global scene. It does so by examining how the narratives have changed over time and in response to shifts at the regional and global level, such as the end of the Cold War and the bipolarity of the international system. It also seeks to capture any mismatch between 'what actors say' and 'what actors do', thereby checking whether discourse and reality match. Additionally, the narrative analysis traces the varying scenarios and dynamics across the relevant thematic dimensions of EU-Turkey relations. For example, elements of conflict dominated the identity dimen-

---

35 See Wessels, Wolfgang. Narratives matter: in search for a partnership strategy. IPC-Mercator Policy Brief. Istanbul, April 2020.

sion in recent decades whereas security considerations were prominent during the Cold War period and recently in relation to the rising conflicts in the EU's neighbourhood. Finally, the arguments incorporated within the narrative analysis highlight different desired and/or projected futures for the relationship conceptualised as conflict, cooperation or convergence. More concretely, these narratives may reflect arguments for or against Turkey's EU membership while emphasising alternative forms of collaboration between the EU and Turkey.

The chapter on narratives as well as the one on identity extend their analysis to the late Ottoman Empire (identity) and the 1950s (narratives) in order to substantiate their future-oriented assessment with a historical account of the relevant driving forces. The subsequent analysis of the present developments identifies drivers that have shaped the EU-Turkey relationship since December 1999 when Turkey was granted official EU candidate status at the EU's Helsinki Summit.

Drivers are defined as the ideational, material, structural and agency-related factors that determine a story's outcome. Specifically, they can accelerate or decelerate the process of Turkey's integration into the EU, break up traditional pathways and/or lead to alternative options for the relationship.[36] In concrete terms, drivers can represent conditions, logics, (structural) trends, movements, events, interests, economic flows of capital, labour and knowledge, threat or identity perceptions, actors or certain policies. The aim is not to compare the drivers across all the relevant thematic dimensions but rather, offer a collective evaluation and assess their future relevance. This mapping of the drivers helps formulate the most likely future scenario of EU-Turkey relations.

In terms of evaluating the possible future pathways of EU-Turkey relations, the volume builds on Peter Schwartz's concept of scenario-building[37] for "imagining, delineating and systematising three reference scenarios in order to construct different pathways that might exist in the future, suggesting and informing appropriate scholarly analysis or policy decisions that may be taken along those possible paths".[38] Scenarios predict hypothetical worlds from different angles. They sketch how the drivers are likely to behave based on how they have performed in the past. The same set of drivers may unfold in different ways, following different possible plots.

---

36 See Tocci, Turkey and the European Union: Scenarios for 2023, p. 4.
37 Schwartz, Peter. The Art of the Long View: Paths to Strategic Insight for Yourself and Your Company. Currency Doubleday, 1996.
38 See Tocci, Turkey and the European Union: Scenarios for 2023, p. 4.

Hence, the scenario exercise builds upon a wealth of information about the past and the present before identifying the future patterns. Therefore, different interpretations of the same event can create different expectations for the future. The volume applies a medium-term approach to scenario-building, which means that the projections apply to EU-Turkey relations in the foreseeable future. Beyond that, it becomes difficult to make a reliable assessment based on the current drivers shaping the relations.

Three ideal-type scenarios provide points of reference for structuring the future-oriented analysis. Relatedly, it is possible to categorise likely futures based on whether the relations deteriorate, remain the same while circumstances improve, or fundamentally change for the better.[39] Consequently, the ideal-type scenarios respectively represent growing estrangement between the EU and Turkey, interest-based complementarities that are mutually exploited or maximum possible EU-Turkey rapprochement.[40]

The deterioration of EU-Turkey relations implies the *conflict scenario* which is primarily characterised by growing estrangement between the EU and Turkey that eventually results in the two sides taking competitive and conflictual positions and actions against one another. Such a scenario results from an enduring internal crisis within the EU marked by dissolving member state solidarity, persistent problems regarding the EU's migration and asylum policies as well as the rise of populism and Euroscepticism challenging the EU at its very core. In turn, these developments would cement the anti-Turkey constituency across the Union. On the Turkish side, the country would feature growing centralisation and become increasingly embroiled in problems both at home – for instance, regarding the Kurdish question – and abroad – notably, concerning the Syrian conflict. Long-standing conflicts such as Cyprus would not be resolved and Turkey would not return to its path towards European values. Together, these factors would result in the abandonment of Turkey's EU membership prospects along with persistent clash and competition between the two sides. At the same time, the EU's neighbourhood would continue to be characterised by long-term and multifaceted crises which would involve both the EU and Turkey, albeit in different and at times, contrasting directions. At the global level, the temporary vacuum caused by the structural power shift, coupled with demographic trends and natural resource scarcity, would add to the uncertainty and harbour the potential for further EU-Turkey conflict.

---

39 Schwartz, The Art of the Long View, p. 30.
40 For a detailed description of the three ideal-type scenarios see also Tocci, Turkey and the European Union: Scenarios for 2023.

At the other end of the spectrum, the *convergence scenario* represents the relations' fundamental change for the better. It is predicated on the assumption that Turkey's EU accession process will eventually be completed following the country's full compliance with the Copenhagen criteria and the completion of the membership negotiations. Additionally, the Cyprus question would be resolved and doubts in the EU member states regarding Turkey's EU membership would gradually disappear. Furthermore, if the EU were to become more internally differentiated in the process, Turkey's membership of the EU – but not of its innermost core – would help assuage the 'Turkey scepticism' across several 'core' member states.

The middle ground is occupied by the *cooperation scenario*. Accordingly, the EU and Turkey would aim at exploiting existing complementarities through cooperation rather than Turkey's EU accession track. In a regional and a global scene characterised by profound turmoil, the two sides would seek avenues and instances for functional cooperation as mutual indispensable strategic partner. This might revitalise formerly rejected or unsuccessful concepts such as "privileged partnership",[41] the EU-Turkey positive agenda (2012) and/or associate membership.[42] However, the EU would lose its gravitational pull on Turkey and Turkey's reform path would proceed unanchored to the EU. At the same time, as a key NATO ally, Turkey would not detach itself altogether from the "West" and would even embrace integration with the EU in select policy spheres.

As stated above, the scenario-building exercise builds upon the analysis of the drivers in six thematic dimensions of EU-Turkey relations: identity, politics, security, the economy, energy, and migration. The identity dimension considers EU-Turkey relations' historical legacies as well as future projection in cultural and identity terms.[43] The study of politics[44] and the

---

41 zu Guttenberg, Karl Theodor. Preserving Europe: Offer Turkey a 'privileged partnership' instead. In: The New York Times, 15.12.2004. http://www.nytimes.com/2004/12/15/opinion/preserving-europe-offer-turkey-a-privileged-partnership-instead.html [04.04.20].

42 E.g. Duff, Andrew. The Case for an Associate Membership of the European Union, 2013. http://wp.me/p2MmSR-3dQ [04.04.20].

43 See Aydın-Düzgit, Senem. Constructions of European Identity: Debates and Discourses on Turkey and the EU. London, 2012; Rumelili, Bahar. Identity and desecuritisation: the pitfalls of conflating ontological and physical security. In: Journal of International Relations and Development, 2013, Vol. 18(1), pp. 52-74.

44 See Soler i Lecha, Eduard. The EU, Turkey and the Arab Spring: From Parallel Approaches to a Joint Strate-gy?. In: Tocci, Nathalie et al.: Turkey and the Arab Spring: Implications for Turkish Foreign Policy from a Transatlantic Perspective.

economy[45] addresses, inter alia, issues associated with the Copenhagen criteria, thereby mapping the principal determinants of convergence and divergence between Turkey and the EU. The security dimension discusses Turkey as a foreign policy partner of the EU and a NATO ally while reflecting on the effects of security crises in the neighbourhood.[46] The area of energy, which straddles the economy and security dimensions is gaining increasing salience in light of developments in Turkey and the neighbourhood as well as the rising relevance of EU energy supply security.[47] Finally, Migration touches upon political, economic and ideational dimensions, and enjoys increasing prominence and complexity in the overall EU-Turkey relationship.[48]

Each chapter of the volume studies a different thematic dimension in order to map the key drivers substantiating the most likely scenario in the respective dimension. Hence, the overall task guiding the chapters is the identification of the conditions and logics that would drive the thematic EU-Turkey relations towards conflict, cooperation or convergence. This is done at the three levels of analysis described above, which enables the investigation of factors/drivers originating from both Turkey and the EU as

---

Mediterranean Paper Series, October 2011, Washington; Huber, Daniela. Democracy Promotion and Foreign Policy - Identity and Interests in US, EU and Non-Western Democracies. Basingstoke, 2015.

45 See Erdil, Erkan. ERA-WATCH country reports – Turkey. Brussels: European Commission, 2013.

46 see Ülgen, Sinan. How Turkey wants to reshape NATO Europe's World, 2012, pp. 24-29; Manis, Athanasios. The Middle East at breaking point: Turkey's neighbourhood policy and the need for enhanced 'Soft' Power. Middle East Research Institute. Policy Note, January 2015; Morillas, Pol. Towards a Global Strategy for the EU. CIDOB edicions, 2015, Barcelona.

47 See e.g. Baechler, Laurent. Lessons from the European Union Emission Trading Scheme and Prospects for Linking the EU and Turkey's Climate Strategies. Proceedings Book of the 17th International Energy and Environment Fair and Conference, ICCI Istanbul, 2011; Sartori, Nicolò/ Colombo, Silvia. Rethinking EU Energy Policies Towards the Southern Mediterranean Region, IAI Working Papers, No. 14, 2014; Schröder, Mirja. Turkey's Role in the Southern Gas Corridor. A geopolitical evaluation of EU and USA energy strategies in the region. EU-GLOBAL working paper, 04/2015.

48 See Kale, Başak. Challenges of Integration and Prospects of Divergence of Turkey's Migration Policy with the EU. In: Khader, Bichara (ed.): Les Migrations dans les Rapports Euro-Méditerrannéens et Euro-Arabes, Paris: L'Harmattan, 2012, pp. 217-229; Kaya, Ayhan. Islam, Migration and Integration: The Age of Securitization. London, 2012; Dimitriadi, Angeliki. Managing the Maritime Borders of Europe: Protection through Deterrence and Prevention?. Eliamep Working Paper No. 50, 2014.

well as regional and global developments, which together condition the EU-Turkey relationship. Hence, each chapter outlines the relevant drivers – along with the constellations in which they exist – before subsequently identifying the most prominent drivers within each thematic dimension.

While reflecting on the particularities of each thematic dimension, the analysis of each chapter similarly follows three steps. Firstly, the relevant focal issues[49] are selected for the purpose of pinpointing the clusters of issues within which the specific drivers unfold and shape the relations in each thematic area. These respectively comprise the following:

- Identity: Turkish and European identity constructions in the late Ottoman, modernisation and early Republican periods as well as during the Cold War and the post 1999-period; and the role of religion, secularism and nationalism.
- Politics: Political change (government, leadership and ideology); democracy and human rights; Turkey's democratisation in line with the Copenhagen criteria and public opinion.
- Security: The security dynamics between the EU and Turkey in the context of the Cyprus conflict; the Eastern Neighbourhood; the Caucasus; the unravelling of the order in the Middle East (i.e., Iran, Syria and Iraq) and the global level including the transnationalisation of terrorism or EU-NATO relations.
- Economy: The direction, magnitude and quality of the flows of goods and services, finance and knowledge between the EU and Turkey, as well as between Turkey and the neighbourhood and global actors (notably, the US and the BRICS countries); relevant political economy questions including, inter alia, Turkey's compliance with the economic membership criterion and the implications of the Trans-Atlantic Trade and Investment Partnership (TTIP).
- Energy: The EU's and Turkey's energy and climate strategies, interests and priorities; the Brussels-Ankara-Moscow energy triangle; energy and climate security priorities and challenges in the changing global energy order; energy interests of the EU and Turkey in the Caspian Sea and the Middle East; gas developments in the Eastern Mediterranean as trigger or obstacle of EU-Turkey cooperation.

---

49 As the analysis could not deal with every single driver in each thematic dimension it identifies focal issues that are those issues that structure the thematic dimension and have a relevant impact on EU-Turkey relations.

- <u>Migration</u>: Skilled migration flows between Turkey and the EU; irregular transit migration from Turkey to the EU; Turkish and EU asylum policies.

Secondly, each chapter identifies the principal drivers arising in the respective focal issues. As mentioned above, the drivers – unfolding at three levels of analysis – shape the progression of the EU-Turkey relationship in each thematic area. To give specific examples, the EU level incorporates, inter alia, drivers located in individual member states, which may be of particular salience for the EU-Turkey relationship as a whole. Similarly, in the identity and migration dimensions, the evolution of the debate in Germany on multiculturalism and integration is of broad relevance for the EU-Turkey relationship. Furthermore, bilateral tensions over Ankara's linking of the German and Dutch decisions banning Turkey's campaign attempts (in Germany and the Netherlands) ahead of the April 2017 Turkish constitutional referendum to Nazi practices also strongly affected the relations in the political dimension.[50]

Thirdly, the chapters weigh and rank the drivers in order to delineate the most likely scenario in their respective thematic dimensions. Three variables highlighting the significance of the drivers are decisive in this context.[51] First, the *relevance* of the drivers provides information about the expected scope of their respective impact on the future trajectory of EU-Turkey relations. Drivers can impact either the EU or Turkey or both. If a driver is relevant for both sides, its impact on the relations will be greater than it would be if it was only relevant for one of them. Drivers originating from the neighbourhood or the global level are considered to be of indirect, i.e. contextual, relevance. The second variable is *time*. Drivers can have short-term, medium-term or long-term impact, which factors into their ranking. The third variable is the *probability* of the drivers and it consists of three specific driver categories. *Projections* (knowns) are structural trends in terms of slow-changing phenomena, planned projects or inevitable collisions with respect to, for example, demography, energy dependencies, the eastward shift in economic power, and the strategic interests of both the EU and Turkey. *Uncertainties* (known-unknowns) are foreseeable changes such as the growing destabilisation of the Middle East and the eastern neighbourhood. Finally, the so-called '*wild cards*' (unknown-

---

50 See Soler i Lecha, Eduard et.al. Politics are taking EU-Turkey Relations Hostage. In this volume, pp. 77-102.
51 See Schwartz, The Art of the Long View, p. 122.

unknowns) are improbable yet deeply disruptive events for the EU-Turkey relationship, such as a Russian military attack on the EU.

The greater the relevance (i.e., relevant for both Turkey and the EU), the longer the time perspective of its impact and the higher the probability of a driver, the more it is considered a key driver. The reverse argument holds true for the opposite: The lesser the relevance (i.e., relevant for either Turkey or the EU), the shorter the time perspective of its impact and the lower the probability of a driver, the less it matters for projecting future EU-Turkey scenarios.

Once the individual relationship scenarios are formulated as such in each thematic area, the concluding chapter revisits their findings and relevant drivers in order to pinpoint the most likely scenario for the overall EU-Turkey relationship. In so doing, it assesses the relative relevance of the different areas of EU-Turkey relations (and the drivers within them) within the mixture of EU-Turkey conflict and cooperation, thereby problematising whether some policy areas (e.g., politics, security or identity) are more critical than others (e.g., energy or migration) for potentially shifting the relations towards conflict or convergence. This is an important step for evaluating the relevance of the thematic drivers in the overall relationship. Negative/positive drivers may lead to conflict/convergence in one particular thematic area but if their weight in the broader relationship is not significant, they will not necessarily stir the latter towards conflict or convergence.

4. Outline of the Volume

Chapter 2 conducts a historical analysis of the narratives and provides insights into mutual perceptions of EU-Turkey relations in Turkey and Europe. The narrative analysis by Hauge et.al. reveals that Turkish and European narratives vary considerably in their nature and significance over time. This suggests that different Turkish and European perceptions and judgements on actors, events or relations unfold over time and emerge, endure or vanish in parallel with the milestones and/or historical critical junctures in EU-Turkey relations. Similarly, the identity analysis of Chapter 3 builds upon historical milestones as the main drivers of identity constructions. Aydın-Düzgit and Rumelili highlight the relevance of identity for the future of EU-Turkey relations because identity differences can act as stumbling blocks for the progress of the relationship. They deconstruct general claims that Turkey does not qualify as sufficiently European for EU membership and/or Turkey's self-perception is at best ambivalent towards Europe.

Chapter 4 which addresses the political dimension of EU-Turkey relations is guided by the conviction that it "takes two to tango". Soler i Lecha et. al. argue that developments in the EU are just as important as developments in Turkey for shaping the relations. In particular, they emphasize that beyond the general enlargement fatigue in EU member states, it is possible to detect a particular *Turkey fatigue* which factors into the relations' deterioration. Additionally, they discuss the impact of the politicisation of Turkey's EU membership (in Turkey and Europe). Chapter 5 by Ülgen and Ergün offers a rather grim account highlighting the strong interplay of conflictual trends and the need for EU-Turkey cooperation in the area of security. In contrast, chapter 6 by Erdil and Akçomak tackles the economy dimension and offers the most positive account of EU-Turkey relations among all the dimensions. The flows of capital, goods, services and knowledge generate mutual beneficial effects for both sides and the modernisation of the EU-Turkey Customs Union holds the greatest potential for convergence between the EU and Turkey. Chapter 7 which discusses the energy dimension highlights the differences between Turkey and the EU in terms of energy mixes as well as turbulences in the neighbourhood. Colantoni argues that the cooperation potential is consequently undermined. The chapter on migration (Chapter 8) subsequently emphasises the central role played by irregular migration (i.e., in 2015 and 2016, in the context of the Syrian refugee crisis) in the evolution of EU-Turkey relations. Dimitriadi and Kaya conclude that cooperation necessarily endures in this area despite the simultaneous persistence of conflict.

Together, the individual chapters imply that EU-Turkey cooperation is imperative in all the thematic dimensions notwithstanding rising conflict, particularly in politics, security and energy. Hence, the future most likely scenario for broader EU-Turkey relations is realistically conceptualised as *conflictual cooperation*. This is explained in detail in the conclusions in chapter 9 where Saatçioğlu synthesises the findings of the thematic chapters and reflects on the future pathways that could sustain EU-Turkey relations amidst conflictual cooperation.

Key Dynamics and Future Scenarios

Narratives of a Contested Relationship: Unravelling the Debates in the EU and Turkey

Ebru Ece Özbey, Hanna Lisa Hauge, Atila Eralp and Wolfgang Wessels

1. Introduction

The debate on EU[1]-Turkey relations has historically reflected an oscillation between rapprochement and estrangement, mirroring the relations themselves. Recently, the diplomatic crises and escalation of tension between Turkey and the EU, including its institutions and various member states, seem to indicate an all-time low in the relationship. This chapter, therefore, focuses on the ways in which Turkish and European actors have experienced and chronicled the temporally connected, continuously interacting events of the past and unravels the recurrent patterns along with specific features of the parties' rhetoric over the years. Through a narrative approach, it provides an overview of the key stories on EU-Turkey relations since the early 1960s as told by the actors involved and investigates their implications for the future of this troubled relationship.

The chapter's main premise is that the dynamics between Turkish and EU narratives are closely interlinked with the general course of this relationship. In other words, the state of relations at any given moment determines the trends of convergence and divergence between Turkish and EU narratives and vice versa. For instance, if an actual set of events is mutually favourable to the parties, their accounts about each other and the fate of their relationship itself are expected to be positive and synergetic. Concurrently, corresponding and clashing narratives have different repercussions for the overall relationship. If the dominant narratives in the EU and Turkey share the same goal and there is a certain harmony between the constitutive elements used in the stories on the both sides, the relationship is more likely to develop in a positive direction because these collective stories are intrinsically constructive and persuasive. They alter the ways in

---

1 Although the institution in question is referred to as 'European Union' throughout this chapter for ease of reading, it should be noted that it is specified as the 'European Economic Community' from 1957 to 1992 and the 'European Community' from 1992 to 2007.

which audiences perceive, interpret and respond to the actors, structures, connections as well as critical developments surrounding them. Hence, mapping actors' mind-sets and priorities for the present and the future alongside real-life interactions between the actors can contribute to a deeper understanding of EU-Turkey relations.

This chapter draws several conclusions through qualitative analysis of a broad textual corpus of 282 official statements, speeches and documents, which were manually coded by the authors using a joint codebook for both Turkish and European sources. Firstly, it reveals that Turkish and European narratives vary considerably in their nature. All Turkish narratives identified share the same goal of full membership while differing in their plots and lines of argumentation. The EU narratives identified, however, vary both in their plot and projected *finalité* for the relationship. Most of them do, however, share a perception of Turkey as an important (geo)strategic partner for the EU. Secondly, our study exhibits the time factor for and within narratives. It demonstrates how different perceptions and judgements (on actors, events or relations) unfold over time and how they emerge, endure or vanish in parallel with the milestones, or historical critical junctures, in EU-Turkey relations. It also shows how time has become an important element pursuant to the arguments used in the Turkish narratives, especially those appearing later. Finally, it asserts that since the 1960s, there has been an increase in the number of competing narratives on both sides and debates have become more divergent.

Concerning present and future trends, this chapter contends that, although conflict appears as a cyclical, relational pattern between Turkish and European narratives since the outset of official relations, recent years have witnessed a unique, heightened aggravation of tension between the parties. Current narratives that dominate debates in Turkey and the EU comprise a combination of conflictual elements paired with arguments emphasising the necessity of cooperation. Assuming that both of these – seemingly controversial – trends within the narratives persist, Turkish narratives' unrequited goal of membership, which is not reciprocated on the European side, will continue to preclude the possibility of convergence, signalling instead "conflictual cooperation"[2] as the most likely scenario in the near future.

The remainder of this chapter proceeds as follows: The next section gives a short account of the conceptualisation and operationalisation of the

---

2 See Ergun, Doruk/ Ülgen, Sinan. EU-Turkey security relations: Key drivers and future scenarios. In this volume, pp. 103-120.

term 'narrative'. Section 3 summarises the most significant narratives identified for the EU and Turkey.[3] Section 4 assesses the elements of continuity and change in debates over time, simultaneously paying attention to the dynamics between Turkish and European narratives. The chapter concludes by discussing the relationship's future prospects based on these results.

2. A Narrative Approach to the Analysis of EU-Turkey Relations

Several studies have so far investigated discourses,[4] perceptions,[5] narratives,[6] identity constructions,[7] and historical legacy of the Ottoman Em-

---

3 For a more detailed analysis of the narratives, including representative examples and excerpts from the documents, see Hauge et al. Narratives of a Contested Relationship. Unravelling the Debates in the EU and Turkey. FEUTURE Online Paper No. 28, February 2019, https://feuture.uni-koeln.de/sites/feuture/user_upload/Onli ne_Paper_No_28.pdf [21.08.20].

4 See for example Aydın-Düzgit, Senem. European Parliament 'doing' Europe. Unravelling the right-wing culturalist discourse on Turkey's accession to the EU. In: Journal of Language and Politics, January 2015, Vol. 14, No. 1, p. 154-171; Macmillan, Catherine. Discourse, Identity and the Question of Turkish Accession to the EU. Through the Looking Glass. Farnham, 2013; Aydın-Düzgit, Senem. Constructions of European Identity. Debates and Discourses on Turkey and the EU. Basingstoke, 2012; Çağatay-Tekin, Beyza. Representations and Othering in Discourse. The construction of Turkey in the EU context. Amsterdam and Philadelphia, 2010; Wimmel, Andreas. Beyond the Bosphorus. Comparing Public Discourses on Turkey's EU Application in the German, French and British Quality Press. In: Journal of Language and Politics, September 2009, Vol. 8, No. 2, pp. 223-243.

5 See for example Eralp, Atila/ Torun, Zerrin. Perceptions and Europeanization in Turkey before the EU Candidacy. In: Tekin, Ali/ Güney, Aylin (eds). The Europeanization of Turkey. 1st ed., London, 2015; Müftüler-Baç, Meltem/ Süleymanoğlu-Kürüm, Rahime. Deliberations in the Turkish Parliament. The External Perceptions of European Foreign Policy. In: Journal of Language and Politics, January 2015, Vol. 14, No. 2, pp. 258-284.

6 See for example Levin, Paul T. Competing Narratives. Images of Turkey in the European Parliament (1996-2010). In: Levin, Paul T. (eds). Turkey and the European Union. New York, 2011.

7 See for example Aydın-Düzgit, Senem et al. Turkish and European Identity Constructions in the 1946-1999 Period. FEUTURE Online Paper No. 15, March 2018; Lindgaard, Jakob et al. Turkey in European Identity Politics: Key Drivers and Future Scenarios. FEUTURE Online Paper No. 19, April 2018; Aydın-Düzgit, Senem et al. Turkish and European Identity Constructions in the 1815-1945 Period. FEUTURE Online Paper No. 4, July 2017; Yılmaz, Gözde. From Europeanization to De-Europeanization. The Europeanization Process of Turkey in 1999-2014. In:

pire[8] within the context of EU-Turkey relations. This study contributes to the existing literature by simultaneously exploring and comparing the European and Turkish narratives for the period between 1958 and 2017 based on a systematic qualitative coding of a broad data set, providing insight into potential future narratives and related scenarios for the future of the EU-Turkey relationship.

While the definition of narrative adapted here is tailored to the specific research design and questions of this study, it is based on the main approaches of narrative analysis, particularly as applied in the field of political science.[9] Narratives here are defined as interpretations by political ac-

---

Journal of Contemporary European Studies, May 2016, Vol. 24, No.1, p. 86-100; Özkural Köroğlu, Nergiz. Neo-Ottomanization vs. Europeanization. Turkey-EU Relations. In: Ankara Avrupa Çalışmaları Dergisi, 2014, Vol. 13, No. 2, pp. 111-131; Cautrés, Bruno/ Monceau, Nicolas. La Turquie en Europe. L'Opinion des Européens et des Turcs. Paris, 2011; Rumelili, Bahar. Turkey: Identity, Foreign Policy, and Socialization in a Post-Enlargement Europe. In: Journal of European Integration, March 2011, Vol. 33, No. 2, p. 235-249; Ergin, Melz. Otherness within Turkey, and between Turkey and Europe. In: Gifford, Paul/ Hauswedell, Tessa (eds). Europe and Its Others. Essays on Interperception and Identity. Oxford, 2010; Schneeberger, Agnes. Constructing European Identity through Mediated Difference. A Content Analysis of Turkey's EU Accession Process in the British Press. In: Journal of Media and Communication, July 2009, Vol. 1, No. 1, p. 83-102; Müftüler-Baç, Meltem/ Taşkın, Evrim. Turkey's Accession to the European Union. Does Culture and Identity Play a Role. In: Ankara Review of European Studies, January 2007, Vol. 6, No. 2, pp. 31-50; Rumelili, Bahar. Negotiating Europe. EU-Turkey Relations from an Identity Perspective. In: Insight Turkey, February 2008, Vol. 10, No. 1, pp. 97-110; Casanova, José. The Long, Difficult, and Tortuous Journey of Turkey into Europe and the Dilemmas of European Civilization. In: Constellations, June 2006, Vol. 13, No. 2, pp. 234-247; Lundgren, Asa. The Case of Turkey. Are Some Candidates More 'European' Than Others. In: Helene Sjursen (Eds.). Questioning EU Enlargement. Europe in Search of Identity. New York, 2006; Nas, Çiğdem. Turkish Identity and the Perception of Europe. In: Avrupa Araştırmaları Dergisi, February 2001, Vol. 9, No. 1, pp. 177-189.

8 See for example McDonald, Deniz Bingöl. Imperial Legacies and Neo-Ottomanism. In: Insight Turkey, Fall 2012, Vol. 14, No. 4, pp. 101-120; Kaya, Ayhan/ Tecmen, Ayşe. Turkish Modernity. A Continuous Journey of Europeanisation. In: Ichijo, Atsuko (Eds.). Europe, Nations and Modernity. Identities and Modernities in Europe. London, 2011.

9 See for example Jones, Michael et al. (Eds.). The Science of Stories. Applications of the Narrative Policy Framework in Public Policy Analysis. Basingstoke, 2014; Hyvärinen, Matti. Analyzing Narratives and Story-Telling. In: Alasuutari, Pertti et al. (Eds.). SAGE Handbook of Social Research Methods. Los Angeles, 2008; Shenhav, Shaul. Political Narratives and Political Reality. In: International Political Science

tors of the nature, evolution, drivers[10] and end-goals of EU-Turkey relations.

Because narratives do not necessarily emerge as complete stories in the documents analysed, we, as the coders, (re)constructed and identified them by collecting and classifying individual data elements and organising them into a complete story.[11] Thus, a trajectory is pursued following the way in which actors think about the relationship, along with the respective self and other, in a constant effort to understand and reflect the stories as they are being told.

In this regard, narratives were distinguished according to their plot and goal. The elements and arguments constituting the plot, for example, can include narrators' perceptions of each other and other relevant actors. They can also comprise accounts of the existing settings and drivers of the relationship on different levels. The goal indicates the estimated or desired *finalité* for the relationship and, in the case of EU-Turkey relations specifically, can range from full membership at one end of the spectrum to alienation or distancing at the other. Identifying the goal links narratives to different future scenarios of EU-Turkey relations, namely conflict, cooperation and convergence, in two ways. Firstly, it shows each individual narrative's "visions for the future"[12]. Secondly, it reveals the presence or lack of compatibility between the dominant Turkish and European narratives' goals at any given time.

The chapter's narrative analysis is based on a unique and comprehensive dataset compiled by the authors. The document selection for the dataset

---

Review. July 2006, Vol. 27, No. 3, pp. 254-262; Czarniawska, Barbara. Narratives in Social Science Research. London, 2004; Fischer, Frank/ Forester, John. The Argumentative Turn in Policy Analysis. Durham, 1993; Kohler Riessman, Catherine (Eds.). Narrative Analysis. Qualitative Research Methods Series. Thousand Oaks, 1993; Roe, Emery. Narrative Policy Analysis. Theory and Practice. Durham, 1994; Kaplan, Thomas. The Narrative Structure of Policy Analysis. In: Journal of Policy Analysis and Management, Summer 1986, Vol. 5, No. 4, pp. 761-778.
See also for an overview of narrative approaches in political science Gadinger, Frank et al. Politische Narrative. Konzepte, Analysen, Forschungspraxis. Wiesbaden, 2014; Patterson, Molly/ Renwick Monroe, Kristen. Narrative in Political Science. In: Annual Review of Political Science, June 1998, Vol. 1, pp. 315-331.

10 This chapter follows FEUTURE's definition of drivers as the ideational and material, structural and agency-related factors that can either accelerate or decelerate the process of Turkey's integration with the EU or can open up and lead to alternative options.

11 Polkinghorne, Donald E. Narrative configuration in qualitative analysis. In: Qualitative Studies in Education, July 1995, Vol. 8, No. 1, pp. 5-23.

12 Kaplan, Thomas. The Narrative Structure of Policy Analysis.

was based on thirteen milestones (see Table 1) which constitute critical junctures in the history relationship from both European and Turkish perspectives from 1959 to 2016.[13] The years immediately preceding and following the selected milestones were also added to the dataset to trace the changes in argumentation in a more concrete and detailed manner.

Table 1: Milestones in EU-Turkey relations

Selected Year	Milestone
1958 1959 1960	Turkey's application for associate membership in the European Economic Community (EEC)
1962 1963 1964	Ankara (Association) Agreement is signed by Turkey and the EEC
1969 1970 1971	Additional Protocol and the Second Financial Protocol to the Association Agreement are signed by Turkey and the EEC
1973 1974 1975	Sampson Coup and Turkish intervention in Cyprus
1979 1980 1981	Military coup in Turkey
1986 1987 1988	Turkey's membership application to the EU
1988 1989 1990	End of the Cold War and collapse of the Soviet Union
1995 1996 1997	Customs Union between Turkey and the EU comes into force
1998 1999 2000	Helsinki Summit of the European Council grants candidacy status to Turkey
2003 2004 2005	Cyprus becomes an EU member
2004 2005 2006	EU-Turkey accession negotiations begin
2011 2012 2013	Positive Agenda is launched and Turkey freezes its relations with the EU during Cyprus' EU Presidency
2015 2016 2017	EU-Turkey Summit (Migration Deal) and military coup attempt in Turkey

Source: Own compilation.

In total, the dataset includes 138 documents from the EU and 144 documents from Turkey (see Table 2) covering a total of 36 years in the period between the late 1950s and the end of 2017. The documents were collected from web sources and online archives as well as institutional and governmental archives in the EU and Turkey, including a wide array of textual data (ranging from resolutions, conclusions, communications, statements as well as speeches to reports and presentations) so as to reflect the official positions of institutions and actors on both sides.[14]

---

13 For more information on the selection of the milestones see Hauge, Hanna-Lisa et al. Mapping Periods and Milestones of Past EU-Turkey Relations. FEUTURE Working Paper, September 2016.
14 While employing textual data from official documents in order to make comparative and over-time observations on *collective stories*, the authors acknowledge that

Table 2: Overview of the data set

	EU	Turkey
Actors and Types of Documents Selected for Analysis (Time Frame for Milestones:1959-2016); Time Frame for Data Collection: 1958-2017)	European Parliament: resolutions, selected debates European Council: conclusions, statements European Commission: reports, communications Speeches: by leaders of EU institutions	Presidents: speeches, presentations, statements Prime Ministers: speeches, presentations, statements Ministries of EU Affairs and Foreign Affairs: official documents on EU-Turkey relations Economic Development Foundation (IKV): reports, books, articles, newsletters, brief notes
Number of Analysed Documents	138	144

Source: Own compilation.

We manually coded documents selected using Computer-Assisted Qualitative Data Analysis Software (CAQDAS) to facilitate better data access, overview and assessment. We structured the codebook jointly for both EU and Turkish sources so as to ensure the results' comparability, while still providing sufficient flexibility in coding the documents to reflect differences between the discourses of Turkish and EU actors. The codebook was, therefore, developed as a mix of deductive and inductive approaches, with codes included to reflect not only the plot and the goal, but also actors' perceptions of the self and the other, for example in terms of identity (e.g., whether Turkey was perceived as 'European'). As further elements in the plot, our codebook reflected the relationship's drivers as described by the actors. These drivers as part of the actors' argumentations were structured in line with the different thematic dimensions to which they relate, name-

---

documents of official nature might be prone to bias, given that such documents are texts that are "written with distinctive purposes in mind" (Bryman, Alan. Documents as Sources of Data. In: Bryman, Alan (Eds.). Social Research Methods. 4th ed., New York, 2012, p. 555; Atkinson, Paul Anthony/ Coffey, Amanda Jane. Analysing Documentary Realities. In: Silverman, David (Eds.). Qualitative Research. Issues of Theory, Method and Practice. 3rd ed,, London, 2010). Due to their official character, they might deliberately leave certain matters out, or be written in an ambiguous, indirect style. To overcome these mentioned limitations, the authors resorted to a triangulation of sources. They analysed different institutions and actors for each side and consulted the secondary literature as well as other primary sources, like speeches given to different audiences.

ly: politics, economy, security, energy and climate, migration, as well as identity and culture.[15]

3. Past and Present Narratives From the EU and Turkey: An Overview.

Outlining the results of an elaborate empirical study, this section provides an overview of narratives identified for the EU and Turkey. It presents each narrative's plot and goal as well as the ideal-type EU-Turkey relationship scenario and the historical period(s) to which it relates the most. As such, it prepares for the ensuing analysis which will examine how Turkish and EU narratives have converged or diverged over time.

In general terms, this study affirms that there are numerous (not only akin but also contradicting and sometimes even completely dissimilar) narratives coexisting in a polyphonic chorus at any given time. Thus, this overview represents only brief extracts from an 'orchestra of narratives' within the EU and Turkey. In order to shed light on this often cacophonic debate, the chapter focuses on drawing selections which represent the most dominant narratives from 36 out of nearly 60-year-long history of official relations. Hence it disregards the secondary (counter or alternative) narratives that have been adopted by only a limited number of actors or have prevailed only for short periods. Thus, the narratives introduced below have an ideal-type character and are by no means exhaustive and exclusive.

3.1 EU Narratives

The analysis of documents for the EU institutions indicates four main narratives: (1) *Membership*, (2) *Special Candidate*, (3) *Strategic Partner*, and (4) *Distant Neighbour*.

3.1.1 Membership

The *Membership* narrative promotes Turkish accession to the EU as a *finalité* and is thus linked to the convergence scenario. Although there are

---

15 More detailed, specific information on the codebook and data selection is available in Appendix for: Hauge et. al. Narratives of a Contested Relationship.

occasional references to partial or differentiated membership in its plot, a clear commitment to the goal of Turkish membership is ultimately displayed. The drivers that motivate this goal range from geostrategic or economic interests to the prospect of contributing to Turkey's democratisation via the enlargement procedure.

This narrative stresses Turkey's strategic value and European character, considering the country as an eligible candidate for joining the EU. Accordingly, Turkey's accession process is expected to follow the same procedure that would apply to any other EU accession candidate. It is not politicised and is formally based on the Copenhagen Criteria. Consequently, its completion depends on Turkey's fulfilment of the relevant economic, political and *acquis* conditions.

Historically, the *Membership* narrative dominated only in the relationship's early period, namely, during the 1960s and 1970s when most official documents and statements by European institutions included references to the final goal of membership through establishment of the Customs Union. The significance of this narrative seemingly declined in the 1980s against the backdrop of the economic and political challenges that Turkey was facing at the time. Its relevance was briefly revived in debates surrounding the EU's milestone decisions on Turkey's EU candidacy (1999) and the opening of accession negotiations (2005). In 2015, the EU linked the issue of Turkey's accession process with the Migration Deal. Thus, there was a brief phase where a change in the debate towards such a narrative seemed to reach the realm of possibility, although the goal of EU membership for Turkey was not really spelled out. During most of the last two decades, thus, mention of *Membership* has been lacking from EU institutions' political discourses. Although debates on Turkey's differentiated or partial EU membership have emerged in expert and academic circles over recent years,[16] such concepts do not as yet form part of the EU institutions' official discourse.

---

16 See inter alia, Karakaş, Cemal. EU-Turkey: Integration without Full Membership or Membership without Full Integration: A Conceptual Framework for Accession Alternatives. In: Journal of Common Market Studies, Vol. 51, 2013, p. 1057- 1073; Duff, Andrew. The case for an Associate Membership of the European Union. LSE EUROPP Blog, 2013; Müftüler Baç, Meltem. Turkey's Future with the European Union: An Alternative Model of Differentiated Integration. In: *Turkish Studies*. Vol. 18, No. 3, 2017, p. 416-438; Ülgen, Sinan. Avoiding a Divorce: A Virtual EU Membership for Turkey. Carnegie Europe, Brussels, 2012; Saatçioğlu, Beken. The European Union's Refugee Crisis and Rising Functionalism in EU-Turkey Relations. *Turkish Studies*, Vol 21, No. 2, 2019, pp. 169- 187, DOI: 10.1080/14683849.2019.1586542.

3.1.2 Special Candidate

According to the *Special Candidate* narrative, there are certain political and economic conditions that render Turkey a special EU candidate (or a special EU applicant in the relations' earlier period). The narrative includes references to obstacles such as Turkey's difficulties in fulfilling the Copenhagen Criteria and the EU's capacity to absorb Turkey in view of the country's large economy and population. Particularly in the 1960s and 1970s, it also referred to the gap between the Turkish economy and those of member states. As regards accession negotiations, this narrative rather follows the credo of 'pacta sunt servanda' by not abandoning the accession process while stressing that negotiations with Turkey are open-ended and/or long-lasting.

Representations of this narrative usually imply the goal that Turkey remains an accession candidate in an open-ended process. Thus, no specific end goal is formulated, leaving the prospects for the future EU-Turkey relationship rather vague. This narrative is partially linked to the convergence scenario given that the accession process is not explicitly abandoned. However, based on its emphasis on the accession process and negotiations' open-ended character, it also relates to the cooperation scenario.

With few representations during the 1960s and 1970s, the *Special Candidate* narrative gained relevance in the late 1980s. It was institutionalised by the EU's December 1997 Luxembourg Council which put forward a specific "European Strategy" only for Turkey, while recognising the Central and Eastern European applicants as formal EU candidates. Elements of this narrative continue to characterise the EU's discourse even after the opening of accession negotiations in 2005.

3.1.3 Strategic Partner

The *Strategic Partner* narrative starts from a perception of Turkey as an important geostrategic partner, an element which is also present in other narratives. Based on this awareness, it stresses the need for close cooperation with Turkey. The argumentation refers to drivers from various dimensions such as economic security and political issues. Regarding the potential format of EU-Turkey cooperation, this narrative refers to transactional forms of cooperation in certain policy fields (as with the 2016 EU-Turkey Migration Deal). At the same time, it also includes references to more rules-based cooperation such as an upgrade of the EU-Turkey Customs Union. Ongoing accession negotiations with Turkey might not have to be stopped, but they are not top priority on the EU's political agenda. Hence, this narrative's implied goal is a strategic partnership with Turkey falling short of membership, which links it to the cooperation scenario. Turkey's EU accession either cannot be foreseen or the accession process and/or its completion is/are not the EU's prime concern.

Nevertheless, Turkey's geostrategic importance for the EU is a constant motif in its discourse throughout the decades. However, due to Ankara's rejection of any status less than membership, strategic partnership as an official replacement of membership has never been able to gain ground in official EU discourse. That said, official EU statements and resolutions in recent years begin to include references to a strategic partnership being shaped around debates for an upgraded Customs Union and the EU-Turkey Migration Deal.

3.1.4 Distant Neighbour

The *Distant Neighbour* narrative portrays Turkey as an estranged and distant or even hostile neighbour, which may also not share the same democratic values as the EU. In this view, the so-called backsliding in the democratic reform process moves Turkey away from European values. Additionally, with its unreliable foreign policy, Turkey is perceived either as dragging the EU into existing conflicts in its neighbourhood or as an aggressor creating conflicts, for example in terms of its regularly controversial role in Cyprus. This narrative may also include concerns that Turkey is no longer a stable partner of the West. From an identity perspective, representations of this narrative tend to label Turkey as "the Other". Consequently, there is even talk of the EU openly threatening to abandon Turkey's accession process and/or impose sanctions or measures such as a freeze or suspension of relations, with attendant serious implications for the concrete relationship.

This narrative is linked to the conflict scenario, as it entails the EU's distancing and alienation from Turkey in many spheres. More precisely, it may result in the abandonment of Turkey's accession perspective, a freeze and/or suspension of accession negotiations, or at worst, relations in the broadest of terms. The 1980s saw the first phase in the *Distant Neighbour* narrative dominating debate, as a result of the 1980 military coup in Turkey. There were also subsequent instances of conflict, for instance in certain cases of EU disagreement with Turkish foreign policy and disapproval of Turkey's human rights situation during the 1990s. This narrative has gained key relevance over recent years, particularly when Turkey's July 2016 failed coup attempt gave way to extreme emergency rule measures and purges.

3.2. Turkish Narratives

Analysis of the documents for actors and institutions from Turkey indicates five main narratives: 1) *Westernisation*, 2) *Europeanisation*, 3) *Eurasianisation*, 4) *Turkey as the Heir*, and 5) *Turkey as a Great Power*.

3.2.1 Westernisation

Westernisation is the predominant Turkish narrative during the entire history of EU-Turkey relations, a view which is seen to be reinforced by actors with immensely different backgrounds and political positions. This narrative dates back to the outset of the relationship in the 1960s and considers Turkey as a crucial part of the West, an alliance that brings together the EU and several other Western actors. Nourished by insecurity and anxiety stemming from bipolarity and nuclear armament at the height of the Cold War, it places considerable emphasis on Turkey's cooperation, primarily with NATO and the United States, but also with European institutions such as the Council of Europe and the EU. It brings to the fore Turkey's democratic, secular and liberal side, while at the same time underlining the country's geostrategic importance. In this context, Turkey is seen as an asset for the European integration project, indicating that its EU membership is nothing but a rational decision that includes benefits for both sides.

This narrative links to the convergence scenario as it foresees Turkey's EU accession with a focus on the country's rightful place within the Western alliance and institutions. It is dominant throughout the Cold War but especially during the 1960s and early 1970s. As European integration institutionalises and gains political significance along with economic power, the EU becomes increasingly important for Turkey, leading to the emergence and rise of the *Europeanisation* narrative. Although dominance of the *Westernisation* has gradually weakened since the 1990s, it still remains relevant to a certain degree in the last two decades.

3.2.2 Europeanisation

The *Europeanisation* narrative shares many elements and lines of argumentation with the *Westernisation* narrative, but focuses more on Turkey's already achieved as well as potential EU-induced transformation. It sees Turkey as a natural part of continental Europe, due not only to arguably evident geographical reasons but also Turkey's centuries-long interactions and connections with its European neighbours. The presenters of this narrative assert Turkey as a modern, secular and civilised country that is well-integrated into the European economic and political system, praising Turkey's involvement in different European organisations, namely the Council of Europe and the Organisation for Security and Co-operation in Europe. They consider the EU as part of this larger European composition and emphasise Turkey's rightful place within it.

According to this narrative, Turkey and the EU share a common destiny as well as joint interests and concerns over a wide spectrum of issues. They need each other for strategic reasons in the face of multiple challenges arising on different levels. During the Cold War, this need was derived mainly from a turbulent international environment but, starting from the 1990s, it becomes more closely associated with various socioeconomic and sociopolitical struggles as well as opportunities on bilateral and regional levels. The most recent examples, for instance, include the 2015 Syrian refugee crisis, cross-border crime and terrorism, economic and financial instability together with energy challenges. Beyond these cogent grounds for cooperation, though, the parties are said to cherish and defend the same beliefs and norms; expected eventually to come together on the basis of shared values.

This narrative links to the convergence scenario, as it foresees membership for Turkey with a focus on its rightful place within the European institutions. Albeit interwoven with *Westernisation*, the *Europeanisation* narrative can be identified as early as the 1960s. It gains dominance as Turkey engages more and more with the EU through different institutional mechanisms and seemingly reaches its peak with the legal and political harmonisation processes successfully carried out by Turkey in the early 2000s.

The *Europeanisation* narrative initially holds a very positive assessment of the EU, but starting from the 1990s, some assertions of conditionality begin to surface. After marking the transitional stage, official application and candidate status in the relations, Turkish actors perceive EU membership as the obvious next step in the process. As the EU postpones the final phase and continually imposes new preconditions, the sincerity and objectivity of the relations are questioned, with the demand for equal treatment and transparency becoming more explicit. Accordingly, Turkish actors stipulate for respect and impartiality, asserting that Turkey will certainly be an EU member but "only with its head held high"[17]. Despite increasing criticism towards the EU, the end goal of membership persists and the narrative remains to be highly relevant.

3.2.3 Eurasianisation

Emerging in the period immediately following collapse of the Soviet Union, the *Eurasianisation* narrative draws considerable attention to the smaller, newly independent states in post-Soviet Eurasia. It leaves Turkey's one-sided foreign policy orientation toward the West aside and instead promotes Turkey not only as an influential regional power but also a bridge between the West and the East. While acknowledging Turkey's self-evident connection to Europe, it asserts that Turkey is not only a European country but also a prominent and important actor with historical and cultural connections to the promising countries from a wider region. Assuming that the EU would seek political and economic cooperation or even some form of integration with Eurasian actors, this narrative not only sees Turkey as a role model for these countries, but also argues that Turkey's much-delayed EU membership is the first step towards a larger and stronger EU.

This narrative emerged in the early 1990s and remained relevant for nearly a decade thereafter. It links to the convergence scenario as it foresees Turkish membership with a focus on the country's geostrategic importance in the Eurasian region. Furthermore, it envisages EU enlargement towards, or at least growing EU influence in, Eurasia. However, with Russia and Iran (re)gaining power in the region and the EU showing little interest in Eurasia-oriented ventures, the optimism regarding wider-European cooperation has diminished and consequently Turkish actors have stopped addressing Eurasian affairs within the context of EU-Turkey relations, albeit with some exceptions, namely energy and security-related matters. Although there are some references to Turkey's Eurasian nature and devotion to establishing closer relations with the actors from the region in recent years, this narrative seems to have lost its relevance significantly in the new millennium.

---

17 See for example Çiller, Tansu. 51. Cumhuriyet Hükümeti'nin (II. Çiller Hükümeti) Programını Sunuş Konuşması. Türkiye Büyük Millet Meclisi. Ankara, 1995; Demirel, Süleyman. Ondokuzuncu Dönem Beşinci Yasama Yılı Açış Konuşması. Ankara, 1995.

3.2.4 Turkey as the Heir

The *Turkey as the Heir* narrative has been developed as a response to European claims about the so-called clash of Turkish and European identities and debates on Turkey's Europeanness. As a response to European scepticism towards Turkey's EU membership, which purportedly reflects memories of past atrocities and conflicts between the predecessors on both sides, this narrative attempts to initiate a discussion on the parties' common history without subscribing to ancient hatred and prejudices. While embracing memories of Turkey's history, it does not disparage Turkey's Ottoman or Turkic characteristics to the detriment of those considered as European.

In parallel to Turkey's closer relations with Middle Eastern and Central Asian countries under the conservative AKP government during the last 18 years, references to Turkey's imperial legacy and alleged organic links to Turkic dynasties have significantly increased. However, although this narrative envisages Turkey as the grandiose heir and highlights the glory of former empires (starting from the Anatolian *beyliks* from the 11th century), it does not necessarily defend the idea of conflicting identities between Turkey and Europe. On the contrary, it often asserts that Turkey is European *because of* its Ottoman past and accuses European counterparts of exploiting historical divergences between the two parties. Even though it promotes Turkey's greater engagement with countries that were once a part of the Ottoman Empire, the narrative claims that Turkey is nevertheless more European than many EU member states, with an almost thousand-year history on the continent. This is all in support of Turkey's objective to gain full membership to the EU.

Historically, this narrative can be traced back to the 1970s when Turkey's Islamist political forces led by Necmettin Erbakan put forward the idea of the National View, which initially opposed Turkey's involvement in European integration, but later reversed its position. At the beginning, this narrative is neither common among different actors nor does it have any noticeable influence in the face of strong Euro-enthusiasm from the Cold-War period or the overwhelming feeling of optimism immediately thereafter. However, it has gained significance and popularity in the last decade under the AKP government. Although it contains somewhat controversial or conflictual elements and lacks the enthusiasm of the first three Turkish narratives, *Turkey as the Heir* still links to the convergence scenario since it foresees membership for Turkey despite the waning interest of the European partners.

3.2.5 Turkey as a Great Power

The Turkey as Great Power narrative envisages Turkey as a powerful political and economic actor with a pivotal regional role that is associated with various strategic opportunities. It pictures Turkey and the EU as equals, asserting that Turkey's accession negotiations should continue in a more transparent, impartial manner while criticising the EU for not displaying the attention and respect that Turkey deserves. It contains an explicit "Us" vs "Them" rhetoric, which gradually becomes antagonistic as a series of events brings forward the parties' differing and sometimes contradictory interests. While it does not abandon Turkey's EU membership goal, it maintains that the EU and Turkey are at a crossroad in their relationship, suggesting that a fundamental change of attitude towards Turkey is needed on the EU's side in order to maintain a dialogue.

The *Turkey as a Great Power* narrative periodically appears starting with the 1990s, but gains true prominence in parallel with Turkey's economic stability and development achieved under the first (2002-2007) and second AKP governments (2007-2011). Specifically, its dominance has been reinforced by a relatively successful economic performance in the aftermath of the Great Recession in 2008 and improved military capabilities against regional security threats (namely, cross border operations, fight against the ISIS, and active role in the Syrian refugee crisis) as well as the AKP government's durability since 2002.

As with Turkish narratives presented earlier, this narrative also links to the convergence scenario in foreseeing EU membership for Turkey. Yet, it eschews an asymmetrical relationship between Turkey and the EU, emphasising rather the notion of quid pro quo.

4. Progressively Divergent and Increasingly Conflictual: Dynamics Between European and Turkish Narratives

For our analysis, mutual perceptions of the "Self" and the respective "Other" and how they are interlinked with goals associated with different narratives are of specific interest. Three main conclusions have been reached in this regard.

Firstly, the identified Turkish and European narratives vary considerably in their nature:

While Turkish narratives share the same goal but have different plots, the EU narratives differ in both their goals and plots. In Turkey, all the dominant narratives consistently emphasise and aspire to the goal of EU membership. There is no alternative goal proposed in lieu of full integration with the EU. The justification and motives behind this desired goal, though, vary among the different narratives. In the early period of EU-Turkey relations, Turkey viewed the EU as part of the Western alliance rather than a distinct and significant political actor in its own right. Hence, joining the EU was targeted by Turkish political actors primarily against a backcloth of the bipolar international order of the Cold War period. In the 1980s, both normative and strategic values attributed to the EU started to transform and expand. The EU attracted more attention, which gave way to stronger, more pointed, multifaceted ideas and judgments than were emanating from the then Turkish actors.

From the 1990s, the EU gained a distinct identity and started to be treated not only as a noble partnership between civilised nations but also as an actor in itself, within the Turkish rhetoric. This characterisation of the EU had robust and far-reaching consequences in terms of altering the qualities that Turkish actors ascribed to the EU. These actors had hitherto described the EU as a formal mechanism in their deliberations, benchmarking the institutional and structural indicators in Turkey vis-à-vis the EU and focussing on the essential legislative and administrative reforms for enhanced cooperation or, more favourably, integration. With this perception of the EU as a conveyer of identity, Turkish actors came to see the EU as an ally, partner, rival or collaborator, as we observe in subsequent Turkish narratives. This new depiction rendered the multiplicity of European states into one EU (or interchangeably, Europe) as an agent with its own idiosyncratic agenda, intentions, and strategies, which as a consequence enabled finger-pointing and blame-switching in narration. The Turkish actors started attributing human characteristics and behaviour to the EU, including jealousy, hypocrisy, deception, and reluctance.

In this context, although still a stable aim, the meaning of Turkey's membership of the EU also changed. It evolved from "something to be achieved", which underlines the EU's normative superiority over Turkey and Turkey's willingness to work for membership, to "something to be taken", which indicates Turkey's long-expected reward from its equivalent counterpart, the EU. Hence, the fact that all Turkish narratives include the official goal of membership does not necessarily suggest that their respective plots are devoid of conflictual elements. On the contrary, *Turkey as the Heir* and *Turkey as a Great Power* narratives both comprise aggression, resentment, and disappointment towards the EU, albeit their commitment to full integration.

As opposed to Turkish narratives, the EU narratives vary in their goals, ranging from *Membership* (mainly, during the 1960s and early 1970s, as well as the period between 1999 and 2005) to the alienation of and separation from Turkey. In some instances, there are even statements referring to the goal of freezing or ending Turkey's accession negotiations, as was the case, for example, in 2016. Furthermore, in the post-2005 period, EU institutions interestingly seemed to refrain from formulating a concrete goal or *finalité* for the EU-Turkey relationship. They instead referred to an "open-ended" accession process. This terminology is often paralleled with arguments underlining Turkey's unique character as an exceptional accession candidate.

The results also indicate that European references to the EU's partnership with Turkey have increased over time. Such a (strategic) partnership reflects the need for continued cooperation with Turkey in light of the country's immutable geostrategic importance for the EU. However, official EU statements analysed within the aforementioned time frame until 2017 do not specify whether such a partnership would replace Turkey's full membership perspective as the main framework of relations. There were, though, individual voices such as former enlargement commissioner Johannes Hahn who in April 2017 stated that he sought a mandate by the member states for a "realistic" and "rational" alternative to the, in his eyes, "artificial debate" over accession.[18]

At the same time, EU actors' perceptions of Turkish identity are also quite diversified. While some narratives (i.e., the *Membership* narrative) portray Turkey as a European country, others assess Turkey as a neighbour to the EU and focus more on its geostrategic importance. In fact, Turkey's strategic importance for the EU is a perception shared by most narratives. Furthermore, perceptions of Turkey as an increasingly alienated partner moving away from European values mark narratives during the 1980s until the mid-1990s as well as in recent years. This change, of course, also needs to be evaluated in light of the growing scepticism among European political elites and publics in several member states towards enlargement generally and Turkey specifically.

Secondly, the impact of time is observable in the construction and evolution of narratives, initially concerning the role of temporality and then as a driver in itself:

Narratives are no ahistorical constructions. The analyses reveal that when narrating the relationship, actors give sense to their (collective) expe-

---

18 Beesley, Arthur. Brussels pressed to rethink Turkey ties. In: Financial Times, 24.04.2017, https://www.ft.com/content/c5e92e7c-28ee-11e7-9ec8-168383da43b7 [10.09.20].

riences retrospectively and, mostly, in a linear fashion. They draw on the past in making sense of the present. Thus, what these actors agonise over and express from multifaceted reality is time-sensitive. Language of the relationship evolves as the joint EU-Turkey history progresses. Turkey of the 1960s is not the same as Turkey under the National Security Council. Similarly, the EU is a project in the making with a capacity to change with each legislative regulation and/or enlargement process. Above all, the setting in which the parties' stories take place changes, for instance, during the Cold War, after 9/11 or in the wake of the 2008 financial crisis. Thus, the substance of the narration alters, especially at critical moments during temporal development. If there are some time-defying elements that transcend different narratives and milestones, they can be interpreted as essential components that will be conceivably carried into future narratives (and not necessarily as universal truth).

The temporal aspects of narratives can most easily be illustrated by the drivers referred to in the plots. In the Turkish narratives, for instance, the lack of stability and reconciliation in the Middle East as well as North Africa appears as a constant positive political driver that prompts Turkish actors to seek closer relations with the EU. This is a piece of reality that defies time from the Turkish perspective, as it is observable in all identified Turkish narratives from the outset of relations. Opposing parties and zones of conflict in the region change throughout the years, but security-related concerns stemming from this turbulence in the broader area find their way into every story narrated by Turkish actors as part of an embedded, durable argument.

Turkish actors' demand for revision of the 1995 Customs Union Decision, though, is a relatively recent negative economic driver that creates tension and distance between Turkey and the EU. Despite longstanding debates over the Customs Union's added value since the 1970s among certain policy circles in Turkey,[19] the agreement's modernisation has only recently become a driver in Turkish narratives. This is due, in part, to the increasing number of free trade agreements being signed or negotiated between the EU and third parties. Especially in light of the Transatlantic Trade and Investment Partnership (TTIP) negotiations between the EU

---

19 Although not included in the dataset, Bülent Ecevit draws attention to a popular slogan from the 1970s, "They're the partners, we're the market", in a 2004 press release, stating that there were people, both from the right and the left, who were sceptical of Turkey's partnership with the EEC during his time as Prime Minister. See Hürriyet. Bülent Ecevit'ten AB Açıklaması. 19 January 2004, https://www.hurriyet.com.tr/gundem/bulent-ecevitten-ab-aciklamasi-196968 [10.09.20].

and the U.S. along with the trade deal negotiations between the UK and EU after Brexit, these agreements seem to have fuelled the said contextual change. Amongst Turkish actors, concerns have been nurtured about compatibility and growing asymmetry in power relations due to the negative welfare effects that these agreements might convey for Turkey.

The role of temporality is especially important when seeking to predict future narratives. The historical approach of the narrative analysis conducted for this chapter reveals that the historical patterns observed in the flow of argumentation may be useful in forecasting future stories' potential constituents. The examples above demonstrate continuous (i.e., regional instability) and discrete (i.e., modernisation of the Customs Union) elements and drivers mentioned in the narratives. In addition, there are cyclical and cumulative arguments observed within and across the narratives over time. For instance, Turkey's identity as a European country is a matter of debate, which over the years has been portrayed in very different ways, ranging between an image of Turkey as European or rather as "the Other". It has evolved in ups and downs, creating a cyclical pattern in shaping how Turkey is perceived and, implicitly, altering the plots and goals of the narratives.

Finally, there are certain arguments that increasingly appear in the narratives over time. For example, debates on the EU's trustworthiness, transparency and eagerness for admitting Turkey as a member have been prevalent since the 1990s. In this context, time becomes prominent as a driver in itself. Turkish actors see it not only as a resource that has been expended in the cause of EU membership but also use it as a unit to compare their situation to that of present and former candidates. Having waited at the EU's door for more than half a century, the exhaustion and frustration of the Turkish actors fuel the questioning of the EU as a reliable partner (in the specific context of membership). The more Turkey waits for membership, the more conflictual Turkish actors' narratives become, which makes elapsed time a cumulative, negative driver, supporting an assumption that it may be a possible component of future stories in the absence of concrete behavioural change from the EU side. Thus, it is likely that similar debates will form part of the narratives as potential drivers in the near future.

Thirdly, the earlier official narratives from Turkey and the EU shared significant similarities whereas the denoted plots and goals of subsequent Turkish and European stories have gradually diverged, causing greater plurality in the debate:

The narrative analysis conducted in this study has generated some conclusions concerning the timing of narratives in a historical context. Although mapping their precise timing is not this chapter's main aim (due to the qualitative nature of present research), Figure 1[20] constructs a chronology of Turkish and EU narratives since the late 1950s, thereby illustrating their salience over time.

This figure highlights the historical trends of debates on both sides over time. Looking at the plots and goals of the dominant narratives on both sides, it can be concluded that the 1960s and the early 1970s saw a harmony, or convergence, of narratives from Turkey and the EU. In Europe, Turkey's accession to the European Economic Community was expressed as the final goal of the association agreement and the Customs Union. When compared with the current context of EU-Turkey relations, it is surprising to observe how clearly European actors voiced their support for Turkey at the time. However, this kind of rhetoric has to be interpreted against a background of the Cold War and Turkey's strategic importance as a NATO ally. Similarly, Turkish actors argued along the lines of *Westernisation* and *Europeanisation* narratives during this time. Hence, narratives from the EU and Turkey did converge around the goal of Turkey's accession.

With the 1980 military coup in Turkey, the debate became more differentiated, in that we can identify an end to harmonious narratives. Elements of the conflict-related *Distant Neighbour* narrative – particularly, European criticism of Turkey's military rule and human rights violations – infiltrated EU's discourse, entering a certain degree of alienation into the relationship. While Turkey went back to civilian rule in 1983 and submitted an (unsuccessful) application for membership in 1987, EU's attention at the end of the 1980s and in the 1990s was instead targeting states from Eastern and Central Europe for future enlargement. Turkey was rather perceived as a special EU applicant state. Hence, the formal goal of membership dropped out of the official European discourse.

---

20 A more detailed version of this figure, which indicates whether at any given time narratives in debates converge, cooperate or conflict with each other (as outlined in the three ideal-type scenarios could be found in Hauge et al. Narratives of a Contested Relationship.

Figure 1: Timeline

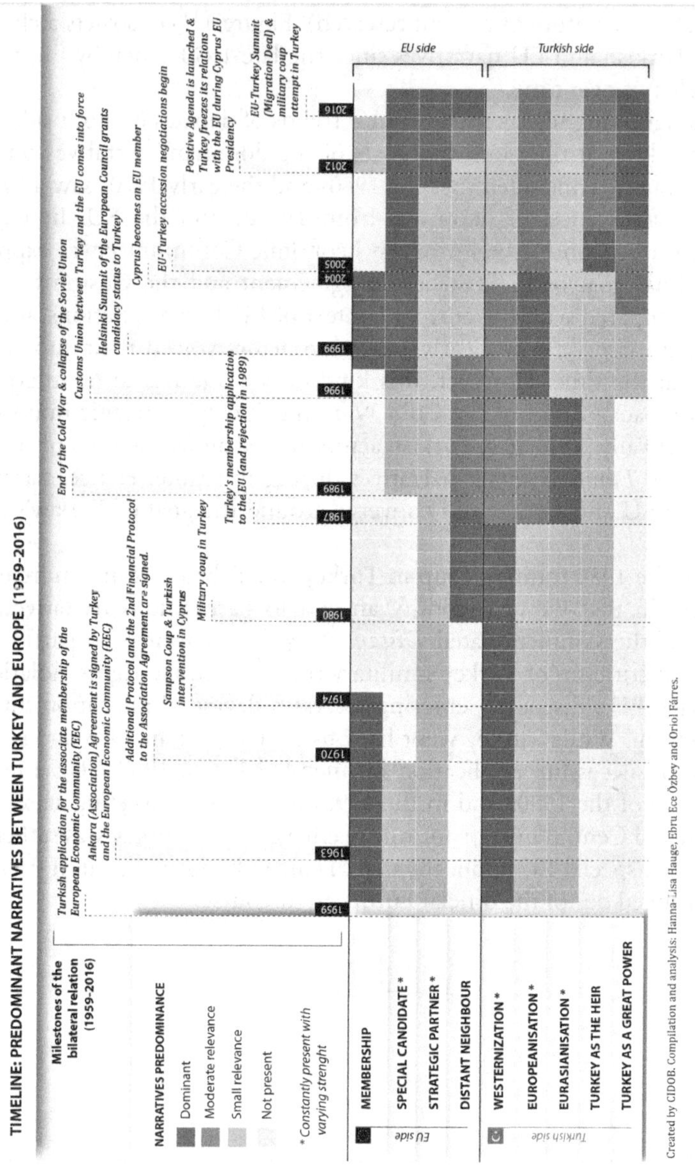

TIMELINE: PREDOMINANT NARRATIVES BETWEEN TURKEY AND EUROPE (1959-2016)

Created by: CIDOB. Compilation & analysis: Hanna-Lisa Hauge, Ebru Ece Özbey & Oriol Farrés.

In Turkey, global changes following the Soviet Union's collapse also influenced discourse, seeing especially the rise of *Eurasianisation* narrative. In particular, following the Luxembourg European Council's decision to deny Turkey candidacy status in 1997, Turkey's hopes for an influential role as a future Community member were crushed. At the same time, *Turkey as a Special Candidate* narrative started to dominate European politics, as illustrated by the "European Strategy" that was specially proposed for Turkey.

A turning point was the EU's 1999 Helsinki Decision granting Turkey candidacy status, which drastically changed narratives and led to a short period of greater harmony. On the EU side, *Membership* narrative regained lost ground, at least temporarily, until accession negotiations officially began in 2005. Despite their post-Luxembourg disappointment and frustration about EU's sincerity for Turkish accession, Turkish actors went back to voicing their enthusiasm for membership. Unfortunately, this positive atmosphere did not last long as the Cyprus conundrum triggered a (still persistent) deadlock in accession negotiations.

Since then, European and Turkish narratives have become increasingly conflictual, particularly in recent years. The EU's perception of Turkey moving away from democratic values has solidified, generating official criticism especially following the purges ensuing the July 2016 attempted coup. Overall, increasing representations of *Distant Neighbour* narrative have characterised EU discourse in the period since 2016. At the same time, European arguments linking to *Turkey as a Strategic Partner* narrative have persisted and gathered momentum as Turkey is still perceived as a highly important (geo-)strategic partner, at least as much as it has been in the preceding decades.

In Turkey itself, narratives testifying conflictual elements have increased. As demonstrated by *Turkey as the Heir* and *Turkey as a Great Power* narratives, Turkish actors have been perceiving the EU's image to have changed radically and for the worse. Notions such as normative superiority of the West or the EU no longer mark these narratives. The Union's trustworthiness and credibility are being questioned, which makes Turkish actors' discourse more intolerant and aggressive towards the EU, with the EU-Turkey relationship itself being seen as more fragile. In parallel with Turkey's prolonged EU candidacy, the increasing number and variety of drivers along with the persistent lack of a clear roadmap for membership, antagonism and polarisation have gradually gained prominence in the narratives. The rhetoric of "Us" vs "Them", which positions Turkey and the EU on opposing sides (as opposed to one common front pursuing one joint goal) has grown. Consequently, despite the repeated official emphasis on Turkey's indispensable and indisputable EU membership goal, stories provided by the Turkish actors' discourses are indicative of conflict rather than convergence.

5. Conclusion: A Mix of Conflict and Mutual Dependence

This chapter has inquired EU-Turkey relations with a novel, empirical and narrative-based approach relying on a comparative qualitative analysis of a uniquely comprehensive dataset from the EU and Turkey. It has paid a particular attention to the analysis of continuity and change in Turkish and EU narratives, which is guided by the assumption that enduring issues, perceptions, or arguments, should they be identified in the past and present narratives, would also be likely to remain constituents of future narratives due to their persistent relevance.

Linked to that, an important question that arises is whether one narrative has dominated over time and will therefore likely do so in the future. Indeed, there are several historical patterns in the flow of argumentation in both Turkish and European narratives. Yet, while there are certain persistent elements within the identified narratives (i.e., goals or perceptions), the analysis does not confirm the presence of one singular and comprehensive enduring dominant narrative on either side. On the contrary, the study shows that debates on both sides have rather grown more divergent and multifaceted.

On Turkey's side, the most important continuous element is seen as a proclamation of EU membership as the official goal. What does this suggest for the relationship's future? Primarily, it indicates that membership is likely to endure as a cornerstone of future Turkish narratives. Additionally, this makes a potential transformation of the EU's official narrative from Turkish membership towards some other form of strategic partnership or cooperation more problematic. No alternative end goal proposed by the EU in lieu of accession is anticipated to resonate on the other side, in that Turkish actors will persist with their perpetual goal of membership.

On the EU side, despite the shifting goals expressed by EU actors concerning a future relationship framework, the perception of Turkey's geostrategic significance has historically featured heavily in discourse, which is therefore likely to persist in the future, along with a resulting realisation that cooperation with Turkey is a necessity. Indeed, our analysis demonstrates that in recent years, representations of Turkey as a *Strategic Partner* narrative have remained influential despite growing dismay and conflict between the EU and Turkey. Notwithstanding EU criticism of political developments in Turkey, European institutions still stress Turkey's importance as a key collaborator and partner.

Another critical factor that is likely to influence the future is the constellations of present narratives. In other words, do the EU's and Turkey's present narratives link to any of the ideal-type scenarios (conflict, cooperation, or convergence) for the future of EU-Turkey relations? A key conclusion to be drawn from this research with repercussions for future debates is that since 2015 the political rhetoric on both sides has turned relatively contentious in comparison to the earlier period of EU-Turkey relations. Observers are aware that relational conflict is nothing new, and the "rocky"[21] and "cyclical"[22] character of EU-Turkey relations has, in part, become normality for some time now. Elements of conflict and diplomatic crises can come and go given that an "oscillation and coexistence between conflict and convergence captures the very essence of the (un)steady state of Turkey's place in Europe"[23].

Yet, the level of escalation since 2015 is high and seems likely to persist into the near future, particularly in the light of the recent socio-political turmoil and economic hardship in Turkey, which have been paralleled by rising populism and opposition to Turkish membership within the EU institutions as well as member states. Being limited to a dataset that ends in 2017, this study lacks the systematic analysis of the European and Turkish stories from the last couple of years. Notwithstanding these limitations, both the developments and the concurrent discourses on both sides seem to be in line with the study's conclusions. While the European Parliament's resolution demanding a suspension of accession in March 2019[24] represents arguably the highest level of escalation in EU institutions' discourse, Turkish actors also exhibit a growingly aggressive approach, hence more antagonistic "Us" vs "Them" language. This indicates, with a note of caution, that narratives on both sides are likely to feature conflict for some time. Further investigation of the post-2017 narratives could help us to establish a greater degree of accuracy on this matter.

---

21 Müftüler-Baç, Turkey's future with the European Union, p. 1.
22 Narbone, Luigi/ Tocci, Nathalie. Running in circles? The cyclical relationship between Turkey and the European Union. In: Journal of Southern Europe and the Balkans, November 2009, Vol. 9, No. 3, p. 233-246.
23 Tocci, Nathalie. Beyond the Storm in EU-Turkey Relations. FEUTURE Voice No. 4, January 2018, p. 2.
24 European Parliament. European Parliament resolution of 13 March 2019 on the 2018 Commission Report on Turkey. 2018/2150(INI), Strasbourg, 2019.

In closing, this chapter concludes that a mixture of conflictual and pro-cooperation elements is likely to mark both sides' future debates. Despite recurring escalating tensions, which have also characterised the relationship's history, results from our narrative analysis indicate that the EU and Turkey ultimately perceive each other as key partners, with emphasis on the need to cooperate in a variety of policy fields.

Contested Identities: Historicising and Deconstructing Representations in EU-Turkey Relations

Senem Aydın-Düzgit, Bahar Rumelili

1. Introduction

One fundamental, if not the most significant, issue which underlies the EU-Turkey relationship is identity. Far too often, academics and policy-makers have highlighted perceived identity differences as stumbling blocks in relations between the two sides. It was widely claimed that Turkey is not sufficiently European for membership in the EU and/or Turkey's self-perception was at best ambivalent towards Europe.

In this chapter, we aim to deconstruct and contest these generalising claims. We adopt a post-structuralist conception of identity where identity is not a fixed set of objectively given characteristics that actors possess, but it is rather produced through the ways in which they discursively represent each other. We claim that these mutual identity representations in the case of Turkey and Europe[1] have been and continue to be contested within both settings, across different time periods and in relation to different focal issues which arise in the context of key political and cultural drivers. A historical perspective is indispensable in the identity and culture realm for two reasons. Firstly, scenarios about the future of EU-Turkey identity and cultural relations that are based solely on contemporary discourses are likely to be misleading. Recent public discourses in Europe characterise Turkish and European identities as dichotomous and in opposition. However, this assessment is based on a fixed and static understanding of identity that does not take into account the extent to which identities are multi-layered and changing. Secondly, a historical outlook is necessary because identity representations draw from both past and present repertoires in their construction. This is particularly the case for relations between Turkey and Europe where identity-based perceptions have been a key component since the 18th century.

---

1 Since our analysis covers the evolution of mutual identity perceptions both before and after the formation of the EU, we refer to relations between Turkey and Europe rather than Turkey and the EU.

We conducted a historical analysis of representations from 1839 to 1999, which allowed us to identify evolutionary discourse patterns in the form of structural path dependencies, critical junctures and incremental changes through layering. Overall, this analysis attests to the fluidity and frequent ruptures in identity representations on both European and Turkish sides, thereby providing a corrective to simplistic readings of the relationship as one of continuous differentiation and exclusion, mainly on cultural and religious grounds. It also allows us to highlight the link between a wider set of drivers and scenarios, thus identifying highly unlikely but deeply disruptive events – so-called 'wild cards'. In this way, we can also assess the time period of impact (short-term or long-term) for the different categories of drivers. The contemporary analysis of post-1999 representations focuses on processes which have impacted the relationship more recently and are likely to do so in the near future. Our analysis of regional and global representations indicates the broader frameworks of meanings that structure the identity and culture dimension of EU-Turkey relations.

In this chapter, scenarios for the future of EU-Turkey relations are defined with respect to particular identity representations that dominate European and Turkish discourse. Firstly, the conflict scenario entails reciprocal representations of the Other as homogeneous, inherently and antithetically different, socially distant and threatening to Self. Secondly, the cooperation scenario generates reciprocal representations of the Other as heterogeneous, non-threateningly different in a way that allows for co-existence and mutual recognition. Thirdly, the convergence scenario comprises reciprocal representations of the Other as (the existing or on the path to becoming) part of a common/shared identity and thus validating of Self. These are ideal-type scenarios, since identity representations are always contested and hence can never exist in pure form.

Our historical analysis reveals that dialectical transitions between these three sets of representations (from conflict to cooperation or convergence and vice versa) have occurred on many occasions over time in response to different political and cultural drivers. Such transitions are facilitated by ongoing contestation over identity representations both in Turkey and Europe. While one set of representations is dominant, others remain dormant in the cultural repertoire, ready to be activated when conditions are ripe. Contemporary analysis shows, for instance, that after 2013 the conflict representation set has become dominant in EU-Turkey relations. Hence, by linking findings from the historical and contemporary analyses, a relevant question in identifying futurescenarios is when we can expect the next transition to the cooperation or convergence representation sets (as indicated by historical patterns). Which set of drivers are likely to steer continuity of the conflict representation set in the foreseeable future and possibly beyond? Furthermore, which set of events are likely to drive the dialectical transition towards cooperation or convergence?

This chapter adopts the concept of driver to denote key political and cultural events that have triggered and shaped identity representations, given that in line with our post-structuralist conception we claim that identities are instantiated through discursive representations. Hence, we consider events that trigger identity debates and discussions in EU-Turkey relations as identity drivers. Hence, our study has analysed identity representations triggered by twenty key events in the history of Turkey-Europe relations. Focal issues are those with respect to which Europe (or Turkey) constitutes its identity by comparing itself with and/or differentiating itself from its significant Other, that is Turkey (or Europe). We have identified that the mutual identity representations in Turkey-Europe relations, triggered by different political and cultural events, have predominantly focused on four focal issues, namely: nationalism, status in international society, state-citizen relations and civilisation. We have analysed how different drivers have triggered the differentiation of Turkish and European identities from one another with respect to civilisation, status in international society, nationalism and state-society relations. Yet, the definition and salience of these focal issues have varied over time and in relation to the drivers involved. A particular event (X) may trigger identity representations where Europe and Turkey compare their identities and establish their differences around focal issue A, while another event (Y) may trigger representations that focus on other issues (B, C). In this sense, the events which are treated as drivers were found in conceptual terms to have a bearing on at least one of these focal issues.

In the next section, historical drivers and their links with ideal types and future scenarios will be discussed. Subsequently, contemporary drivers at EU-Turkey, regional and global levels will be identified. The penultimate section will link our findings from the historical and contemporary analyses.

2. Historical Drivers

2.1 Focal Issues and Scenarios

Our historical analysis is based on the study of identity representations surrounding a total of twenty key events. We start with proclamation of the Tanzimat Edict in 1839, which was a major reform step towards aligning state-society relations in the Ottoman Empire with European standards of civilisation. We then analyse identity representations pertaining to the relatively extensive and domestically controversial 1856 Reform Edict that was proclaimed just prior to the Paris Conference that concluded the Crimean War, during which England and France had allied with the Ottoman Empire. Our third event is Abdülaziz's visit to Europe in 1866, which was the first peaceful visit of an Ottoman Sultan to Europe. Thereafter, we evaluate identity representations around the Cretan Insurrection of 1866-69, where European states supported Ottoman territorial integrity against Greek rebels. Our fifth event features acts of violence committed against the Armenian population during 1894-96, known as the Hamidian massacres, which triggered a turn toward negative representations of the Ottoman Empire in Europe, although Ottomans at the time insisted on their sovereign right to discipline unruly subjects. The final event in this Ottoman period is the March 31st revolt which was suppressed by the Committee of Union and Progress. This subsequently led to the deposition of Abdülhamid II.

Following the establishment of the Republic of Turkey, we have analysed how the radical Europeanising reforms of Kemal Atatürk shaped Turco-European identity representations in the context of events surrounding the abolition of the Caliphate in 1924 and adoption of the Latin Alphabet in 1928. We also assessed the effects of Turkey's progress in gender equality on identity representations, focusing on events such as a Turkish woman's victory in the 1932 Miss Universe contest and the convening of an international women's rights congress in Istanbul during 1935. Considering the rise in European nationalism which led to the Second World War, we looked at how identity representations were affected by: Turkey's successful gaining of control over the Straits through international legal means presented by the 1936 Montreux Convention; and the annexation of Austria by Nazi Germany.

In the early post-war period, we analysed Turkey's membership within the Council of Europe in 1949 as a marker of Turkey's commitment to European integration and the military coup of 1960 as an instance of domestic political instability in Turkey. Subsequently, we studied identity debates surrounding the 1978 release of the American film Midnight Express, whose negative depiction of the Turks and Turkish prison systems provoked widespread anti-Western nationalist reactions in Turkey. In 1981, the attempted assassination of Pope Jean Paul II by Turkish national Mehmet Ali Ağca served to differentiate Turkish and European identities along religious lines. Accordingly, by looking at subsequent events such as the Madımak hotel fire in 1993 and the Islamist Welfare Party's success in the December 1995 general elections, we analysed how the division of Turkish politics into Islamist and secular camps resonated in Europe. In this period, we also focused on how the rise of anti-immigrant xenophobia in Europe shaped identity constructions in Turkey and Europe by evaluating the 1993 arson attack against Turkish workers in Solingen, Germany. Finally, the 1995 Bosnian Genocide in Srebrenica constitutes the last major event triggering widespread identity debates before declaration of Turkey's EU candidacy in 1999.

Table 1: Historical Analysis of Identity and Culture Drivers in Terms of Relevance, Impact and Scenarios

Date	Drivers	Relevance	Impact[2]	Focal Issue	Ideal-type scenario
1839	Tanzimat Edict	TR/Europe	LT	civilisation state-society	convergence
1856	Reform Edict and the Paris Conference	TR/Europe	LT	civilisation status in IS[3]	convergence
1866-7	Sultan Abdülaziz's visit to Europe	Europe/TR	ST	civilisation status in IS	convergence
1866-9	The Cretan insurrection	TR/Europe	ST	state-society status in IS	cooperation
1894-6	The Hamidian massacres	Europe/TR	LT	state-society civilisation	conflict
1909	Abdülhamit's deposition	TR/Europe	ST	state-society nationalism	conflict
1924	Abolition of the Caliphate	TR/Europe	LT	civilisation state-society status in IS	convergence/ cooperation
1928	Adoption of the Latin Alphabet in Turkey	TR/Europe	LT	civilisation status in IS	convergence/ cooperation
1932	Keriman Halis' victory in the Miss Universe competition	TR/Europe	ST	civilisation nationalism status in IS	convergence/ cooperation
1935	Congress of the International Alliance for Women held in Istanbul	TR/Europe	ST	civilisation state-society	convergence

---

2 LT and ST refer to long-term and short-term impact, respectively.
3 IS stands for International Society.

Date	Drivers	Relevance	Impact	Focal Issue	Ideal-type scenario
1936	Montreux Convention	Europe/TR	ST	nationalism status in IS	cooperation
1938	Nazi Germany's Annexation of Austria	TR	ST	nationalism status in IS	cooperation
1949	Turkey's membership in the Council of Europe	Europe/TR	LT	civilisation status in IS	convergence/ cooperation
1960	Military Coup in Turkey	TR/Europe	ST	state-society status in IS	cooperation
1978	Release of the film Midnight Express	TR/Europe	LT	nationalism civilisation status in IS	conflict
1981	Attempted assassination of Pope Jean Paul II by Mehmet Ali Ağca	Europe/TR	ST	civilisation nationalism status in IS	conflict/ cooperation
1993	The Solingen arson attack against Turkish workers	Europe/TR	LT	nationalism civilisation status in IS	conflict
1993	Madımak Hotel fire in Turkey	Europe	ST	state-society nationalism	conflict
1995	Welfare Party's electoral success	Europe/TR	LT	civilisation nationalism	conflict
1995	The Bosnian Genocide	TR	LT	civilisation nationalism status in IS	conflict

Source: Own compilation.

Table 1 indicates our assessment of: (1) relevance - whether the event had relevance for identity representations in Turkey, Europe or both, (2) the event's short- or long-term impact, (3) focal issues invoked by the event, (4) the nature of identity representations invoked by the event in terms of our three futurescenarios. Regarding relevance, all twenty events were found to be concerned with identity debates on the European and/or the Turkish side, as indicated by the extent of identity representations triggered by this event in European and Turkish newspapers at the time. While some events sparked identity representations only in Turkey (TR) or Europe, the majority (in total, seventeen) had relevance in terms of (re)producing identity representations on both sides. In terms of impact, our analysis reveals both a shorter-term and a longer-term relationship between events as drivers, focal issues and ideal-type scenarios. In the shorter-term relationship, each event drives identity representations in a certain direction within its own historical context, with varying degrees of relevance and impact. Some events, though, also have a longer-term, cumulative effect on focal issues and continue to be invoked in the identity debates triggered by later events which are linked to the same focal issues. Such events are indicated as long-term drivers in Table 1. Additionally, all of these events were found to relate conceptually to at least one of the four focal issues of civilisation, nationalism, status in international society and state-society relations. As Table 1 demonstrates, the focal issues which are invoked in Turco-European identity debates change over time and in the context of different events. Furthermore, instead of a unilinear evolution toward conflict or convergence, there have been a number of shifts from conflict to cooperation and convergence, along with the reverse, within this timeframe.

2.2 Patterns and Shifts

Our historical analysis reveals that identity representations oscillate between the two extreme poles of conflict and convergence, while cooperation is relatively rare. In other words, Turkish and European identity representations are more likely to portray the Other as either antithetically different and threatening or as sharing a common identity rather than viewing each other as a partner that is non-threateningly different. As underlined by the key international relations literature on identity construction,[4] identity is constituted in relation to difference, which is also the case in Turco-European identity relations. Thus, Turkey is discursively constructed as a significant Other for Europe, with Europe being constructed as a significant Other for Turkey. Whilst not intrinsically related to identity concerns, our analysis reveals that political and cultural events ranging from military coups to beauty contests have on occasions triggered identity differentiations between Turkey and Europe. Yet, issues from which the differences were constructed and the relationship of superiority/inferiority/equality thereby bestowed on Turkey and Europe, varied considerably across time and space. While some events triggered representations of Turkey in Europe as antithetically different from Europe, others portrayed Turkey as becoming European. Conversely, while some events engendered

---

4 Rumelili, Bahar. Constructing Identity and Relating it to Difference. Understanding the EU's Mode of Differentiation. In: Review of International Studies, January 2004, Vol. 30, No. 1, pp. 27-47.

representations of Europe in Turkey as the model to emulate, others created representations of Europe as a threat. Thus, either party's dependence on the Other's difference in order to construct its identity fostered either conflict or convergence, depending on the constructed difference's nature.

That most analysed events were relevant in identity terms both in Europe and Turkey is a product of the political and cultural intimacy between the two parties. As political and cultural relations intensify, events that have little bearing on the bilateral relationship and concern only one side can trigger identity discussions and differentiation in both parties. Indeed, identity debates have become increasingly interactive and dialogical so that either side is aware of how its identity is being portrayed by the Other and responds accordingly. This also supports the polarisation of the Turco-European identity relationship either towards conflict or convergence. In most of the events being studied, identity representations in Turkey and Europe were reciprocal, leading to their simultaneous support of the conflict or convergence scenarios.

As indicated in Table 1, there have been four major transitions in identity representations. Firstly, a transition from convergence to conflict occurs in response to the Hamidian massacres and is sustained with Sultan Abdülhamit's deposition. Secondly, conflict gives way to cooperation/convergence in the period after the establishment of the Turkish Republic and remains intact well into the 1970s, as observed in the mutual representations incurred over key events such as: adoption of the Latin Alphabet; Keriman Halis' victory in the Miss Universe Contest; the Montreux Convention; Germany's annexation of Austria *(Anschluss)*; Turkey's membership in the Council of Europe; and the 1960 military intervention. Thirdly, convergence/cooperation shifts back to conflict in the 1970s and lasts until the late 1990s through key cultural events such as release of the film Midnight Express, sustained later by political events such as the attempted assassination of the Pope, the Solingen tragedy and the rise of political Islam in Turkey. Fourthly, conflict turns to convergence/cooperation following Turkey's receipt of EU candidacy status in 1999.

Rapid shifts in identity representations from conflict to convergence or vice versa occurred mainly against the backdrop of major geopolitical changes or shifting patterns of alliances. Cooperation between Europe and Turkey against a common enemy generated a shift toward convergence or cooperation. This was the case during the Crimean War when the Ottoman Empire allied with Britain and France against Russia, as well as during the signing of the Montreux Convention in 1936. We evaluate the former in regard to the driver, 'Reform Edict and the Paris Conference'. Such cooperation was most visible during the Cold War when there was more institutionalised and stable political collaboration as well as security coop-eration between Turkey and European states within the framework of NATO, the Council of Europe and Turkey's membership bid to the EU, which are analysed in relation to the driver, 'Turkey's membership in the Council of Europe'.

Conversely, a lack of European support for Turkey against security threats concerning its territorial integrity, facilitated shifts towards con-flictual identity representations in Turkey. For example, Turkish percep-tions of European involvement in the Hamidian massacres fostered repre-sentations of Europe as a potential destabiliser to the Ottoman/Turkish Self on the basis of political and territorial concerns.[5] This shows that when Ottoman security was not served by cooperation with European states, internal debates about the suitability and risks of European civilisa-tional intrusion become paramount. In fact, similar debates erupted in Turkey during the late 1960s and 1970s over the Cyprus conflict and the same pattern was observed in relation to Turkey's intensifying conflict with the PKK in the 1990s.

We have found that the key issue of civilisation lies at the forefront of Europe-Turkey relations. Over time, conceptions of civilisation in mutual relations have changed. During Sultan Abdülaziz's visit to Europe in 1866-1867, civilisation was conceived as a single notion joining Europe with Turkey. However, following the First World War, a gradual transition to a conception of multiple civilisations positioning Europe and Turkey in different cultural spheres emerged. The differentiation of Turkish and European identities on the basis of civilisation can support conflict or co-operation, depending on the way in which it is employed. The conflict sce-nario appears, for instance, when a binary civilisationist discourse is trig-gered by key events such as: Islamist terror attacks in the West; the rise of fundamentalism, violation of religious freedom in Muslim countries; racism towards Muslim immigrants in Europe/West; and humanitarian crises in Muslim countries that are overlooked in Europe/West. A notable example is the post-Cold War rise of the "clash of civilisations" paradigm[6], which was strengthened by conflicts in the Balkans and the rise of political Islam in Turkey. Analysis of events such as the 1981 attempted assassina-tion of Pope Jean Paul II and the Welfare Party's 1995 electoral success

---

5 Aydın-Düzgit, Senem et al. Turkish and European Identity Constructions in the 1815-1945 Period. FEUTURE Online Paper No. 4, July 2017.
6 Bottici, Chiara/ Challand, Benoit. The Myth of the Clash of Civilisations. New York and Abingdon, 2010; Huntington, Samuel. The Clash of Civilisations and the Remaking of the World Order. 1st ed., New York, 1996.

highlights how far this paradigm strengthened the salience of the civilisational focal issue in both Turkish and European identity representations and helped construct the identities of 'Christian' Europe and 'Muslim' Turkey as mutually incompatible and antagonistic. Later, the same civilisational paradigm was also promoted by certain political circles in Europe and Turkey insisting that Turkey's membership of the EU is necessary to prevent a clash of civilisations, thus in support of closer relations between Europe and Turkey.[7] Regardless of whether civilisation is invoked to distance Turkey from Europe or to promote closer relations with Turkey, the multiplicity of civilisations is highlighted, with Turkey being situated within a different Eastern civilisation.

Like civilisation, status in international society is remarkably persistent as a focal issue in Turco-European identity debates. How each side perceives the other's status within international society in material and normative terms is a constant theme in identity representations. When Turkey's normative status in international society is questioned as in the Hamidian Massacres or during the 1978 release of Midnight Express, this gives way to the conflict scenario by triggering representations in Turkey of Europe (and also the West in general) not only as inimically opposed to Turkey, but also constituting a threat.[8] However, the recognition in Europe of Turkey's equal normative status, as in cases where prominent Turkish figures are granted European/international awards (e.g., Keriman Halis' victory in the Miss Universe beauty contest),[9] triggers positive representations of Europe as a model in Turkey.

While most of the identity comparisons between Turkey and Europe have focused on Turkey's status in international society, crises in Europe have historically triggered representations of Europe as a declining actor in Turkey. For example, the rise of nationalism in Europe prior to the Second World War (analysed with regard to the drivers of Germany annexing Austria and the Montreux Convention) led to increasingly negative perceptions in Turkey of the European Other as weaker and inferior to the Turk-

---

7 Baban, Feyzi/ Keyman, Fuat. Turkey and Postnational Europe. Challenges for the Cosmopolitan Political Community. In: European Journal of Social Theory, February 2008, Vol. 11, No. 1, pp. 107-124.

8 Aydın-Düzgit, Senem et al. Turkish and European Identity Constructions in the 1945-1999 Period. FEUTURE Online Paper No. 15, March 2018.

9 Aydın-Düzgit et al., Turkish and European Identity Constructions in the 1945-1999 Period.

ish Self.[10] In the early 1990s, racist attacks toward Turkish immigrants in Germany and European inaction during the Balkan conflict (analysed respectively with regard to the drivers of the Solingen arson attack and the Srebrenica Massacre)[11] similarly triggered representations of Europe as a declining power in Turkey.

The historical analysis also reveals that nationalism became increasingly salient as a focal issue in Turco-European identity relations over time. During the early republican era, pro-European nationalism was the dominant form in Turkey and, as evident in the identity representations triggered by events such as the 1928 adoption of the Latin Alphabet, this form of Turkish nationalism promoted identity convergence between Europe and Turkey. In contrast, the post-1950 transition to multi-party politics and the post-1970 left-right polarisation in Turkey resulted in a growing divergence of Turkish views on Europe, leading to the transition from pro-European to anti-European nationalism supported by both the radical left and right. Consequently, the invocation of nationalist tropes and myths in Turkey was accompanied with representations of the European Other as inherently antagonistic towards Turkey. Anti-European nationalism in Turkey has been triggered at times by alienation from Europe/West, as happened when Midnight Express was released. Nationalism in Europe has been a relevant key issue in identity representations both during the interwar period and following the rise of anti-immigrant nationalism directed mainly against the Turkish migrants in Germany in the 1980s and early 1990s.[12] As shown by the analysis of drivers such as Germany's Annexation of Austria and the Solingen arson attacks, nationalism in Europe has hardened identity differentiation between Turkey and Europe, and generated Turkish perceptions of Europe as morally inferior.

Finally, the salience of state-society relations as a focal issue in Turco-European identity representations has varied in line with the extent of domestic discontent and polarisation in Turkey. As evident in the analysis of drivers such as the Hamidian Massacres, the 1960 military coup and the Madımak hotel fire, political instability, civil conflict, and identity-based tensions within Turkey have given way to identity representations in Europe that depict Turkey as a country torn between conflicting identities and

---

10 Aydın-Düzgit et al., Turkish and European Identity Constructions in the 1815-1945 Period.
11 Aydın-Düzgit et al., Turkish and European Identity Constructions in the 1946-1999 Period.
12 Kaya, Ayhan. Sicher in Kreuzberg. Constructing Diasporas. Turkish Hip-Hop Youth in Berlin. Bielefeld, 2001.

as inferior to Europe in terms of democratic standards, sometimes verging on the barbaric. As is also the case today, the level of domestic contestation over Europe[13] has always risen with domestic discontent and polarisation in Turkey during different historical periods. As mentioned above, the post-1950 transition to multi-party politics and post-1970 left-right polarisation in Turkey have resulted in a growing divergence of views on Europe. The transition from pro-European to anti-European nationalism in this period was supported by both the radical left and right which also took part in fragile coalition governments at the time. As the Turkish political scene diversified with the rise of right-wing nationalism and political Islam, so the essentially conflictual representation of Turkish and European identities rose, which was illustrated by Turkish reactions to Midnight Express, Srebrenica and Erbakan's rise to power.[14] However, domestic contestation and polarisation can support the conflict or the convergence scenario, depending on shifting power dynamics in Turkish politics and society. At times, the anti-European rhetoric adopted by the government has triggered a pro-European discourse among oppositional forces in society.[15]

3. Contemporary Drivers

In the post-1999 period, multiple events have driven identity debates in EU-Turkey relations and hence our analysis has highlighted various categories of drivers on the Turkish and European sides. These drivers show the continuing relevance of the four focal issues. In regard to shaping European representations of Turkey,[16] important triggers include the domestic debates on integration, security, religion and identity, especially in the post-9/11 era. These debates in turn are often reflected in specific representational stances. This shows the endurance of civilisation as a focal issue in the contemporary era, shaped around an understanding of multiple and

---

13 Erdoğan, Emre/ Uyan-Semerci, Pınar. Fanusta Diyaloglar. Türkiye'de Kutuplaşmanın Boyutları. İstanbul, 2018.
14 Aydın-Düzgit et al., Turkish and European Identity Constructions in the 1946-1999 Period.
15 Aydın-Düzgit, Senem. Legitimising Europe in Contested Settings. Europe as a Normative Power in Turkey. In: Journal of Common Market Studies, October 2018, Vol. 56, No. 3, p. 612-627.
16 Ergun, Doruk et al. The Role of the Middle East in the EU-Turkey Security Relationship. Key Drivers and Future Scenarios. FEUTURE Online Paper No. 20, May 2018.

incompatible civilisations. Furthermore, European discussions about the direction of Turkish foreign policy and its alignment with European foreign policy objectives have triggered identity-related representations of Turkey. Especially significant were the representations in European foreign policy discourse of Turkey as a 'model' country to the Caucasus in the 1990s, a non-violent Muslim majority country after 9/11, a well-functioning market economy following the 2008 Euro crisis and a model secular democracy to the Arab Spring countries in 2011, all of which have bestowed Turkey with a liminal identity as a "bridge", "gate" or "alliance" between civilisations.[17] Until 2013, this went hand in hand with Turkey's rising status in international society as an emerging economy and a soft power. Additionally, identity-related European representations of Turkey were shaped by debates on the EU's future. Accordingly, those countries in continental Europe that are in favour of deeper integration have been sceptical about Turkish identity and its possible place within the Union in comparison to others such as the UK, which have supported a wider and more porous cooperation.[18] This deepening and widening debate is linked with the question of Europe's status in international society. Finally, events pertaining to domestic conflict and instability in Turkey have impacted European identity-related representations of Turkey. Similar to the results of the historical analysis, such developments engendered differentiations of Turkish and European identities on the basis of key issues such as 'state-society relations' and 'status in international society'. Most notable is the steep increase in perceptions of differing political cultures, especially following the highly publicised Gezi protests of 2013. Similarly, Turkish tendencies towards majoritarianism and outright authoritarianism were perceived as incompatible with Europe's political culture.[19]

---

17 Rumelili, Bahar. Modeling Democracy. Western Hegemony, Turkey and the Middle East. In: Morozov, Viatcheslav (eds). Decentering the West. The Idea of Democracy and the Struggle for Hegemony. Abingdon, 2013; Rumelili, Bahar. Liminal Identities and Processes of Domestication and Subversion in International Relations. In: Review of International Studies, April 2012, Vol. 38, No. 2, p. 495-508.

18 Tocci, Nathalie. Conditionality, Impact and Prejudice in EU–Turkey Relations. Rome, 2007.

19 For some examples of texts, where such representations figure prominently, see Aydın-Düzgit, Senem. Türklük, Müslümanlık, Doğululuk. AB'nin Türkiye Söylemleri. İstanbul, 2015.

In Turkey, identity-related representations of Europe have in turn been driven by a number of contemporary developments.[20] Firstly, domestic debates on the roles of politics and religion in Turkish society have been a key driver. Initially, conservative backers of the Justice and Development Party (AKP) government saw the EU as a source of religious freedom — especially for women to wear the headscarf (the türban) at university and in public jobs — while the old Kemalist elite perceived the EU as the catalyst for rising Islamism in Turkey. This later changed due to a growing sentiment in the new AKP elite that Europe was an exclusivist "Christian club".[21] Particularly instrumental in perpetrating this view was the European Court of Human Rights' (ECtHR) 2005 decision on the Leyla Şahin case and scathing EU criticism of a 2007 Turkish attempt to criminalise adultery. Secondly, domestic political contentions surrounding implementation of the EU's membership conditions have engendered identity representations. Turkey's secular nationalists have seen in the EU accession process' conditionality a re-enactment of the "Sèvres Syndrome",[22] a fear that Western countries are plotting against Turkey's national integrity through the support of internal collaborators such as the Kurds and non-Muslim minorities as they allegedly did with the 1920 Sèvres Treaty. At first aloof from this fear, the AKP has also arguably adopted (and adapted) this position. These two drivers are associated with anti-European nationalism in Turkey. Thirdly, Turkey's turns on foreign policy constitute a key driver of identity-based representations by the EU.[23] This was evident after the advent of the 2002 AKP government in the form of closer relations with the Middle East and as a result of more recent reversals in the AKP's foreign policy outlook, such as its frequent overtures towards Russia.

The identity dimension of EU-Turkey relations is also shaped by representations at regional and global levels.[24] These have been analysed in terms of seven key events in EU-Turkey relations covered in the Egyptian,

---

20 Lindgaard, Jakob et al. Turkey in European Identity Debates. Key Drivers and Future Scenarios. FEUTURE Online Paper No. 19, April 2019.

21 Kaya, Ayhan/ Marchetti, Raffaele. Europeanization, Framing Competition and Civil Society in the EU and Turkey. Rome, 2014, p. 8.

22 Yılmaz, Hakan. Euroscepticism in Turkey. Parties, Elites and Public Opinion. In: South European Society and Politics, February 2011, Vol. 16, No. 1, pp. 185-208.

23 Rumelili, Bahar. Turkey. Identity, Foreign Policy, and Socialization in post-Enlargement Europe. In: Journal of European Integration, February 2011, Vol. 33, No. 2, pp. 235-349.

24 Louis, Justin et al. Identity Representations of Turkey and Europe in Foreign Media. Regional and Global Perspectives on EU-Turkey Relations. FEUTURE Online Paper No. 14, March 2018.

Georgian, Russian and American press, namely: (1) the declaration of Turkey's candidacy status to the EU at the Helsinki Summit in 1999; (2) the start of EU-Turkey accession negotiations in 2005; (3) Orhan Pamuk's 2006 Nobel Prize in literature; (4) Sarkozy and Merkel's stance on Turkish accession (2007-2012); (5) the 2011-2012 French parliament's bill on mass killings of Armenians; (6) the 2016 EU-Turkey migration deal; and (7) the July 2016 failed coup attempt in Turkey. This analysis has shown civilisation to be the most pertinent key issue in post-1999 representations of the identity relationship between Turkey and Europe. In both the Eastern and Southern neighbourhood as well as Russia and the US, religious and cultural differences are the most recurrent reasons advanced to explain why Turkey has remained at Europe's doorstep. Overall, identity representations in Egyptian and American media tend to be more critical of Europe for distancing Turkey on cultural grounds whereas in Georgian and Russian media, the spotlight is on Turkey's cultural characteristics which are represented as making the country unfit for EU membership. In Egyptian representations of EU-Turkey relations, there is significant empathy with Turkey on cultural and religious grounds, explaining the impossibility of Turkey's accession due to identity and religious differences with the EU. Reflecting the US official position as a fervent supporter of Turkey's EU bid, the American representations either depict Turkey as a 'positive' Other whose religion could be an asset or implicitly criticise the EU for delaying its accession process for cultural or religious reasons. Conversely, Georgian and Russian discussions of EU-Turkey relations portray Turkey as an outsider due to its culture and religion, quite often negatively claiming that Turkey's accession would spoil Europe's identity and values.[25]

In the US and Russia, both holding the status of global powers, the media pays close attention to the issue of 'status in international society'. Both countries tend to consider the EU as a declining actor. When it comes to Turkey, the US media rather encourages Turkey's EU bid due to the country's status as a crucial NATO ally while Russian articles tend to praise Turkey's shift toward the East.[26] Regarding 'state-citizen relations', an issue also widely covered, the texts unanimously regard Turkey as inferior to Europe in terms of political, economic, human and minority rights. While Georgia negatively focuses on the gap that exists between Turkey and Europe, the Egyptian and US sources praise Turkey's early reform efforts. Fur-

---

25 For relevant texts that contain these depictions, see Louis et al. Identity Representations of Turkey and Europe in Foreign Media.
26 Ibid.

thermore, the US media considers that it is Europe's mission and responsibility to help Turkey democratise. Finally, whilst nationalism is the least covered issue in the texts under scrutiny, coverage that does exist consistently signifies greater divergence between Turkey and Europe.[27]

4. Linking Historical and Contemporary Drivers with Levels of Analysis: Implications for Future Scenarios

Linking the historical analysis with contemporary drivers reveals a number of patterns which may be relevant in predicting the identity dimension's future in EU-Turkey relations. Our historical analysis shows that dialectical transitions between the three sets of representations (from conflict to cooperation or convergence and vice versa) has occurred at various times in response to different political and cultural drivers. Thus, while contemporary analysis shows that after 2013 the conflict representation set has dominated EU-Turkey relations, it is reasonable to expect that the weight and impact of contemporary drivers will vary over time. Historical and contemporary analyses, therefore, suggest that the identification of future scenarios will largely depend on how contemporary drivers will change and under what conditions the next transition to a cooperation or convergence representation set, as indicated by historical patterns, will materialise.

Not all of the contemporary drivers shaping identity representations of Turkey in Europe and vice versa are likely to have long-term impact. For example, the discourse on Turkey as a 'model' has already proven its short-term impact by being eliminated soon after the Arab Spring turned sour. Similarly, it can be argued that the classic debate on EU widening and deepening is increasingly being side-lined in favour of a more complex discussion on the future shape of differentiated integration in the EU,[28] suggesting that the former debate's impact may be short-lived and subject to conditions structuring the fate of institutional integration. On the Turkish side, foreign policy orientations can also be expected to have short-term impacts, with flexible alliances increasingly gaining prominence.

At the same time, domestic European debates on integration, security, religion and identity can be expected to have a longer-term impact. Histor-

---

27 Ibid.
28 European Commission. White Paper on the Future of Europe. Reflections and Scenarios for the EU27 by 2025. COM(2017) 2025, Brussels, 2017; Müftüler-Baç, Meltem. Divergent Pathways. Turkey and the European Union. Berlin, 2016.

ically, the differentiation of Turkish and European identities on the basis of civilisation has proven resilient over two centuries.[29] In light of the wave of right-wing populism in Europe and Turkey, it is thus highly probable that the civilisationist discourse will continue to be employed to denote Europe and Turkey as distinct and even antagonistic civilisational entities in the near future.

Similarly, nationalism in Europe and Turkey is likely to continue driving conflictual identity representations, as illustrated by its heavy relevance and influence as a focal issue in the past. For both Europe and Turkey, representations of the Other have been routinely employed by political actors to score domestic political gains. In the Turkish context, the rise of anti-European nationalism fuelled by the governing party is likely to have a relatively short-term impact. The historical account has shown that it can be transformed into a pro-European nationalism through an elite-driven discourse and that positive representations of Europe as a model are just as effective in political competition for empowering the opposition. The most recent example was the case of the AKP which espoused a pro-European narrative during its initial years in power, leading to the emergence of positive attitudes towards the EU across its constituency that was hitherto known to harbour largely Eurosceptic sentiments.[30] Yet, for Europe the impact may be longer-lasting and thus, medium-term since public perceptions are generally resilient to elite manoeuvring in contrast to Turkey.

The growing authoritarianism within state-society relations in Turkey strengthens European perceptions of the widening gap between European and Turkish political cultures. As shown by the historical analysis, the differentiation of Turkish and European identities on the basis of state-society relations has been a consistent representational practice in the context of different events marking the relationship. Representations of Turkey as inferior to Europe in terms of democratic standards and at times as barbaric, have also undermined Turkey's status in international society and led to its stigmatisation. Historical patterns have revealed that such negative representations trigger calls in Turkey for independence from Europe and the West. Consequently, the more Turkey detaches itself from democracy and fundamental freedoms, thereby facing European criticism, the more

---

29 Aydın-Düzgit et al., Turkish and European Identity Constructions in the 1815-1945 Period; Aydın-Düzgit et al., Turkish and European Identity Constructions in the 1946-1999 Period.

30 Çarkoğlu, Ali/ Kentmen, Çiğdem. Diagnosing Trends and Determinants in Public Support for Turkey's EU Membership. In: South European Society and Politics, August 2011, Vol. 16, No. 3, pp. 365-379.

strongly it may aspire to detachment from Europe and its normative framework. While Turkey's current political dynamics reinforce this mutually reinforcing cycle of European criticism and Turkish detachment in the short-term, it is also possible that any future shift in the country's domestic power constellations may push the pro-European rhetoric back into favour, consequently allowing a more pro-European agenda to come to the fore.

At the same time, Europe's multiple crises since 2008 and the rise of new global powers have allowed Turkey to represent itself as a country with high status in international society. Contemporary Turkish representations of global politics point to the rise of regional actors such as Turkey, at the expense of traditional powers such as Europe and the US.[31] While Europe's perceived decline serves to justify Turkey's growing detachment from European norms and order, comparable episodes in history suggest that the impact will be rather short-term. Indeed, representations of Europe in decline were also common place during the interwar period, as shown when we analysed Germany's Annexation of Austria, but shifted radically once Europe started to recover after the Second World War. Whether this dynamic will intensify in the near future largely hinges on developments both in the European integration project and the general regional/global order.

Historically, the lack of European support for Turkey against its security threats, especially concerning territorial integrity, facilitated shifts towards conflictual identity representations in Turkey. In the current security context where Turkey faces potential spill-over effects from its Kurdish conflictfollowing the Syrian civil war, this pattern may be expected to continue. Indeed, the perceived lack of EU support in fighting the Gülenist movement after Turkey's attempted coup of 15 July 2016 generated similar representations. Historical patterns also suggest, though, that this driver's impact hinges on the intensity and resilience of any security threat faced by the Turkish state as well as European stances taken towards it. As such, strong rebounds to cooperative relations can easily be seen to follow.[32] Re-

---

31 Aydın-Düzgit, Senem. De-Europeanisation through Discourse. A Critical Discourse Analysis of AKP's Election Speeches. In: South European Society and Politics, March 2016, Vol. 21, No. 1, pp. 45-58.

32 For example, while the Cyprus conflict in the 1970s and Kurdish conflict in the 1990s fuelled negative representations of European states and the EU as threatening, following the declaration of Turkey's candidacy in 1999, such representations receded to the background. See Aydın-Düzgit et al., Turkish and European Identity Constructions in the 1946-1999 Period.

cent tensions between Turkey and Cyprus in the Eastern Mediterranean and ensuing EU sanctions on Turkey, which were reciprocated by the latter's suspension of the EU-Turkey statement on migration – the so-called refugee deal – show how unforeseen security-related issues (here the discovery of oil in the Eastern Mediterranean) can also foster conflict in EU-Turkey relations.

Historically, Turkey's support for European states against key security threats in the past fostered cooperative and even convergent identity representations between Turkey and Europe, as illustrated by the interwar period. Recently, this trend has additionally been demonstrated by the 2016 EU-Turkey refugee deal, whereby Turkey's accommodation of European demands in managing the refugee crisis as well as counterterrorism assistance fostered cooperation at a time when the country's accession prospects had lost credibility. Yet, with uncertainty surrounding the future of migration trends and the refugee deal itself, it is questionable whether or not cooperation on migration control will sustain cooperative identity representations in Europe.

This analysis of historical drivers allows us not only to identify 'known-unknowns', in other words historical patterns likely to be repeated in the future, but also to appreciate the possibility of the 'unknown-unknowns' impacting the identity dimension of EU-Turkey relations. As shown by the historical analysis, rapid shifts in identity representations from conflict to convergence or vice versa have mainly occurred in the context of major geopolitical changes or shifting patterns of alliances. While the end of the Cold War produced an increasingly volatile relationship between Turkey and the West, within the uncertain contemporary geopolitical context, co-operation between Europe and Turkey against a common enemy could potentially emerge and have a fundamental effect on the relationship or then again simply never occur. For example, a sudden growth in Russian aggression towards Europe could force Turkey to re-evaluate its allegiances and potentially side with Europe as a NATO member. Similarly, any potential conflict between Turkey and Russia over the Syrian quagmire, in part triggered by Turkey's troubled relations with the US, could also make the country turn towards Europe. At domestic level, a potential wild card would be the change of power constellations in Turkish politics, where a relatively pro-European government could spearhead renewed convergence with Europe through more positive representations of the European Other, particularly via political reforms concerning democracy, the rule of law and fundamental freedoms.

5. Conclusion

This analysis of contemporary identity drivers in EU-Turkey relations suggests that we are approaching a more conflictual orientation in the foreseeable future, coupled with potential for a certain degree of cooperation. The worst-case scenario would be that where mutual identity representations are constructed as binary and antagonistic through all focal issues, with little scope for cooperation or convergence and decreased interaction between the two sides. In contrast, the best-case scenario would be that where increased intimacy (as a result of a pro-European power constellation in Turkey and a more cosmopolitan political set-up in most of Europe) accompanies mutually positive identity representations which would in turn foster more productive interactions consolidating positive representations in a virtuous cycle. Yet, we believe that the most likely future scenario seems to fall somewhere in the middle of these two ideal types. One can expect the rise of nationalism and civilisational discourse on both sides to fuel conflict. Conversely, Turkey's cooperation in tackling perceived security threats to Europe (for instance, migration and ISIS terrorism), as well as any potential European signals that can be interpreted as a recognition of Turkey's status in the international system, such as visa facilitation or liberalisation granted to Turkey, can support a certain degree of cooperation, if not convergence, between the two sides.

Yet, our historical analysis suggests that identity representations do not lead to a static state of affairs where a given scenario dominates for long periods. Indeed, we have observed just the opposite picture where conflict, convergence and/or cooperation constantly alternate in response to specific drivers over time. This leads us to conclude that although contemporary drivers point towards the conflict scenario, we expect that ultimately the EU-Turkey relationship's contested nature will create openings for alternative scenarios to emerge in the future.

Politics are Taking EU-Turkey Relations Hostage: Explaining the Ups and Downs in the Political Dimension of the Relationship

Eduard Soler i Lecha, Melike Sökmen, Funda Tekin

1. Introduction

The relationship between Turkey and the European Union (EU) has been a rollercoaster ride.[1] Whilst both parties have come dangerously close to divorce, they are nevertheless at the same time aware that this would be tantamount to reaching a point of no return. Within this permanent state of crisis, it could rightly be claimed that politics has taken the relationship hostage. This implies that political drivers, conceptualised as ideational, material, structural and agency-related factors, push the EU-Turkey relationship away from convergence towards conflict, hence limiting the political need for cooperation in relevant thematic dimensions.[2] However, this has not always been the case (see Figure 1). The current phase of Turkish reforms backsliding was preceded by a phase of stagnation. Indeed, there was even a phase in which relations were becoming stronger and the idea of EU membership was a realistic option. The 1999 Helsinki Summit granted Turkey EU candidate status and accession negotiations started in October 2005. During this period, politics – elections in Germany, the Greek-Turkish détente and the succession of reformist governments in Ankara – drove relations towards greater convergence. Political incentives offered by the EU motivated Turkey to implement major reforms which, in turn, increased support for this transformative force, both in Turkey and the EU.

---

1 Tekin, Funda/ Wessels, Wolfgang. German-Turkish Relations. Think Ahead. In: Turhan, Ebru (eds). German-Turkish Relations Revisited. 1st ed., Baden-Baden, 2019, pp. 269-279.
2 For detailed definition of the terms drivers as well as convergence, cooperation and conflict see Tekin, Funda. The future of EU-Turkey relations. In this volume, pp.11-28.

Figure 1: 20 years of EU-Turkey relations: from optimism to mutual disappointment

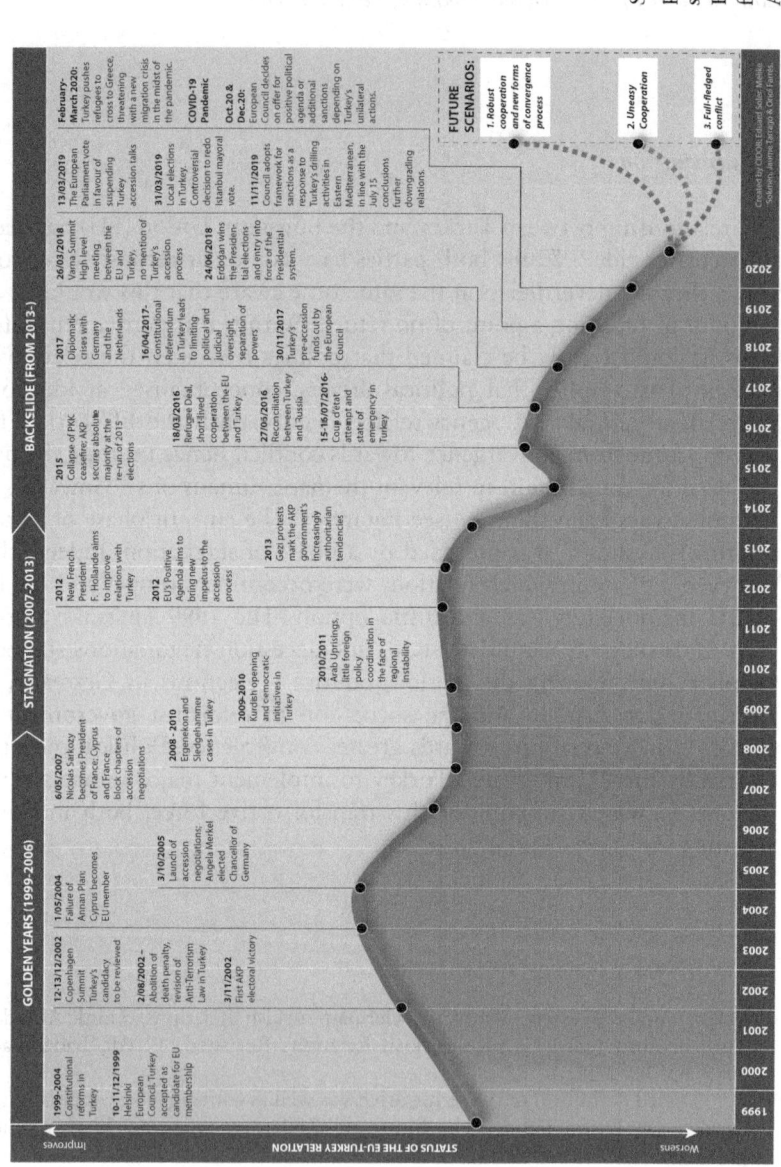

Source: Own compilation with the support of Barcelona Centre for International Affairs.

This chapter looks at why political drivers have turned what once was seen as a virtuous cycle of incentives and reforms into a vicious cycle characterised by mutual frustration. It further discusses the most likely future scenario for EU-Turkey relations in the political dimension.

The long history of EU-Turkey relations helps to put into perspective the current stalemate, in which accession negotiations are de facto suspended, the EU has introduced sanctions against Turkey and tensions over Turkey's actions in Syria, the Eastern Mediterranean and Libya are increasing. This relationship has repeatedly encountered and recovered from critical moments, for instance in 1974 (following Turkey's intervention in Cyprus), 1980 (in the wake of the coup d'état and the subsequent wave of repression in Turkey) and 1997 (when the EU's Luxembourg Council excluded Turkey from the group of twelve states that were granted EU candidacy and Turkey consequently unilaterally suspended political dialogue with the EU). Although the current situation does not seem to be a temporary crisis, the existing stalemate is not impossible to overcome, as discussed in this chapter.

The critical state of EU-Turkey relations coincides with major political transformations and challenges in Turkey and the EU, as well as regional and global developments.

In Turkey, certain developments such as two years of emergency rule after the failed coup attempt of 15 July 2016 or the adoption of a hyper-presidential system in 2017 in a national referendum and its implementation in 2018[3] contributed to an accumulation of power and resources by President Recep Tayyip Erdoğan. At the same time, the 2013 Gezi Park protests, the Justice and Development Party's (AKP) loss of an absolute majority in the June 2015 elections and their waning success at municipal elections – particularly in Istanbul –, led to the governing party's loss of support. The emergence of alternative leaders in the opposition as well as in the AKP itself during 2019 arguably attest to the vulnerability of the President's rule.

The EU has also become increasingly exposed over the last decade. The 2008 global financial crisis mutated into a sovereign debt crisis that compromised the Eurozone's sustainability. Furthermore, its priorities had to be reoriented in view of the United Kingdom's decision to leave the Union

---

3 Batalla, Laura/ Joppien, Charlotte. Turkey's new presidential system. What implications for EU-Turkey relations. November 2018, https://eu.boell.org/en/2018/11/1 5/turkeys-new-presidential-system-what-implications-eu-turkey-relations-1 [09.09.20]; Rose-Ackerman, Susan et al. Hyper-Presidentialism. Separation of Powers without Checks and Balances in Argentina and the Philippines. In: Faculty Scholarship Series, November 2010, Vol. 29, No. 1, pp. 246-333.

(Brexit) in 2016. Rising populism and Euroscepticism as well as the perception of being surrounded by a troubled and troubling neighbourhood – from Ukraine to Syria – turned the EU's ring of friends into a ring of fire. Migration and Russian aggression in the neighbourhood emerged as major concerns and, consequently, Turkey's position on both issues gained further relevance. Globally, challenges to multilateralism, the disruptive effects of US President Donald Trump's election in 2016 and Putin's defiance have ambivalent effects on EU-Turkey relations. In principle, this should have motivated Turkey and the EU to join forces in defence of multilateral institutions and commitments, but this has not translated into any meaningful practical initiatives.[4]

Adding to an already turbulent and complex environment, 2020 has witnessed the spread of a pandemic significantly altering global dynamics and having a strong impact in both the EU and Turkey. COVID-19 is a crisis not only in terms of health, but also its consequential strong social, economic and geopolitical impacts. While it is still too early to assess the depth and direction of its impact in EU-Turkey relations, the pandemic does seem to have acted as a catalyst for deeper integration in the EU, and has further revealed economic vulnerabilities in both Turkey and the EU. It remains to be seen whether or not this realisation will alter political strategies and lead Turkey to look for profit from reshoring or nearshoring processes in a context in which European economic and political actors advocate cutting the supply chain reliance on China.

One of the big questions underlying the political relationship is the credibility and feasibility of Turkey's membership prospects. From the outset, Turkish accession to the EU has been a contested issue. Turkey has claimed that its eligibility for membership was established with the 1963 Ankara Agreement. However, unlike previous enlargement rounds, Turkey's accession negotiations were explicitly defined as open-ended[5] and slowed down soon after their opening in 2005. So far 16 out of 35 negotiation chapters have been opened, of which only one has been provisionally closed (Chapter 25 – Science and Research). Additionally, 14 chapters are

---

4 See also Ergun, Doruk/ Ülgen, Sinan. EU-Turkey security relations: Key drivers and future scenarios. In this volume, pp. 103-120.

5 European Commission. Negotiating Framework. Brussels, 2005, p. 1 https://ec.eur opa.eu/neighbourhood-enlargement/sites/near/files/pdf/turkey/st20002_05_tr_fram edoc_en.pdf [19.08.20].

blocked – 8 by the EU Council[6] and a further 6 by the Republic of Cyprus.[7] Recently, negotiations have come to a full stop. In June 2018, the EU's General Affairs Council noted that Turkey's accession negotiations had "effectively come to a standstill" and "no further chapters can be considered for opening or closing and no further work towards the modernisation of the EU-Turkey Customs Union is foreseen."[8] One year later, in reaction to "Turkey's continued and new illegal drilling activities" in the Eastern Mediterranean, the Council further suspended meetings of the EU-Turkey Association Council and EU-Turkey high-level dialogues, deciding to reduce pre-accession assistance to Turkey for 2020 while inviting the European Investment Bank to review its lending activities in Turkey.[9] Since then, the situation has deteriorated further. In November 2019, the Council decided to set up a framework for restrictive measures in response to Turkey's illegal drilling activities in the Eastern Mediterranean. In July 2020, ministers concluded that EU-Turkey relations were under strain, tasking the High Representative with exploring further paths that could contribute to lowering tensions. During all these years, though, while on the one hand the EU has acknowledged the deterioration in relations, emphasising that Turkey has been "moving away from the EU",[10] on the other hand it has also repeatedly referred to Turkey as a "key partner".[11] European leaders also discussed about Turkey in the October and December 2020 European Council meetings, condemning and qualifying Ankara's actions as unilateral and provocative and studied the possibility of applying new sanctions, a compromise that did not meet the expectations of an ever harsher stance advocated by France, Greece and Cyprus.

---

6 Chapters 1 – Free movement of goods, 3 – Right of establishment and freedom to provide services, 9 – Financial services, 11 – Agriculture and rural development ,13 - Fisheries, 14 – Transport policy, 19 – Social policy and employment, 30 – External relations.

7 Chapters 2 – Freedom of movement of workers, 15 - Energy, 23 – Judiciary and fundamental Rights, 24 – Justice, freedom and security, 26 – Education and culture, 31 – Foreign, security and defense Policy.

8 Council of the European Union. Enlargement and Stabilisation and Association Process. Council conclusions. 10555/18, Brussels, 2018, p. 13.

9 Council of the European Union. Conclusions – 20.06.2019. EUCO 9/19, Brussels, 2019.

10 European Commission. Turkey 2018 Report. SWD(2018) 153 final, Brussels, 2018, p. 3.

11 European Commission. Turkey 2019 Report. SWD(2019) 2019 final, Brussels, 2019, p. 3; European Commission. Turkey 2018 Report, p. 3; European Commission. Sixth Report on the Progress made in the implementation of the EU-Turkey Statement. COM(2017) 323 final, Brussels, 2017.

In an attempt to make projections about the future, we analyse the political drivers in the EU-Turkey relationship since 1999. There will be a focus on three key issues (political change, democracy and human rights along with public opinion) and four levels of analysis (the EU, Turkey, the neighbourhood and the global scene). We identify the circumstances under which internal political changes in Turkey, the EU (including individual member states) the neighbourhood and at the global level have altered EU-Turkey relations. While the analysis of democracy and human rights focuses mainly on developments in Turkey, it has also become increasingly relevant for the EU in view of recent developments in some member states (e.g. the Commission launching the Article-7 TEU procedure against Hungary and Poland). The key issue of public opinion calls for analysis both in Turkey and the EU so as to elucidate whether or not changing patterns in Turkish and European public opinion have correlated with changes at a decision-making level in the EU, the member states and Turkey, and vice versa.

We argue that politics define both the tone and upper limits of the overall relationship. This implies that convergence at the overall EU-Turkey relationship level – understood here as Turkey becoming an EU member or drawing closer to that goal[12] – can become possible only through political convergence (i.e. Turkey's full compliance with the EU's Copenhagen political membership criteria). At the same time, the perception that compromising cooperation in areas of mutual dependency such as energy, migration, security and the fight against terrorism is a political risk for all parties has served to mitigate such political tensions.[13]

The chapter proceeds as follows. Section 2 analyses the drivers from a perspective of three focal issues: political change, democracy and human rights together with public opinion. Section 3 looks at the current state of Turkey-EU relations in light of these drivers. Our final section evaluates the most likely scenario, explaining why political drivers entail a tailor-made approach for framing the future EU-Turkey relationship.

---

12 For a concise definition of the three ideal-type scenarios of convergence, cooperation and conflict see Tekin, Funda. The future of EU-Turkey relations. In this volume pp. 11-28.

13 See the other chapters in this volume.

2. *Political Drivers of EU-Turkey Relations: It Takes Two to Tango*

While it is tempting to attribute the current stalemate in EU-Turkey relations merely to Turkish political developments, the picture emerging from this chapter's analysis is more complex. Political drivers in both Turkey and the EU continue to have a tremendous impact on the relationship, which is why we borrow the metaphor 'it takes two to tango' to refute those analysts who explain the relationship simply as a result of one party's behaviour.[14] Additionally, while political drivers from the neighbourhood or the global level may not be strong enough to reverse the dominant trend in EU-Turkey relations (from convergence to conflict or from conflict to convergence),[15] they are meaningful in increasing or lowering the incentives for cooperation between the two parties.

2.1 *Tracing Turkey's Move Away From the EU*

Political changes in Turkey stem mainly from the AKP's consolidation as Turkey's dominant party coupled with the evolution towards a hyper-presidential system. Add to this the country's political as well as legislative reforms, the redefinition of goals and strategies in foreign policy together with the attitudes, hopes and frustrations observed in Turkish public opinion. All of this can be seen as constituting key drivers in relations with the EU. Until recently, these elements were pointing towards a declared aim of greater convergence.[16] During its early years in government, the AKP saw the EU as a potential ally for executing domestic reforms and notwithstanding its diversified foreign policy, EU membership was an indisputable goal.[17] Public opinion was largely favourable towards membership (partic-

---

14 Soler i Lecha, Eduard et al. It Takes Two to Tango. Political Changes in Europe and their Impact on Turkey's EU Bid. FEUTURE Online Paper No. 17, April 2018, https://feuture.uni-koeln.de/sites/feuture/user_upload/Online_Paper_No._17_D2.2..pdf [21.08.20].

15 Tekin, Funda. The Future of EU-Turkey Relations. In this volume, pp.11-28.

16 Soler i Lecha, Eduard. EU-Turkey Relations. Mapping landmines and exploring alternative pathways. FEPS Policy Paper, September 2019.

17 Hauge et al. Narratives of a Contested Relationship. Unravelling the Debates in the EU and Turkey. FEUTURE Online Paper No. 28, February 2019, p. 22.

ularly around 2004-2005) despite high scepticism regarding its likelihood.[18]

The same drivers now point in the opposite direction. The AKP government and Erdoğan's willingness to preserve power fuelled by the failed military coup of July 2016 pushed Ankara to implement policies contradicting the EU's reform demands. Additionally, the government is adamant in its pursuit of a foreign policy strategy that widens the distance with its European and Western allies.[19] Proof can be found in Erdoğan's inconsequential suggestion of holding a referendum on EU membership[20] or repeated references to a possibility of joining the Shanghai Cooperation Organisation if EU negotiations are not revamped.[21] Yet, contradictory messages have also been sent such as Erdoğan's reiteration in November 2020, that Turkey's future was in Europe and that the country was part of Europe.[22] These mixed messages reflect a larger state of opinion in the country, as in addition to a persistent support for the accession process, scepticism regarding the likelihood of membership has been increasing over the past years.[23]

2.1.1 The AKP Government's Political Calculations Shifting from the EU and the 'Erdoğan-Factor'

The ruling elites in Turkey have always utilised the EU accession process as an important point of reference to legitimise their political action in

18 Şenyuva, Özgehan. Turkish Public Opinion and the EU Membership. Between Support and Mistrust. FEUTURE Online Paper No. 26, October 2018, p. 9.

19 Eralp, Atila et.al. Political Changes in Turkey and the Future of Turkey-EU Relations. From Convergence to Conflict? FEUTURE Online Paper No. 12, December 2017, p. 12; Seufert, Günter. Foreign Policy and Self-image. The Societal Basis of Strategy Shifts in Turkey. SWP Research Paper, September 2012.

20 Euractiv.com. Erdogan says he will consider referendum on Turkey's EU bid. 05.10.2018, https://www.euractiv.com/section/global-europe/news/erdogan-says-he-will-consider-referendum-on-turkeys-eu-bid/ [19.08.20].

21 Hurriyetdailynews.com. President Erdoğan: EU not everything, Turkey may join Shanghai Five. 20.11.2016, https://www.hurriyetdailynews.com/president-erdogan-eu-not-everything-turkey-may-join-shanghai-five-106321 [19.08.20].

22 See Daily Sabah. Turkey to build its future with Europe, Erdoğan says. 21 November 2020, https://www.dailysabah.com/politics/diplomacy/turkey-to-build-its-future-with-europe-erdogan-says [21.12.2020].

23 Aydin, Mustafa et al. Türkiye Eğilimler Araştırması 2019. Istanbul, January 2020, https://www.khas.edu.tr/sites/khas.edu.tr/files/inline-files/TE2019_TUR_BASIN_1 5.01.20%20WEB%20versiyon%20powerpoint_0.pdf [19.08.20].

Turkey.[24] During its early years in power, the AKP government also invoked the EU process as a signifier of its democratic, reformist and modern aspects.[25] The party instrumentalised this process as a way of enlarging the space for religious freedoms (in Turkey's secular context), whilst at the same time weakening the ethno-nationalist and hard-line secularist forces represented by the high judiciary, the military and other Kemalist state bureaucracy that it perceived as a threat to its existence as an Islamist party.[26] In particular, AKP reforms diminishing the military's political role has led to a public perception of the AKP as an agent of democratic transformation, in turn fostering convergent trends in the EU-Turkey relationship.

Meanwhile, the credibility of EU membership has been a crucial component within the AKP's political calculations, which establishes a direct correlation between the reform momentum and Turkey's prospect for accession to the EU.[27] Over the years, though, the AKP government has increasingly lost trust in the EU's membership promise. Moreover, political calculations have become increasingly 'Erdoğanised', in terms of the party becoming primarily an instrument for achieving the leader's personal ambitions. This can be traced along the following lines: In 2014, Erdoğan became Turkey's first directly elected president. In 2015 he called for snap elections in order to secure the AKP single party government. Erdoğan's opponents or other strong AKP leaders such as Prime Minister Ahmet Davutoğlu were eventually forced to clear the field. Finally, the constitutional reform of 2017 and elections in 2018 secured Erdoğan's increased powers within the hyper-presidential system. Hence, preserving political power is one of the determining factors of Erdoğan's political calculations. This has been reinforced in 2019 by parts of the AKP starting to dissociate

---

24 Hauge et al. Narratives of a Contested Relationship.
25 Deniz, Yesil/ Tekin, Funda: Tracing Ebbs and Flows in Political and Legislative Reforms in Turkey in View of EU-Turkey Relations. FEUTURE Online Paper No. 30, March 2019, p. 10; Eralp et al. Political Changes in Turkey; Saatçioğlu, Beken. AKP's 'Europeanization' in Civilianization, Rule of Law and Fundamental Freedoms. The Primacy of Domestic Politics. In: Journal of Balkan and Near Eastern Studies, January 2014, Vol. 16(1), p. 86-101; Börzel, Tanja/ Soyaltin, Didem. Europeanisation in Turkey. Stretching a Concept to its Limits. KFG Working Paper No. 36. Berlin, February 2012.
26 Deniz/ Tekin, Tracing Ebbs and Flows, p. 12.
27 See for example Schimmelfennig, Frank et al. Cost, Commitment and Compliance. The Impact of EU Democratic Conditionality on Latvia, Slovakia and Turkey. In: Journal of Common Market Studies, May 2003, Vol. 41, No. 3, p. 509.

themselves from the president, leaving the party with ambitions to form new political parties.[28]

2.1.2 Political Reforms (or the Lack Thereof)

The EU's political membership criteria require Turkey to adopt transformative political reforms inter alia in the areas of democratisation, civil-military relations and the Kurdish question.[29] By analysing these reforms, one can trace the fluctuations and identify points of contention in the EU-Turkey relationship. Co-opting the Kurdish and liberal segments of society, for instance, made the early AKP governments (namely, before 2013) appear to be on track towards convergence with the EU. Yet, the government's initial constructive approach to the Kurdish issue through the so-called "Kurdish opening"[30] in 2009 and envisaged democratic reforms in 2013, with electoral changes and broadening of language rights, has given way to hard-line nationalist discourse in 2015, thereby creating tension in EU-Turkey relations.

After the 'golden years' of political reforms in Turkey between 2000 and 2007, the pace of reforms started to slow down almost to the point of stagnation. In 2013 the AKP government intensified its efforts to strengthen its grip on power. Since then, EU-Turkey relations have been less affected by a lack of reforms as was so in the previous period, but more by the content and direction of larger reform projects in Turkey that have driven both sides further apart.[31] For instance, immediately after the July 2016 coup attempt, some consideration was given to reintroducing the death penalty, a move which would have put an immediate end to Turkey's accession vocation.[32] Additionally, the prolonged state of emergency following the coup attempt as well as Turkey's drilling efforts in the Eastern Mediter-

---

28 Coskun, Orhan. Former Turkish PM Davutoğlu forms new party in challenge to Erdoğan. In: Reuters.com, 12.12.2019, https://in.reuters.com/article/turkey-politic s/former-turkish-pm-davutoglu-forms-new-party-in-challenge-to-erdogan-idINKB N1YG197 [21.08.20].

29 Eralp, Atila et al. Political Changes in Turkey, p. 4.

30 Cagaptay, Soner. "Kurdish Opening" closed shut. In: Foreignpolicy.com, 28.10.2009, https://foreignpolicy.com/2009/10/28/kurdish-opening-closed-shut/ [21.08.20].

31 Deniz/ Tekin, Tracing Ebbs and Flows, p. 21.

32 Süddeutsche.de. Juncker warnt Türkei vor der Todesstrafe. 08.05.2016, https://ww w.sueddeutsche.de/politik/wiedereinfuehrung-geplant-juncker-warnt-tuerkei-vor- der-todesstrafe-1.3495418 [19.08.20].

ranean since 2019 has had immediate detrimental effects on the EU's pre-accession assistance for Turkey. Finally, constitutionalising the executive presidency system was strongly criticised by both the EU and the Venice Commission of the Council of Europe.[33]

2.1.3 Fragility of the Rule of Law in Turkey

The rule of law and human rights are the principal pillars of Turkey's EU trajectory. Following a period of reforms in these areas with an eye to EU membership in the early 2000s, the AKP's electoral victories together with its strategy of eliminating opposition perceived as a threat to AKP's ideological project (e.g. Ergenekon, Sledgehammer and KCK trials) contributed to changes in Turkey's power balances.[34] The more the AKP consolidated domestic political power, the less it needed the EU, which led to greater selectivity in its pursuit of reforms.[35] To the EU, Erdoğan and the AKP government went from being a much-needed model of democracy during the Arab Spring in 2011 to a government responsible for the crack-down on Gezi protesters in 2013, among others.

Particularly since the coup attempt of 15 July 2016, "Turkey has been moving away from the European Union".[36] Yet even before that, reforms in Turkey had not necessarily produced solid democratisation, despite a fast-paced reform process particularly on issues such as civilian control over the military or various constitutional reform packages in the early 2000s. A visible lack of fundamental rights and the rule of law[37] seriously jeopardises Turkey's EU candidacy and certainly rules out its EU membership in the foreseeable future,[38] representing a strong driver towards the emerging conflictual relationship. In fact, we can clearly link the European

---

33 European Commission. Turkey 2018 Report; Venice Commission. Turkey. Opinion on the Amendments to the Constitutions adopted by the Grand National Assembly. CDL-AD(2017)005, Strasbourg, 2017.
34 Deniz/ Tekin, Tracing Ebbs and Flows, p. 17.
35 Saatçioğlu. Europeanization.
36 European Commission. Turkey 2017 Report; European Commission. Turkey 2018 Report.
37 Saatçioğlu, Beken. De-Europeanisation in Turkey. The Case of the Rule of Law. In: South European Society and Politics, March 2016, Vol. 21(1), p. 133-146.
38 For detailed overview of political and legislative reforms see Deniz/ Tekin, Tracing Ebbs and Flows.

Parliament's (EP) demands for suspending Turkish accession negotiations to weaknesses in the rule of law and democracy.[39]

At the same time, there does not seem to be sufficient evidence for concluding that a comprehensive reform package fully aligning Turkey with the EU's acquis and democratic requirements would necessarily be enough to result in Turkey's full membership. In retrospect, Turkey's 'golden years' of Europeanisation motivated EU member states to open accession negotiations in 2005, albeit not without accommodating the doubts and objections of hesitant member states such as Cyprus and Austria. Consequently, the potential for political and legislative reforms which would be sufficient to drive EU-Turkey relations towards a convergence scenario also depends on political drivers in the EU and overall domestic politics in Turkey. Hence, Turkey's democratic reforms would alone be insufficient to move the EU-Turkey relationship forward.

2.1.4 The EU as Part of Turkish Foreign Policy Strategies

Turkey's reforms in the early 2000s coincided with the EU's preparations for ten plus two new member states' accession into the Union during 2004/2007. Turkish security, foreign policy and economic interests in this period were generally aligned with those of the EU, with the concept of a "New Turkish Foreign Policy" also gaining in popularity under the then Foreign Minister Ahmet Davutoğlu.[40] As well as foreign policy ambitions, this also aimed at diversifying the country's priorities, instruments and partners. Key concepts included Turkey's strategic depth, rhythmic diplomacy, zero-problems with neighbours together with greater use of mediation and public diplomacy as foreign policy tools.[41] During this period,

---

39 European Parliament. Parliament wants to suspend EU accession negotiations with Turkey. Brussels, March 2019.
40 See for example Aras, Bulent. The Davutoğlu Era in Turkish Foreign Policy. In: Insight Turkey, August 2014, Vol. 16, No. 4; Alessandri, Emiliano. The New Turkish Foreign Policy and the Future of Turkey-EU Relations. Documenti IAI. Rome, February 2010, Vol. 19, No. 3; Bilgiç, Ali/ Bilgin, Pinar. Turkey's "New" Foreign Policy toward Eurasia. In: Eurasian Geography and Economics, May 2011, Vol. 52(2), p. 173-195.; Öniş, Ziya. Multiple faces of the "new" Turkish foreign policy. Underlying dynamics and a critique. In: Insight Turkey, January 2011, Vol. 13, No. 1; Soler i Lecha, Eduard. The conceptual architecture of Turkish foreign policy: An update in light of regional turbulence. Documentos CIDOB, Barcelona, June 2012, No. 18.
41 Davutoğlu, Ahmet: Stratejik Derinlik. Turkey, Istanbul, 2014.

while the EU remained Ankara's declared policy priority (consistent with the country's adherence to multilateralism and peace-building), Turkey's foreign policy vision was strongly multidimensional. However, following attempts to revamp Turkey's EU accession track via the EU-Turkey statement on Migration in March 2016 and Davutoğlu's forced resignation in May 2016 a severe rupture happened in the new foreign policy outlook. This fed into Erdoğan's growing prominence in Turkey's foreign policy-making, occasionally coupled with his aggressive rhetoric vis-à-vis the EU.[42] Although this does not exclude the possibility of EU-Turkey collaboration over areas of mutual interest, the general atmosphere is one where Turkey follows its own path, caring little about the advantages of EU convergence on foreign and security policy matters.

2.1.5 Turkish Public Opinion On the EU

In Turkey, public support for Turkey's EU membership has moved in waves over recent years, reaching 70% in 2004, falling below 50% in 2010 and bouncing back up to 53% in 2014.[43] Turkish attitudes towards the EU are hence "highly volatile and subject to extreme backlashes" and "the major spikes are very much linked with political developments in Turkey, in Europe and between Turkey and the EU".[44] Despite deteriorating relations and reduced hopes for membership, more than 50% of the society was still supporting joining the EU, according to an early 2019 poll.[45] Yet, by the end of 2019, this support had sharply declined reaching an all-time low of 27%.[46]

In order to project the direction the EU-Turkey relationship will take in future, it is important to understand that the Turkish people's perception of EU membership and its likelihood in part reflects views expressed by their politicians. In recent years, mistrust and disappointment with the EU

---

42 See for example France 24.com. Erdoğan warns Europe to expect 'millions' of migrants after Turkey opens borders. 03 March 2020, https://www.france24.com/en/20200303-erdogan-warns-europe-to-expect-millions-of-migrants-after-turkey-opens-borders [19.08.20].

43 Raisher, Joshua/ Stelzenmueller, Constanze. Transatlantic Trends. Key findings 2014. September 2014, https://www.gmfus.org/transatlantic-trends [09.09.20], p. 53.

44 Şenyuva. Turkish Public Opinion, p. 2, 5.

45 Aydın, Türkiye Eğilimler Araştırması.

46 European Commission. Public Opinion in the European Union. Standard-Eurobarometer 92. EB92.3, Brussels, 2019, p. 105.

have increased even among pro-European segments of the population. One indication for this general atmosphere is the level of net trust, in other words the difference between how many people tend to trust and not to trust the EU. By 2014 this indicator had reached an all-time low of 49%.[47] The EU-Turkey Statements on migration in 2015 and 2016 temporarily boosted the popular trust levels, but could not reverse the general trend of scepticism that Turkey would ever join the EU, which reached a level of 81% among Turkish public opinion polls in 2017. Additionally, about 32% believed that the EU would not keep its promises made in the EU-Turkey migration deal.[48] In 2017, the AKP government and Erdoğan's campaign for a constitutional referendum on the presidential system together with the run-up to general elections in several EU member states culminated in Ankara's diplomatic rows with the Netherlands and Germany. This further increased the mistrust among Turks towards any EU process. Indeed, 24% of the Turkish population considered that the EU posed the biggest threat to Turkey, ranking it third after the US (66.5%) and Israel (37.4%). In short, public opinion has both contributed to and been affected by the conflictual turns in EU-Turkey relations.

2.2 The European Union Not Showing Its Hand

Fluctuations in EU-Turkey relations cannot be analysed through Turkey's political dynamics alone. In 1998, political changes in Germany served to shift the EU's attitude regarding Turkey from denying to recognising its status as an EU candidate. Angela Merkel's election in Germany in 2005 followed by Nicolas Sarkozy in France in 2007, Cyprus' EU membership since 2004, as well as increasing political opposition to and public debates about Turkey's EU membership in Europe have all played major roles in the stagnation of relations ever since Turkey and the EU embarked on formal accession negotiations in 2005. More recently, the EU is being subjected to new challenges such as Brexit, the so-called refugee crisis in 2015, the rise of Eurosceptic and populist movements, and the lingering effects of an economic crisis aggravated by the COVID-19 pandemic. All have significantly reduced the Union's appetite for further enlargement.

---

47 Şenyuva, Turkish Public Opinion, p. 2.
48 Aydın. Türkiye Eğilimler Araştırması; Aydin, Mustafa et al. Research on Public Perceptions on Turkish Foreign Policy. Istanbul, July 2019.

2.2.1 Enlargement (Or Turkey) Fatigue

The EU's 2004 and 2007 enlargements led to a coining of the term 'enlargement fatigue'. This refers to the Union's unwillingness to grant membership to any additional country based on fears of overstretching and concerns about the Union's absorption capacity and its transformative power.[49] Regarding Turkey, an argument countering enlargement submitted that the country was "too big, too poor and too different", which was also interpreted as "too Muslim".[50] If in the long-term Turkey was to become a member state, it would represent more than 20% of the EU's population.[51] This would make Turkey very influential not only in the EU Council, but also in the European Parliament, where Turkish MEPs would constitute the largest national group, together with German MEPs. Additionally, Turkey would not only be the second largest member state but also the only Muslim-majority country in the Union. The Turkish currency and debt crisis that started in 2018 has provided an opportunity for opponents of Turkey's EU accession to question the benefits of its membership. Coupled with a general halt to EU enlargement under the 2014-2019 Juncker Commission and the veto against the opening of accession negotiations with North Macedonia and Albania during the autumn of 2019, this 'fatigue' seems to have deepened within the EU.[52]

2.2.2 The Undermined Principle of EU Conditionality

The EU's enlargement procedure builds on candidates fulfilling the principle of membership conditionality.[53] Following a utility-based logic, the

---

49 Szolucha, Anna. The EU and Enlargement Fatigue: Why has the European Union not been able to counter enlargement fatigue. In: Journal of Contemporary European Research, May 2010, Vol. 6(1).

50 See for example Lamb, Scott. The Pros and Cons. In: Spiegel.de, 16 December 2004, https://www.spiegel.de/international/turkey-and-the-eu-the-pros-and-cons-a-333126.html [19.08.20].

51 Estimation for the year 2030 based on: Urmersbach, Bruno. Gesamtbevölkerung in der Türkei von 1980 bis 2018 und Prognosen bis 2024. April 2020, https://de.statista.com/statistik/daten/studie/19318/umfrage/gesamtbevoelkerung-in-der-tuerkei/ [19.08.20].

52 For extensive explanation of the rationale behind Turkey fatigue see Soler i Lecha et al. It Takes Two to Tango.

53 For an academic discussion of this principle that relates to the EU's ability to transfer its norms and values to accession candidates facilitating their internal

Union pursues a strategy of imposing this conditionality by what is called "reinforcement by reward".[54] Applied to Turkey, this suggests that its political actors would engage in reforms only if the material benefits outweigh the costs. However, a number of other challenges have jeopardised the country's membership prospects, hence undermining the principle of conditionality. Firstly, each member state has the right to veto all relevant decisions concerning accession, such as granting candidacy status, opening of accession negotiations and individual negotiation chapters along with the completion of the accession agreement between the EU and Turkey. So far, Austria, France and Cyprus have unilaterally blocked the opening of certain negotiation chapters at different points. These vetoes represent political decisions that do not relate to the EU's conditionality framework and hence are even more difficult to overcome. Secondly, there have been debates in the EU about alternative forms of linking Turkey to the EU through variations involving a "privileged partnership".[55] Yet the open-ended nature of Turkey's accession negotiations as defined in the 2005 Negotiating Framework and the prospect of excluding Turkey permanently from certain parts of the acquis in case of accession[56] have together damaged the credibility of Turkey's membership.

2.2.3 Crises Damaging European Integration

The EU seems to have a formidable capacity to accumulate crises without really resolving any of them and yet still remaining resilient to their effects. The COVID-19 pandemic is the latest litmus test for European integration. Despite the initial hesitation and controversies between the so-called frugal countries and those that requested a more generous and am-

---

transformation processes see Aydın-Düzgit, Senem. Legitimizing Europe in Contested Settings. Europe as a Normative Power in Turkey. In: Journal of Common Market Studies, October 2017, Vol. 56(1), p. 612-627; Müftüler-Baç, Meltem. Judicial reform in Turkey and the EU's political conditionality. (Mis)Fit between domestic preferences and EU demands. MAXCAP Working Paper No. 18, Berlin, January 2016; Schimmelfennig, Frank et.al. Cost, Commitment and Compliance.

54 Schimmelfennig, Frank/ Sedelmeier, Ulrich: Governance by conditionality. EU rule transfer to the candidate countries of Central and Eastern Europe. In: Journal of European Public Policy, August 2004, Vol. 11, No. 4, pp. 662.

55 Pope, Hugh. Privileged Partnership Offers Turkey neither Privilege nor Partnership. In: Crisisgroup.org, 23 June 2009.

56 See European Commission, Negotiating Framework.

bitious response, the way COVID-19 has been dealt with points towards greater integration reflexes.

Before the pandemic, the EU had already faced a constitutional crisis in 2005, the 2008 global financial crisis, the 2015 refugee crisis, Brexit and the rise of populist and Eurosceptic political movements. Three effects of these crises on EU-Turkey relations are worth mentioning. Firstly, they have substantially reduced the Union's appetite for enlargement in general and towards Turkey in particular for various reasons. The constitutional crisis prevented the EU from taking the comprehensive step of 'deepening,' which was deemed necessary for the subsequent 'widening'. In turn, the financial crisis required the prioritisation of reforms in the Economic and Monetary Union, whilst additionally weakening those member states that were generally in favour of Turkey's accession, namely Italy, Spain and Portugal. Secondly, these crises led to the politicisation of a claim at the government level in Turkey that the EU was a declining (economic) power, leading to reduced enthusiasm for joining the EU. Thirdly, crises can trigger a revitalisation of EU-Turkey relations. Yet, having a glimpse at the mutual benefits of functional cooperation necessary for solving a major problem – such as the refugee crisis – is not necessarily sufficient for revitalising accession negotiations or accomplishing visa liberalisation for Turkish citizens in the Schengen area.[57] The complexity of the 2016 EU-Turkey Statement on migration, its poor implementation and the quarrel over funds under the EU's Refugee Facility for Turkey turned the deal into a bargaining chip within EU-Turkey relations.[58] Turkey's unilateral decision to open its border with Greece to the refugees' passage in March 2020 (aimed at putting pressure on the EU) offers further proof of this.

2.2.4 Differentiated Integration Diversifying EU-Turkey Relations

Seven consecutive enlargement rounds have made it difficult for EU member states to reach consensus. This was mainly because the EU became more diverse and not all members continue to be politically willing or ob-

---

57 Tekin, Funda. Turkey and the EU. From accession to estrangement. In: Orient, Deutsche Zeitschrift für Politik, Wirtschaft und Kultur des Orients, 2019, Vol. 3, pp. 39-45.
58 Saatcioğlu, Beken. The European Union's Refugee Crisis and Rising Functionalism in EU-Turkey Relations. In: Turkish Studies, March 2019, Vol. 21, p. 169-187; Üstün, Çiğdem/ Senyuva, Özgehan. A Deal to End "the" Deal. Why the Refugee Agreement is a Threat to Turkey-EU Relations. German Marshal Fund, July 2016.

jectively able to participate in further integration steps. Additionally, rising nationalist and Eurosceptic movements in both old and new member states have further amplified these problems. Hence, differentiated integration is likely to represent the 'new normal' in European integration.[59] This can affect the EU-Turkey relationship in terms of diversifying different options for future relations between convergence and conflict. Currently, Turkey is one of the most integrated non-members to the EU. At the same time, according to the current treaty framework, there is no such thing as partial membership. With greater EU differentiation both internally and externally, the scope, nature and form of membership as such will also transform, which will narrow the separation between EU members and non-members, hence creating new frameworks for institutionalising the EU-Turkey relationship.[60]

2.2.5 Public Opinion as a Driver of Conflict

European public support for Turkey's EU membership has been declining over recent years. In 2016, support was as low as 7%, and given the EU's general enlargement 'fatigue' and a pandemic dominating most political agendas, European support for enlargement is unlikely to pick up in the foreseeable future.[61] A host of variables have driven this trend forward, including what has been deemed socio-economic utility, perceived cultural differences, the presence of Turkish background minorities in a given country, a tendency towards bi-partisan scepticism towards Turkish EU membership, historical alliances and animosities, political leadership, current bilateral relations, stances on migrants and terrorism, along with perceptions of human rights and democracy in Turkey. This declining support coupled with the relative success of populist politics across the EU is likely to see European public opinion on Turkish EU membership act as a

---

59 European Commission. White Paper on the Future of Europe. Reflections and Scenarios for the EU27 by 2025. COM 2017(2025), Brussels, 2017; Tekin, Funda: Differentiated Integration. IEP Online Paper, Berlin, March 2017; Schimmelfennig, Frank/ Winzen, Thomas. Ever Looser Union. Differentiated European Integration. Oxford, 2020; Peers, Steve. Trends in Differentiation of EU law Lessons for the Future. PE 510.007, Brussels, 2015.

60 Tekin, Funda. Differentiated Integration. An Alternative Conceptualization of EU-Turkey Relations. In: Reiners, Wulf/ Turhan, Ebru (eds). EU-Turkey Relations – Theories, Institutions and Policies. Pallgrave Macmillan, 2021, forthcoming.

61 Lindgaard, Jakob. EU Public Opinion on Turkish EU Membership. Trends and Drivers. FEUTURE Online Paper No. 25, October 2018, p. 19.

driver that will pull Turkey-EU relations towards a more conflictual orientation before too long.[62]

2.2.6 The Politicisation of Turkey in European Debates

National elections in Europe have implications for the EU and its foreign policy. Politicising the topic of Turkey in European elections has frequently driven EU-Turkey relations towards episodic conflicts and is likely to continue to do so in the future. This was the case in 2017, when Turkey's constitutional referendum coincided with a crowded electoral cycle in the Netherlands, France, Germany and Austria.[63] Yet, full-fledged confrontation was still avoided as a certain level of cooperation has always been maintained due to the intensity of mutual interests, particularly at a bilateral level. Turkey is likely to remain a politicised issue in member states and the EU (particularly in the European Parliament). This translates into political resistance towards the Customs Union upgrade and visa liberalisation processes. It also favours the imposition of EU sanctions on Turkey (as has already happened following the Turkey-Cyprus gas drilling controversy in the Eastern Mediterranean). Forthcoming elections in Germany (2021) and France (2022) could further reinforce this trend.

2.3 The Neighbourhood and the Global Level Balanced Between Cooperation and Conflict

At the neighbourhood and global level, there are mismatches between the EU and Turkey regarding what each perceives as threats or opportunities. Yet, there is still room for cooperation, even if only pragmatically. The turbulent geopolitical environment in the Southern and Eastern neighbourhood, the re-assertion of Russian power in its immediate neighbourhood and beyond, shifting global powers and a contested liberal international order induce potentially conflictual or cooperative outcomes for EU-Turkey relations.

---

62 See Lindgaard, EU Public Opinion 2018, p. 2.
63 Soler i Lecha et.al., It Takes Two to Tango; Turhan, German-Turkish Relations Revisited.

2.3.1 A Defiant Russia

For the EU, Russian interventionism is a crucial concern, as both parties' relative influence on Eastern European states and the Caucasus are mutually exclusive. From Turkey's standpoint, Russian involvement in neighbouring countries has not been as significant as long as it has not threatened Turkey's own territorial integrity. This can create conflict in EU-Turkey relations if Turkey supports Russian actions in the neighbourhood or lead to cooperation if Turkey is threatened by and opposes Russian interventionism.[64] When it comes to relations with Russia, Turkish foreign policy stands between two approaches: Russia as a security threat to Turkey as a NATO ally and Russia as a strategic partner from the perspective of the AKP government.[65] Conflict between the EU and Turkey has already been exacerbated following Turkey's purchase of the S-400 missile defence system from Russia, the construction of the Turkstream energy pipeline and Russian engagements in building Turkey's first nuclear power plant in Akkuyu. So far, Russia exerts significant negative impact on Ankara's ability to partner with the EU.[66]

2.3.2 The Southern Neighbourhood

Turkish foreign policy in the EU's Southern neighbourhood has in the past prompted EU member states to adopt a more positive attitude towards Ankara's EU bid. This may no longer be the case. While political drivers triggered Turkey's estrangement from the EU, the intervening migration and security drivers emanating from the Middle East and North Africa were conducive to maintaining a certain level of cooperation.[67] Looking particularly at the Turkish Parliament's decision in January 2020 to deploy troops in Libya in support of the Tripoli-based internationally recognised government and the prior signature of a bilateral deal between

---

64 Clifford, Benett et al. Politics and Turkey-EU Relations. Drivers from the Southern and Eastern Neighbourhoods. FEUTURE Online Paper No. 11, December 2017.
65 Morillas, Pol et al. EU-Turkey Relations in the Midst of a Global Storm. FEUTURE Online Paper No. 7, November 2017.
66 See also Lindgaard, Jakob et al. The Impact of Global Drivers on the Future of EU-Turkey Security Relations. FEUTURE Online Paper No. 24, July 2018.
67 For a detailed analysis, see Ergun, Doruk/ Ülgen, Sinan. EU-Turkey security relations: Key drivers and future scenarios. In this volume, pp.103-120.

Tripoli and Ankara delimitating their respective economic exclusive zones at the expense of Greece, the assertive policies of Turkey demonstrated here have changed the perception of Turkey's role in the EU's southern neighbourhood. Turkey is seen as an actor with growing geopolitical ambitions that could collide with EU member states – France being the clearest example – and whose policies could be at odds with those of the EU, e.g. regarding the arms embargo in Libya. In parallel, some EU member states (France, Greece and Cyprus) are increasingly embedded in their alliances in the Middle East with countries such as Egypt, the United Arab Emirates and Saudi Arabia that perceive Turkey as a regional rival. Should this trend persist, the Southern neighbourhood could well reinforce conflictual rather than cooperative trends in EU-Turkey relations, while individual EU member countries' interests in the region clashing with the Turkish state's interests can permeate EU-Turkey relations (just as the conflict between Turkey and France has spilled over to NATO) in many negative forms, including sanctions.

2.3.3 The Global Shift of Power and the Contested Liberal International Order

Globally, the shifting balance of power from West to East and a contested liberal international order both have served to undermine the EU's normative power. This has increased the Turkish government's tendency to look for alliances that do not require normative commitments as is the case with the EU, with recent examples being Russia and China.

All in all, a void in multilateral governance has emerged, which is simultaneously characterised not only by the EU's reduced influence in the foreign policy sphere, but also the lack of a durable replacement.[68] Despite the EU's recovery efforts from the COVID-19 pandemic have been seen as a success in terms of the Union's strength and unity, the EU's capacity to provide global leadership has been severely damaged due to the accumulation of crises. At present, the EU's diminishing capacity to act as a 'force for good' in international affairs – a trend reinforced by the pandemic – coupled with Turkey's will to emerge as a regional actor, which is currently playing out in the Eastern Mediterranean, is likely to increase conflictual dynamics between Turkey and the EU. The new US-administration under the leadership of President Biden and Vice-President Harris that will take

---

68 Tocci, Nathalie. The Demise of the International Liberal Order and the Future of the European Project. IAI Commentaries. Rome, November 2018.

office in January 2021 represents a new driver at the global level. Yet, even though the Biden administration will be more multilateral-oriented it is less likely that it will strongly re-engage in the region terminating the vacuum accumulated over the past years.[69]

3. Present State of EU-Turkey Relations: Backsliding and Beyond

The degrading political situation in Turkey, the EU's sustained 'Turkey fatigue' coupled with a general halt on enlargement from 2014 onwards,[70] increasing politicisation of EU-Turkey relations due to electoral cycles on both sides in 2017 and turmoil in the neighbourhood and on the global scene have pushed the relationship towards an all-time low.

Winning the first presidential elections in 2014 by receiving more than 50% of the votes amplified Erdoğan's majoritarian rule. Additionally, the EU's sharp criticisms concerning human rights, the rule of law and fundamental freedoms put Turkey under the spotlight. Repression of the Gezi protests, the purges and the severe curtailment of fundamental freedoms following the 2016 coup attempt, and the erosion of checks and balances with a hyper-presidential system entering into force in 2018 raised concerns not only among Turkey's democratic forces, but also across the EU. However, with the accession process halted, the EU was left with little leverage over the Turkish government.

These developments triggered clear reactions in the EU. The European Commission's Turkey Report – no longer referred to as a 'progress report' – has reiterated that Turkey has been moving away from the EU since 2017.[71] In November 2017 and June 2019, the European Council decided to cut Turkey's pre-accession funds. The EP has repeatedly called for a suspension of accession negotiations with Turkey. The March 2019 call for suspension was also supported by MEPs who traditionally advocated Turkey's EU accession negotiations, but now increasingly question the Turkish government's commitments to reforms. It is worth noting that while the Socialists and Democrats (S&D) group in the EP supported the idea of suspending negotiations, they opposed an amendment backed by

---

69 See Tocci, Nathalie. Peeling Turkey Away from Russia's Embrace: A Transatlantic Interest. IAI Commentaries. Rome, December 2020.

70 Juncker, Jean-Claude. A new start for Europe, Opening Statement in the European Parliament Plenary Session. Strasbourg, July 2014.

71 European Commission. Turkey 2018 Report; European Commission. Turkey 2019 Report.

some in the European People's Party (EPP) calling for the termination of negotiations and the accession process itself. Although the EP's decision is not binding, it was indicative of the state of mind within European mainstream parties.

These decisions and statements are often instrumentalised by President Erdoğan, who expresses his distrust of European and Western partners.[72] Erdoğan has also previously stated that he would consider holding a referendum on whether to end the accession process[73], though this has never materialised.

Despite the generally negative turn since 2013, Turkey and the EU increasingly need each other. In fact, they managed to leave political differences aside when confronted with the risk of destabilisation. The 2015-2016 migration crisis and Turkey's 2018 currency crunch are two examples of this. In such critical moments, confidence-building messages become more frequent and mutual pragmatism gains ground. The EU-Turkey Statements on Migration of 29 November 2015 and 18 March 2016 exhibited such 'Realpolitik' in establishing functional cooperation[74] geared towards solving the migration crisis and facilitating a revitalisation of Turkey's accession negotiations and visa liberalisation. At the same time, continuous EU-Turkey bargaining over the incentives promised by the refugee deal has also heightened tension between the two sides, as evident in Turkey's latest move to open its border with Greece to the refugee movements towards Europe.[75]

In the neighbourhood and Syria, Ankara's foreign policy became increasingly predicated on the war morphing into a Kurdish issue with consequences for Turkey's domestic politics. The recalibration of Turkey's Syria policy has concurrently strained Ankara's relations with the US and to a lesser extent, certain European countries. In Libya, Turkey's and France's assertive policies have added to the already existing disputes with Greece and Cyprus in the Eastern Mediterranean, which is likely to affect not only bilateral relations but also those within the EU sphere. Turkey's current isolation, which is facilitated by the waning influence of Islamist political parties, is not tilting the country back toward the EU.

---

72 Şenyuva, Turkish Public Opinion.
73 Euractive, Erdoğan says he will consider referendum on Turkey's EU bid.
74 Ibid.; Dimitriadi, Angeliki/ Kaya, Ayhan. EU-Turkey relations on migration: Transactional partnership. In this volume, pp. 167-186; Saatcioğlu, The European Union's Refugee Crisis.
75 See Dimitriadi, Angeliki/ Kaya, Ayhan. EU-Turkey relations on migration: Transactional partnership. In this volume, pp. 167-186.

Russia's re-assertion on the international stage in the same period has further multiplied the conflictual elements in EU-Turkey relations. Turkey's frustration with its Western allies within the EU and NATO as well as with the US following the July 2016 coup attempt has accelerated Turkish-Russian rapprochement.[76] Turkey's military cooperation with Russia – particularly, its purchase of the S-400 missile defence system – also triggered political cooperation, particularly in determining Syria's future (outside the auspices of the EU and US), and has made the Turkish government dependent on Moscow.[77]

4. Conclusion

The analysis of how political drivers have impacted EU-Turkey relations indicates that there are some trends which are unlikely to be reversed. Turkey's political and reform trajectory seems to evolve in the opposite direction to EU expectations. In a context where Erdoğan has increased his powers, precisely because he feels politically vulnerable, the Turkish government is likely to adopt policies and actions that will push the country further away from the EU. An EU that is distracted with its many crises is not likely to revamp Turkey's accession prospects, even if Ankara's attitude would change significantly. Global trends such as the contested liberal international order, shifting power balances and increased instability in the neighbourhood will not, by themselves, induce a more conflict-ridden EU-Turkey relationship but they will not favour convergence dynamics either.

Hence, in view of the analysis of political drivers, convergence is not an applicable scenario in a mid-term perspective. On the contrary, most recent developments in reaction to the tensions in the Eastern Mediterranean region have increased hostility between the two sides as well as between Turkey and individual EU member states and hence increased conflict within EU-Turkey relations. Generally, political drivers do not seem to hinder the need for maintaining a certain level of cooperation between Turkey and the EU. This implies that for the time being, cooperation on a transactional basis can continue in areas of mutual interest. Having already invested a great extent into institutional integration (mainly through the

---

76 For a detailed discussion, see Ergün, Doruk/ Ülgen, Sinan. EU-Turkey security relations: Key drivers and future scenarios. In this volume, pp. 103-120.

77 Ergun, Doruk et al. The Role of the Middle East in the EU-Turkey Security Relationship. Key Drivers and Future Scenarios. FEUTURE Online Paper No. 20, May 2018, p. 15.

Customs Union) neither the EU nor Turkey would want to take a step towards breaking these existing institutional ties due to the accompanying costs, nor would the bureaucratic mechanisms allow for an abrupt break. However, conflictual trends in the relationship seem to be very likely to increase in the near future with the potential to still drive the relationship towards a breaking point. In order for maintaining a scenario of conflictual cooperation the two sides have to acknowledge the need to break the mutual escalation ladder of tensions focussing on the areas of mutual interdependencies that might be able to mitigate conflict and tensions.

Why are alternative scenarios less provable? A convergence scenario would require radical political changes both in Turkey and the EU. The EU has not yet resolved its other crises and the current government in Turkey does not have enough incentives to converge with the EU politically on issues such as the rule of law and fundamental rights. At the same time, Turkey's geopolitical and strategic importance with its large population, the intensity of its economic and investment links with the EU and their common interests will buffer the risk of a complete breakdown in relations. The EU's capacity to overcome its crises together with the evolution of Turkish politics could potentially act as game-changers in the future, while political transformations in the neighbourhood or at the global level can reinforce either cooperative or conflicting attitudes in the relationship.

While politics have driven relations away from convergence and more recently towards conflict, a certain level of cooperation has still been preserved. EU-Turkey relations have proven resilient. This resilience, though, cannot be taken for granted and is not directly related to political drivers either, but rather to the depth and breadth of strategic interests keeping Turkey and the EU together.

EU-Turkey Security Relations: Key Drivers and Future Scenarios

Doruk Ergun, Sinan Ülgen [1]

Introduction

The multifaceted relationship between the European Union (EU) and Turkey has undergone significant trials and tribulations over the last two decades. The security facet of the relationship has been especially variable, given the major transformation of the international security environment after the end of the Cold War. With the new millennium, this transformation has accelerated and intensified. The 11 September 2001 (9/11) attacks on the United States (US) marked the transnationalisation of terrorism making conflicts in distant lands homeland security issues for Western states. In 2002, the revelations about Iran's nuclear program heightened inter-state competition, whereas the US intervention in Iraq the following year triggered the unravelling of the order and status quo in the Middle East. Cyprus' membership to the EU in 2004, shortly after the rejection of the Annan Plan, dashed hopes that the issues between the two sides of the island, Turkey and Greece, could be solved anytime soon and further complicated Turkey's prospects for membership to the EU as well as EU-NATO cooperation. Meanwhile, the global financial crisis in 2008 rocked European economies and boosted scepticism about the European project and globalisation – thus forming the backbone of populist tides currently threatening to undermine the EU – as exemplified by Brexit. The so-called 'Arab Spring' further unravelled the state order in the Middle East against its early promises. This resulted in entrenched conflicts in Syria, Libya, Yemen, and others, creating suitable conditions for armed non-state actors

---

1 This chapter was originally written in May 2018 as part of the Centre for Economics and Foreign Policy Studies' contributions to the FEUTURE project and has been updated with the authors' permission. The views and opinions expressed in this chapter are those of the authors and do not reflect the position of any of the organisations that the authors are affiliated with. The authors would like to thank Beken Saatçioğlu and Funda Tekin for their kind support in reviewing and updating the analysis.

to flourish, and giving rise to spill overs affecting both EU member states and Turkey. The international affairs and security dynamics of today are markedly different from merely a decade ago, with hybridisation of war, rising cyber challenges, the gradual shift of economic and geo-political capital to the East, rising weight of non-state actors, and growing conflictual multipolarity that characterises the EU's and Turkey's shared neighbourhood. Reacting to unfolding global and regional events as well as recalibrating their interests accordingly, Turkey and EU member states have undertaken contradictory policies as much as complementary ones over the last two decades.

Against this background, this chapter first identifies the drivers that have guided and will likely guide the various aspects of the EU-Turkey security relationship.[2] It then discusses how these drivers have affected or might affect the relationship in producing three idealised scenarios in the area of security. The first is convergence, which we define as harmony between Ankara's and Brussels' strategies, and the development of institutional mechanisms to sustain cooperation, that may or may not accelerate Turkey's accession to the EU. The second is cooperation, which refers to any form of collaboration or alignment between Turkey and the EU that falls below the threshold of 'institutionalised' cooperation, occurring, for instance, via Turkey's ad hoc participation to various Common Security and Defence Policy (CSDP) missions. The final scenario is conflict, which consists of cases where EU member states and Turkey adopt incompatible stances on a given security issue, either competing to accomplish disparate goals or undertaking actions that detrimentally affect the relationship. In this sense, conflict does not necessarily mean an armed conflict between the EU and Turkey but can cover escalations like in the case of Turkish and Greek "gunboat diplomacy" in the Eastern Mediterranean Sea in late summer 2020[3] – and if violent conflict was deemed as a possibility, it would also fall under the conflict scenario. The chapter concludes that the relationship between Turkey and the EU has increasingly shifted from a 'cooperation bordering convergence' scenario in the turn of the millennium to a 'conflictual cooperation' scenario where the two sides cooperate on a transactional basis in areas of overlapping interest and necessity while

---

2 For a general definition of drivers see Tekin, Funda. The Future of EU-Turkey Relations. In this volume, pp. 11-28.

3 See Tuysuz, Gul. NATO allies are facing off in the Eastern Mediterranean. The conflict could entangle the entire region. CNN, 26.08.2020, https://edition.cnn.com/2020/08/25/europe/greece-turkey-eastern-mediterranean-tension-intl/index.html [02.09.20].

exhibiting frequent 'conflict' due to diverging interests. Under current security and political parameters, we hypothesize that conflictual cooperation will characterise the future EU-Turkey security relationship in the foreseeable future. Accordingly, neither anticipated drivers of conflict will be sufficient for shattering the relationship nor those of convergence and cooperation will be enough to force the two sides to make amends and bridge their differences. Consequently, the relationship will display elements of both conflict and cooperation, with convergence being a slim possibility and limited to thematic areas.

The chapter proceeds as follows. The first section provides a chronological analysis of internal, regional and international dynamics that have served as drivers for the EU-Turkey security relationship. As a testament to how rapid the security environment has changed, the analysis focuses on intervals of five years starting from 1999. In the second section, the chapter makes projections for the next five years and beyond, outlining the potential opportunities and fault lines for the relationship. It concludes by presenting recommendations on issues that may increase the prospect of cooperation against a rising tide of competing interests.

1. Scenes from a Memory: A Chronological Overview on EU-Turkey Security Relations

1.1 1999: A New Hope

The dissolution of the Soviet Union marked an end to the dynamics that characterised regional and international geopolitics after the end of World War II (WWII). Yet, the optimism of the victors of the Cold War in the "Free World" was soon marred with conflict in the Balkans, the first instance of large-scale armed conflict in Europe since the end of WWII. The Caucasus was likewise plagued with conflict during the first half of the 1990s, which, instead of producing an uneasy resolution like the Dayton Peace Agreement, remained protracted and 'frozen' in time. For Ankara the support and freedom of movement that the Kurdistan Workers' Party (PKK) found in Turkey's immediate neighbourhood in the Middle East including the refuge it found in Iraq became a growing source of concern. As Turkey's fight against the PKK terror group raged in full motion, human rights concerns across European capitals became a thorn in EU-Turkey relations. Yet perhaps more problematic were developments in the Eastern Mediterranean, with tensions flaring between Greece and Cyprus on the one and Turkey on the other side over wide-ranging issues including the Aegean territorial disputes, the stationing of S-300 missiles in Cyprus and the support that Greece provided to the PKK leader Abdullah Öcalan.[4]

By the end of the 1990s, however, the majority of these dynamics had improved. While the Kosovo War had dashed hopes that the Dayton Agreement brought stability to the Western Balkans, NATO's operation marked the end to the conflict in June 1999 and highlighted Turkey's positive contribution to European security as a NATO ally. Subsequently, NATO's 1999 enlargement, that included former Warsaw Pact countries – the Czech Republic, Hungary, and Poland – and fostered amiable relations with the Russian Federation, proved promising for Europe's eastern neighbourhood. After going as far as to mobilise against Syria, Turkey managed to capture PKK leader Öcalan in 1999, finding some respite after two decades of bloody conflict that had claimed over 30,000 lives. Although tensions remained in the Mediterranean, the diplomatic outreach between Greece and Turkey, which was initiated by their Foreign Ministers George Papandreou and İsmail Cem and facilitated by mutual popular sympathy following the twin earthquakes that hit both countries in 1999, was also an encouraging development. By the end of the year, on 12 December 1999, Turkey received official candidacy status to the European Union, turning a new leaf in EU-Turkey relations.[5]

1.2 1999-2004: United Against Shifting Global Dynamics

The optimism of the new millennium was soon crushed by the most lethal terrorist attacks in history that happened on 11 September 2001. The attacks compelled NATO to invoke its Treaty's Article 5 for the first time in its history in order to counter al-Qaeda and the Taliban in Afghanistan. Although Afghanistan's security and stability remain a complex and elusive challenge for NATO, its Operation Enduring Freedom in the country provided an important avenue for security cooperation between Turkey and EU member states. Turkey's predominantly Muslim identity also emerged

---

4 CIA. Fiasco in Nairobi. Greek Intelligence and the Capture of PKK Leader Abdullah Ocalan in 1999. Washington, 2009, https://www.cia.gov/library/center-for-the-st udy-of-intelligence/csi-publications/csi-studies/studies/vol53no1/fiasco-in-nairobi.ht ml [02.09.20].
5 European Council. Helsinki European Council 10 and 11 December 1999. Presidency Conclusions. Strasbourg, 1999, https://www.europarl.europa.eu/summits/he l1_en.htm# [02.09.20].

as a soft power tool that improved local receptivity towards the NATO operation.

The 9/11 attacks also highlighted the increasing lethality and disruptive capacity of armed non-state actors and the threat of transnational terrorism, exacerbated by technological developments, urbanisation and increasing complexity of infrastructures that societies rely upon.[6] Indeed, the distant conflict in Afghanistan quickly presented terrorism challenges to the EU and Turkey as al-Qaeda struck Istanbul in 2003, Madrid in 2004 and London in 2005, prompting further collaboration between law enforcement and intelligence agencies across Europe and Turkey.

Similarly, the Rose Revolution in Georgia in 2003 and the Orange Revolution in Ukraine in 2004 as well as the 2004 enlargement of both the EU and NATO, which brought several former Soviet Union and Warsaw Pact countries into the transatlantic political-security architecture, served to cement the security cooperation across European capitals and Ankara. Further to the east, progress towards the Baku-Tbilisi-Ceyhan pipeline constructed between 2003 and 2005, also contributed to Europe's energy security and Turkey's potential role as a transit country in reducing Europe's hydrocarbon dependency on Russia.

In this period, the principal development which negatively impacted EU-Turkey relations was Cyprus' admission into the EU in 2004. In fact, it could be argued that the unresolved Cyprus issue constituted the biggest obstacle to a convergence scenario in EU-Turkey security relations in the 1999-2004 timeframe. On the whole, however, the relationship was still characterised by cooperation, as exemplified by Turkey's security sector reforms, Europe's recognition of the PKK as a terrorist organisation and increasing EU-Turkey counterterrorism cooperation especially in response to al-Qaeda attacks in Europe and Turkey.

1.3 2004-2009: Beginnings of a Divide

In the 2004-2009 period, the EU-Turkey relationship mainly moved along a cooperative path while also featuring the beginnings of diverging foreign policy and security outlooks in Ankara and Brussels.

---

6 Dutka, Diane L. Violent Non-State Actors in World Politics. Their Formation, Actions, and Effects. Pennsylvania, 2006.

On the global scale, the 2008 financial crisis and its ramifications for Europe reduced Brussels' appetite for enlargement[7] and triggered a more independent foreign policy in Ankara. After 2009, under the guidance of Foreign Minister Ahmet Davutoğlu, Ankara's foreign policy orientation drifted further away from European capitals. At the same time, Turkey's domestic developments, notably, its democratisation process, were viewed positively across Europe.[8] On the security level, the most visible ramifications of this process included the transformation of civil-military relations in Turkey and Ankara's growing vision towards reaching a peaceful resolution to the longstanding Kurdish issue, dubbed the 'Kurdish Opening', which subsequently paved the way for the so-called 'Peace Process'.

As in the previous period, the enduring Cyprus conflict continued to be a stumbling block in EU-Turkey security cooperation. In December 2006, the EU Council blocked the negotiation of eight chapters in Turkey's membership talks over Turkey's refusal to extend the Additional Protocol to the Ankara Agreement to the Republic of Cyprus. In 2009, the Republic of Cyprus unilaterally blocked six other chapters, including Chapter 31 (Foreign, Security and Defence Policy). In turn, as a NATO member, Turkey raised obstacles to the deepening of NATO EU cooperation, particularly via impeding the Berlin Plus process.

On the positive side, Turkey's increasing capital to play a constructive role in the Middle East in the 2004-2009 period proved a welcome development. Ankara managed to establish relations with all political actors in Iraq, initiate a rapprochement with Syria, cooperate with EU member states through the United Nations Interim Force in Lebanon (UNIFIL) in southern Lebanon, mediate between Syria and Israel and assert itself as a complementary actor to the diplomatic processes vis-à-vis Iran's nuclear program. Still, there were visible cleavages such as Ankara's decision to recognise Hamas' electoral victory in 2006 in contrast to the EU's move to blacklist the organisation as a terrorist group in 2003 and subsequently boycott it alongside the United States, Russia and United Nations.

---

7 See Soler i Lecha, Eduard et.al. Politics ist taking EU-Turkey relations hostage. In this volume, pp. 77-102.
8 See for example European Commission. Turkey. 2006 Progress Report. SEC (2006) 1390, Brussels, 2006; European Commission. Turkey. 2005 Progress Report. SEC (2005) 1426, Brussels, 2005.

1.4 2009-2014: A Widening Gap

Against the largely cooperative atmosphere of the previous five years, the 2009-2014 period was characterised by rising conflict in EU-Turkey security relations, particularly exacerbated by developments in the Middle East and eastern Europe.

Most importantly, the Syrian civil war presented a complex picture. Although Turkey and the EU agreed in their opposition to the Bashar al-Assad regime, Ankara became increasingly frustrated in the failure of its attempts to convince its European partners and the US to support a military operation against Assad, e.g., through the imposition of no-fly zones. Nonetheless, after Assad's forces downed a Turkish F-4 Phantom jet in June 2012 and Turkey evoked NATO Treaty's Article 4 in response, Germany, the Netherlands, and later, Spain, stationed Patriot missile batteries in Turkey under the NATO umbrella. By the end of 2014, a series of critical incidents such as Turkey's limited border security enforcement against militants and arms crossing into Syria, the rise of the Islamic State of Iraq and the Levant (ISIL), and Turkey's reservations about supporting the Democratic Union Party (PYD) in Kobane came to sow further seeds of conflict in EU-Turkey relations.[9]

Simultaneously, tensions and escalations surrounding hydrocarbon exploration activities in the Eastern Mediterranean further plagued the EU-Turkey relationship.[10]

Further up north, Russia's 2014 annexation of Crimea and the broader hybrid warfare surrounding Ukraine marked a new phase in European security, escalating the dormant competition between the two camps of the Cold War.[11] In particular, Ankara's reluctance to participate to EU econo-

---

9 See for example: Ergun, Doruk et al. The Role of the Middle East in the EU-Turkey Security Relationship. Key Drivers and Future Scenarios. FEUTURE Online Paper No. 20, May 2018, https://feuture.uni-koeln.de/sites/feuture/user_uploa d/D4.5_Online_Paper_No_20.pdf [31.08.20]; European Commission. Kobane refugee crisis. EU steps up assistance. Brussels, October 2014; European Parliament. Kobane: MEPs call on Turkey to do more to help Syrian city under threat by IS. 22 October 2014, http://www.europarl.europa.eu/news/en/headlines/eu-affa irs/20141017STO74417/kobane-meps-call-on-turkey-to-do-more-to-help-syrian-city -under-threat-by-is_[31.08.20].

10 See Colantoni, Lorenzo. So near and yet so far: conflictual cooperation for EU-Turkey energy relations. In this volume, pp. 145-166.

11 See for example Forsberg, Tuomas. Russia and the European security order revisited. From the congress of Vienna to the post-cold war. In: European Politics and Society, November 2018, Vol. 20, No. 2, pp. 154-171; Barry, Ellen/ Myers, Steven

mic sanctions and its muted criticism against Russia constituted yet another source of divergence in the security and foreign policy priorities of the EU and Turkey.[12]

1.5 2014-2019: A Conflictual Partnership

The 2014-2019 timeframe saw the worsening of almost all security threats surrounding Turkey and the EU. Both parties have been the target of numerous terrorist attacks inspired or coordinated by ISIL, including high profile attacks in France, Belgium, Germany, the United Kingdom, Sweden, Spain and Turkey throughout 2015-2017. Consequently, the sides have gradually improved their intelligence and border security cooperation, especially to counter the threats posed by returning foreign fighters. Another by-product of regional conflict, the refugee crisis of 2015, also pushed the EU and Turkey to collaborate more closely on security matters. In this respect, joint efforts aimed at securing the Aegean against illegal migration and smuggling by establishing improved coast guard capabilities and a NATO-led mission.

Yet, Turkey has not found a willing partner in Brussels in tackling other terrorism threats that it encountered. Following the collapse of the 'Peace Process' and the reignition of conflict with the PKK, Ankara was left frustrated in the face of the limited European support it received in its fight against the PKK's terror campaign. Moreover, the EU has strongly criticised Turkey's security operations against the PKK and its affiliates.[13] The 15 July 2016 failed coup attempt which Ankara attributes to the Gülen network (Fethullahist Terrorist Organisation – FETO, as recognised by Turkey) and its aftermath have constituted additional sources of political friction between Turkey and the EU. Ankara has criticised European capitals for lack of support against a coup attempt and an existential threat,[14]

Lee. Putin Reclaims Crimea for Russia and Bitterly Denounces the West. In: Nytimes.com, 18 March 2014, https://www.nytimes.com/2014/03/19/world/europe/ukraine.html [02.09.20].

12 See for example: Hellquist, Elin. Either with us or against us. Third-country alignment with EU sanctions against Russia Ukraine. In: Cambridge Review of International Affairs, October 2016, Vol. 29, No. 3, pp. 997-1021.

13 European Commission. European Commission. Turkey 2016 Report. SWD(2016) 366 final, Brussels, 2016.

14 BBC. Turkey-Germany. Erdogan urges Merkel to extradite Gulen 'terrorists'. 28 September 2018, https://www.bbc.com/news/world-europe-45684390 [02.09.20].

and the EU has expressed concerns about Turkey's disregard for human rights and the rule of law in the process.[15]

In Syria, another key irritant in EU-Turkey security policies concerned the PYD which Turkey equates with the PKK terrorist organisation. This stands in sharp contrast to the support that the PYD has received from not only the US but also some EU member states.[16] Turkey's more recent cross border operations in Syria in 2018 and 2019 (Olive Branch and Peace Spring) targeting the PYD have further deepened the divide between Turkey and the EU, as exemplified by the European Parliament's resolution in March 2018 demanding Turkey to withdraw its troops from Syria[17] as well as the European Parliament resolution of 24 October 2019 on the Turkish military operation in northeast Syria and its consequences.

However, in 2016, Turkey restructured its interests in Syria so as to adopt a predominantly national security-first stance aimed at countering ISIL and PYD as opposed to hastening Assad's deposition. Since Turkey has failed to secure the support of its Western partners for an intervention in Syria, the Operation Euphrates Shield (August 2016 - March 2017) and the subsequent Operation Olive Branch in March 2018 occurred in close cooperation with Russia instead. Turkey's cooperation with Russia, and to some extent with Iran, has also presented it with political capital necessary for influencing the outcome of the Syrian civil war – as illustrated by the diplomatic processes launched in Astana and Sochi. In turn, Russia has further leveraged this short-term national security dependency to forge long-term security cooperation with Turkey, notably through the sale of the S-400 missile defence systems against the staunch opposition of Turkey's NATO partners. As a result, through Ankara's reliance on Russia for its perceived national security interests and broader Syria policy, Moscow has gained the means to spoil future NATO-Turkey relations as illustrated by the risk of Turkey being sanctioned by the US under the Countering America's Adversaries Through Sanctions Act (CAATSA). So far, the US President Trump has used his political weight to postpone CAATSA sanctions but unless Turkey decides to forego the S400 system, the sanctions are likely to be activated.

---

15 European Commission. Turkey 2019 Report. SWD(2019) 2019 final, Brussels, 2019.

16 France24. France's Macron pledges support for Kurd-led Syria force. 30 March 2018, https://www.france24.com/en/20180330-france-macron-pledges-support-kur dish-led-ypg-syria-democratic-forces [02.09.20].

17 European Parliament. European Parliament resolution of 15 March 2018 on the situation in Syria. 2018/2626(RSP), Strasbourg, 2018.

2. The Road Ahead: Projecting the Next Five Years and Beyond

2.1 Potential Scenarios of Convergence

The above review of the last two decades has revealed that in shared threats, convergence scenarios – in terms of Turkey's accession to or deeper engagement with existing EU security frameworks, such as Permanent Structured Cooperation (PESCO), the European Police Agency (EU-ROPOL) or European Border and Coast Guard Agency (FRONTEX) as well as active involvement in discussions surrounding CSDP or the institutionalisation of EU-Turkey security cooperation through the establishment of individual mechanisms between Ankara and Brussels – seldom define the EU-Turkey security relationship. This is because cooperation occurs either under the NATO framework or bi- and multilateral mechanisms involving individual EU member states and Turkey. Furthermore, the possibility of convergence is often undercut by either mutual differences in perceptions, interests or priorities surrounding the security issues at hand or other drivers (e.g., political tensions), which in turn produce cooperation scenarios. Hence, the potential convergence scenarios discussed in this section are indeed *potential scenarios* and should be evaluated with these caveats in mind.

The first issue-area driving the parties towards a convergence scenario is migration. Regardless of how states will structure their individual migration policies, the security dimension of the flow of displaced people to Turkey and Europe will persist as a driver for mutual cooperation (in addition to various prospects for cooperation on migration policy outside of the security domain[18]). This is driven by the increasing prioritisation of the issue in Brussels as underlined by the European Union Global Strategy (EUGS)[19] and recent developments surrounding Turkey's short-lived decision in early 2020 to ease restrictions towards refugee flows through its

---

18 See Dimitriadi, Angeliki/ Kaya, Ayhan. EU-Turkey relations on migration: Transactional partnership. In this volume, pp. 167-186.

19 Indeed, as mentioned in the EUGS: "Together with countries of origin and transit, we will develop common and tailor-made approaches to migration featuring development, diplomacy, mobility, legal migration, border management, readmission and return" see: European External Acition Service. Shared Vision, Common Action: A Stronger Europe. A Global Strategy for the European Union's Foreign and Security Policy. Brussels, 2016, https://eeas.europa.eu/sites/eeas/files/eugs_review_web_0.pdf [11.09.20], p. 27.

border with Greece.[20] From a strictly security perspective, Turkish authorities attribute at least one terrorist attack in Istanbul[21] to ISIL operatives that crossed the border guised as refugees. There are numerous facets to security cooperation in the realm of migration, such as border security, intelligence cooperation, fight against organised crime and trafficking, the protection of migrants' human security, which is of primary importance.

The second potential area for convergence is non-proliferation. Both Turkey and the EU remain committed to preventing the proliferation of weapons of mass destruction (WMD), especially in the Middle East. In the case of Iran, they also converge around the need to find a diplomatic solution to address proliferation concerns and/or deploy political and economic pressure (although Turkey is very reluctant when it comes to sanctions) as opposed to relying on pre-emptive military strikes.

Perhaps an even more salient driver for convergence or at least cooperation is the nexus of terrorism and WMD. Both the EU and Turkey are exposed to the dangers of chemical, biological, radiological and nuclear (CBRN) terrorism, and the Syrian and Iraqi contexts have particularly demonstrated armed non-state actors' inclination to use WMD when presented the opportunity. Indeed, al-Qaeda and ISIL have shown a willingness to acquire WMD capabilities for terrorist purposes.[22] Countering this threat necessitates multilateral cooperation concerning border security, intelligence sharing, fight against smuggling networks as well as improvement of the technical capacity of countries in the eastern neighbourhood and the Middle East to prevent the theft and trafficking of weapons-useable CBRN material. In this context, institutional convergence between the respective agencies in the EU and Turkey, such as Euratom and Turkish Atomic Energy Authority, and law enforcement agencies (e.g. with EUROPOL, FRONTEX and Turkish counterparts) remains a possibility.

---

20 Harris, Chris. Europe's migrant crisis. Why Turkey led refugees head for EU and the link with Syria. In: Euronews.com, 04 March 2020, https://www.euronews.co m/2020/03/03/europe-s-migrant-crisis-why-turkey-let-refugees-head-for-eu-and-the-link-with-syria [31.08.20].

21 Homola, Victor/ Yeginsu, Ceylan. Istanbul Bomber Entered as Refugee Turks Say. In: New York Times, 13. 01.2016, https://www.nytimes.com/2016/01/14/world/eu rope/istanbul-explosion.html [02.09.20];]. Also see for a thwarted attack Milliyet (2017): "Son dakika... Eylem hazırlığındaki 2 DEAŞ'lı Beylikdüzü'nde yaka-landı!", 20.08.2017, http://www.milliyet.com.tr/eylem-hazirligi-yapan-2-deas-li-gu ndem-2505162/ [23.10.2020].

22 Shuster, Simon. Inside the Uranium Underworld. Dark Secrets, Dirty Bombs. In: Times.com, 06.04.2017, http://time.com/4728293/uranium-underworld-dark-secre ts-dirty-bombs/ [02.09.20].

Although the broader issue of terrorism is a common challenge for both sides, disagreements concerning which armed non-state actors fall into the category of terrorist groups (e.g., the above-mentioned disagreement about the PYD), which security threats to prioritise and the means necessary to tackle them have been sources of conflict. Therefore, the broader terrorism challenge falls under the cooperation scenario with a strong emphasis on its potential for further conflict.

Nonetheless, a potential for convergence between the EU and Turkey remains with respect to the development of non-securitised means of fight against terrorism. This can come in the form of joint strategies and institutional setups for countering or preventing violent extremism via steps such as counter-extremism, rehabilitation and reintegration. As a nation facing the threat of violent extremism, Turkey has significant experience in the military and law enforcement dimensions of counter-terrorism but comparatively little experience in preventive approaches. Therefore, with the return of foreign terrorist fighters and non-combatants from the Syrian and Iraqi battlefields, the upscaling of repatriation efforts is increasingly becoming an imperative for both Europe and Turkey, and will constitute an additional avenue of cooperation.

Developments within the transatlantic space may also boost appetite for further convergence. Under the Trump administration, the United States' role in NATO is increasingly questioned, triggering efforts in the EU to gain further independence in addressing its security needs, as exemplified by PESCO, which can in turn create venues for partnership between Ankara and Brussels. The reformulation of the post-Brexit security relationship between the EU and the United Kingdom may also inspire new models for cooperation between the EU and Turkey. Cooperation in defence procurement, the joint development of defence technologies (such as Turkey's partnership with EUROSAM on the SAMP/T Aster-30 NT missile defence system with Italy and France) may form yet another leg of convergence. To be sure, the main caveat here is the increasing divergence of Turkish foreign policy and security strategy from the EU as well as Ankara's attempts to diversify its arsenal, as illustrated by its S-400 procurement. The rising bilateral tension between Turkey and France in 2020 could also potentially handicap EU-Turkey cooperation in defence industries. It is presumed for instance that Turkey's negotiations with EUROSAM have been put on hold as a result of the divergence with Paris.

Emerging threats such as cybercrime, cyber security and cyber warfare may also present an impetus for the EU and Turkey to converge. On the security side of the equation, convergence may take the form of initiatives like joint-capacity development, establishment of joint-response mechanisms, building up the resilience of critical national infrastructure, among others. On the political side, the EU and Turkey may also collaborate in global efforts to set up rules of engagement in the cyber realm, or more broadly, in addressing the question of cyber security governance.

2.2 Potential Scenarios of Conflict

On the opposite side of the spectrum, are issues that continue to be thorns in the EU-Turkey relationship and may be exacerbated in time. Perhaps the most salient among them is Turkey's Kurdish issue which remains unlikely to be resolved through non-securitised measures in the near future. In fact, the opposite is likely to persist, with the Turkish side intent on solving the security dimension of the issue through military means. This includes potential operations against the PYD in Syria, which also has ramifications for the Kurdish issue domestically. In turn, the PYD's role in the fight against ISIL – against Turkey's strong objections – has been a source of tension in recent EU-Turkey relations. Relatedly, the expanding influence of the PKK and its affiliated organisations in the region has regionalised Turkey's domestic Kurdish issue and consequently expanded the likelihood of negative ramifications for EU-Turkey relations.

Turkey's growing tendency to cooperate with new partners, such as Russia and Qatar, either as a result of an interest in reducing reliance on its traditional NATO allies or due to the perceived unreliability of its allies in certain areas – such as in the context of its fight against the PKK – will likely be another driver of conflict. Russia represents one of the most visible drivers. While Turkey continues to perceive threats from Russia, having downed a Russian warplane in November 2015 and having experienced in February 2020 an episode of Russia backed regime offensive in Idlib which led to 34 casualties on the Turkish side, Moscow has increasingly become an ally of convenience for Ankara, delivering results most notably in Syria. Turkey is also seeking Moscow's diplomatic support to reach a cease fire and ultimately a political settlement in Libya. Furthermore, Moscow has leveraged this already asymmetric relationship where Turkey is increasingly more dependent on Russia to address some of its critical economic, national security, foreign policy and energy related priorities, by attempting to create long-term dependencies through strategic defence system procurements – thus far exemplified by the S-400 missile defences. Russia may continue with this policy to drive a wedge between Turkey, the EU and NATO.

Terrorism is another potential source of conflict. While specific aspects of terrorism fall under the scenarios of convergence and cooperation as explained above, the divergence between the EU's and Turkey's respective outlooks towards different entities and disagreement over the justifiable means of effective counterterrorism, will likely remain controversial between the EU and Turkey. In fact, such tension has persisted in EU-Turkey relations and specific security cooperation, and currently continues regarding the Gulen network – FETO - as well as the PYD/YPG as discussed above.

2.3 *Potential Scenarios of Cooperation*

Transnational terrorism and challenges stemming from violent extremist organisations that affect both parties – such as radicalisation and lone-wolf terrorism – top the list of areas for actual and potential cooperation. Against occasional hurdles, the EU and Turkey have cooperated in the real of the intelligence dimension especially in the post-9/11 period, as exemplified by the cooperation agreement signed between EUROPOL and the Turkish National Police in 2004.[23] The rising ISIL threat has been another driver of cooperation (again, in spite of initial differences in opinions on the prioritisation of the fight against the group), with cooperation on intelligence sharing, law enforcement and border control improving in time. In the last couple of years, the focus has shifted from preventing the EU and Turkish citizens from joining ISIL to spotting and addressing the issues related to fighters returning from Syria and Iraq. Even if that threat subsides, Turkey's position as a potential transit route for terrorist operatives moving from the Middle East, the Caucasus and Central Asia will remain an integral driver of cooperation between the EU and Turkey. The aforementioned caveats would likely prevent convergence on counterterrorism, suggesting that there will rather be sustained and deepened cooperation in certain areas – such as intelligence sharing – and in terms of ad hoc issues.

Addressing the root causes of terrorism, namely, promoting regional stability, preventing conflict and supporting good governance practices in the EU's neighbourhood, could also form another area of cooperation for

---

23 Europol. Agreement on Cooperation between Europol and The Republic of Turkey. Warsaw, 2004, https://www.europol.europa.eu/sites/default/files/documents/agree ment_on_cooperation_between_the_european_police_office_and_the_republic_ of_turkey.pdf [02.09.20].

the two partners. The drivers of radicalisation, terrorism and conflict are mostly visible in the Middle East and North Africa (MENA) region and to some degree in the Caucasus, both of which are areas where Turkey and the EU have variegated connections, influence and leverage. However, more recently, the interests of the two parties have often diverged, sometimes quite significantly, in the said regions.[24] Yet, if the sides can agree upon the prioritisation of ensuring stability and preventing conflict, these differentiated relations with stakeholders on the ground, for example through the various state and non-state actors that Turkey and the EU member states are engaged in in Syria, can be used in a complementary way. Should this fail, another area of cooperation for the EU and Turkey is presented by conflict management and post-conflict reconstruction. Especially in Syria and Iraq, there may be significant room for the two sides to collaborate in humanitarian and development assistance, post-conflict reconstruction, peacebuilding, mediation and political reform, among other areas. This scenario, too, would likely play out on an ad hoc basis – as illustrated in the Balkans and Lebanon – instead of producing convergence.

The shifting weight of third parties in regional and global affairs may also motivate Brussels and Ankara to cooperate. While Turkey's relations with Russia represent drivers of conflict with the EU, the collapse of the ongoing understanding reached between Ankara and Moscow remains possible, which would in turn provide an impetus for Ankara to move closer to the transatlantic camp. Furthermore, irrespective of a turn in Turkey-Russia relations, Ankara has already sent signals that it is intent on cooperating with Europe and others in restricting Russia's ambitions, notably in Eastern Europe, by proposing to lead the NATO Spearhead Force and continuing its military cooperation with Ukraine.[25] Turkey has also increased its military cooperation with the US in the Black Sea among others as a reaction to Russia. With regards to global security affairs, there may be room for multilateral security cooperation between EU member states and Turkey on peacebuilding and peacekeeping operations outside their immediate neighbourhood.

Beyond these issues, convergence scenarios discussed above are also equally likely to turn into cooperation scenarios if the institutional flexibil-

---

24 Ergun et al. The Role of the Middle East in the EU-Turkey Security Relationship.
25 Erkuş, Sevil. Turkey Will Lead NATO Spearhead Force in 2021. May 2015, https://www.atlanticcouncil.org/blogs/natosource/turkey-will-lead-nato-spearhead-force-in-2021/ [02.09.20]; Newsweek. Ukraine And Turkey Launch Black Sea Naval Drill Amid RussiaTensions, 07.04.2016, http://www.newsweek.com/ukraine-and-turkey-launch-black-sea-naval-drill-amidst-russia-tensions-444882 [20.10.20].

ities necessary for the emergence of a convergence scenario prove to be politically unfeasible. For instance, the incorporation of Cyprus in PESCO has already precluded any convergence scenarios that could have been focused on the institutional opportunities linked to PESCO.

3. Conclusions: Managing a Conflictual Cooperation

None of the aforementioned security issues that have a bearing on EU-Turkey relations exists in isolation from other security or non-security related matters. Nor do they carry enough weight to single-handedly drive the EU-Turkey relationship in a particular direction. At the same time, against the resilience of the EU-Turkey relationship, we should also acknowledge the significant downturn in the relations over the last decade. Indeed, this may even signal a divergence in the strategic foreign policy and security outlooks of the two parties.[26] While regional trends – including, transnational terrorism, state fragility, non-proliferation, among others – make cooperation between Europe and Turkey imperative,[27] for the short-run, we can foresee that the mismatching strategic thinking in Brussels and Ankara will likely produce more conflict scenarios. Furthermore, the impact of existing areas of contention will be more detrimental to the relationship. The ongoing conflict in the Eastern Mediterranean over the exploration rights of hydrocarbon resources attests to this observation.

Yet, key security issues, especially those that are significant in security terms of both parties, present key drivers for sustained cooperation. Thus, the conflictual drivers will likely not push the two sides irreconcilably apart. Rather, they will reduce what would have been convergence scenarios – had the relationship been more amiable – into cooperation scenarios limiting their scope and sustainability.

If these trends persist, the foreseeable scenario for EU-Turkey relations seems to be one in which the sides are stuck in a loveless marriage – a set-up where the parties cooperate out of mutual need and continue to benefit from existing arrangements, but lack a common vision for the future or a

---

26 Braun-Dorell, Taylor et al. EU-Turkey Relations: Security Drivers from the Eastern Neighbourhood. FEUTURE Online Paper No. 23, July 2018.
27 Lindgaard, Jakob et al. The Impact of Global Drivers on the Future of EU-Turkey Security Relations. FEUTURE Online Paper No. 24, July 2018; Özel, Soli et al. Evolution of the EU's and Turkey's Security Interests, Threat Perceptions and Discourse. FEUTURE Online Paper No. 3, April 2017.

desire to improve and deepen their relationship. As mentioned above, this scenario can be referred to as 'conflictual cooperation'.

It is also important to note that security constitutes only one tenet of the multidimensional EU-Turkey relationship. Indeed, the argument that security affairs represent the main guiding tenet would be a flawed one. Essentially, political and economic drivers form the core of the relationship while other drivers add to the complexity of the equation. In fact, European security has primarily been dealt with under the NATO umbrella, which has in turn lowered the sides' appetite for establishing a separate security framework and pushed them to focus on ad hoc cooperation or bilateral cooperation (between member states and Turkey) instead. Therefore, security relations do not exist in a vacuum as they are negatively or positively impacted by other drivers – and frequently, political ones. Furthermore, by itself, the security dimension has so far been unable to move the EU-Turkey relationship in a certain direction.

Yet, major disruptions in the foreseeable trends have the potential to alter this projection. These include a breakdown of the ongoing partnership between Russia and Turkey and a return to competition, which would drive Turkey closer to Europe. Similarly, the escalation of military tensions in the Middle East, especially one that involves Turkey, may cause Ankara to seek closer ties with its traditional Euro-Atlantic allies. In turn, a military confrontation between Russia and an EU or NATO member country would serve as a litmus test for EU-Turkey relations, pushing it either towards convergence or conflict. Yet, perhaps the most impactful of all would be an armed escalation between Cyprus and/or Greece and Turkey. This would push most areas of cooperation between the EU and Turkey to a grinding halt and carry ramifications for all the layers of the relationship. In contrast, the resolution of the Cyprus issue could alleviate a major obstacle preventing deepened relations between Brussels and Ankara.

On the whole, in the absence of such 'wild cards' in the relationship,[28] conflictual cooperation will likely prevail in the near future. However, there are opportunities that policymakers across Ankara and Brussels may explore to anchor cooperation against turbulences in the relationship. Relatedly, a helping instrument would be to address the deficit of mutual understanding on the drivers of conflict. On the Kurdish issue for example, the EU is challenged in communicating its human rights concerns to Turkey as much as Turkey is challenged in relaying its national security considerations. Similar concerns are also visible when it comes to the topic

---

28 See Tekin, Funda. The future of EU-Turkey relations. In this volume, pp. 11-28.

of Russia. Especially in the midst of political crises the quality of dialogue falters even more, resulting in heightened conflict. Therefore, Turkey and the EU need to step up communication across all levels, aiming to increase frequency, frankness and quality of dialogue. This would also help insulate the security cooperation from the relationships' other undercurrents such as political and economic tensions.

Deepening the military industrial cooperation represents another area of underexplored cooperation. As underlined by the EUGS, the EU has justifiably prioritised the creation of a more competitive European military industry. Turkey is a lead country for both the supply and demand dimensions of the military industry. The creation of more effective linkages between Turkish and European manufacturers can be seen as a mutually beneficial and politically feasible dimension of the cooperative outcome. For instance, an eventual Turkish decision to purchase the EUROSAM ballistic missile defence system, which, in all likelihood, would include a joint production component, would be an example. Additionally, in the past decade Turkish defence industries have developed new capabilities in edge technologies like surveillance and armed drones. As such Turkish military industries can also provide substantial contributions to the further development of European industrial capabilities in security and defence. However, Turkish manufacturers' access to respective EU funding should also be facilitated.

Given the multiplicity of the security dynamics emanating from the neighbourhood, notably the MENA region, the EU and Turkey would also benefit from diversifying their dialogue with a shared perspective focused on foresight and risk analysis. In other words, beyond taking a reactionary approach to issues from the neighbourhood as they arise, thinking ahead and identifying potential areas of cooperation would benefit both parties. In this respect, the first step could consist of taking a closer look into the role that Turkey and the EU can play in promoting peace in all its dimensions, and preventing future conflict in Syria and other areas of present or potential conflict. Beyond the political, diplomatic and military engagement necessary to ensure calm in Syria, there is also a significant need to work towards the country's reconstruction over which the EU and Turkey can cooperate. In order to maximise the effectiveness and sustainability of the response in Syria as well as other future potential conflicts, proper planning and coordination among partners remain key. Therefore, in addition to the military cooperation within NATO (which may also be expanded towards EU-Turkey cooperation in the post-Brexit European security order), Europe and Turkey have the grounds to cooperate more proactively in ensuring peace and realising human security.

Economic Drivers as Anchors of EU-Turkey Relations: Trade, Finance and Knowledge

Erkan Erdil, İbrahim Semih Akçomak

1. Introduction

The economy has long been one of the fundamental areas that has impacted European Union (EU)-Turkey relations. Historically and well before initiating official relations with the EU, Turkey has had economic and trade links with several European countries. Hence, economic ties mark the starting point and, along with political relations resting on Turkey's sufficient compliance with the Copenhagen political criteria, form one of the central aspects of official EU-Turkey relations, as exemplified by key steps such as the 1963 Ankara Agreement and the 1995 Customs Union (CU) agreement. Additionally, among the first chapters opened in accession negotiations several were focusing on economic relations (e.g. Chapters 1-Free Movement of Goods, 3-Right of Establishment and Freedom to Provide Services, 9-Financial Services, 25-Science and Research, 29-CU).

Within the economic dimension of EU-Turkey relations, it is possible to conceptualise three different relationship scenarios: conflict reflecting trends of growing division and competition; convergence implying Turkey's membership in a differentiated Union; and functional cooperation representing the middle ground of engagement without accession.[1] This chapter identifies key economic drivers in EU-Turkey relations since 1999, analysing the flow of goods and services[2] as well as finance[3] and knowledge[4] on the one hand, along with the political economy implica-

---

1 See Tekin, Funda. The future of EU-Turkey relations. In this volume, pp.11-28 and Tocci, Nathalie. Turkey and the European Union: Scenarios for 2023. FEUTURE Background Paper, September 2016, p. 12.
2 Mertzanis, Charialos. Understanding the EU-Turkey Sectoral Trade Flows During 1990-2016. A Trade Gravity Approach. FEUTURE Online Paper No. 8, November 2017.
3 Cömert, Hasan. The Financial Flows and the Future of EU-Turkey Relations. FEUTURE Online Paper No. 9, November 2017.
4 Akçomak, İ. Semih et al. Knowledge Cohesion in European Regions: Convergence and Cohesion with Turkey. FEUTURE Online Paper No. 10, November 2017.

tions of these flows for the EU-Turkey relationship on the other.[5] Aiming for an evidence-based approach, this chapter traces each of the three flows in question and based on these findings identifies key drivers of the economic relationship that may impact the overall EU-Turkey relations. The political economy is considered as creating an umbrella driver that governs the other flows. In looking to propose a future scenario for EU-Turkey economic relations, this chapter addresses three specific questions: What kind of economic drivers are relevant and what constellations exist? What are the most prominent drivers within each flow? Accordingly, what is the likely scenario for EU-Turkey economic relations within a medium-term timeframe? In the conclusion, a table summarises these evidence-based economic drivers considering: their linkage to other thematic dimensions within the EU-Turkey relationship; the timeframe for taking effect; their importance; together with their likelihood and relevance for the EU and Turkey. All drivers are then linked to a proposed scenario of conflict, convergence and cooperation.

Preliminary analysis finds that most drivers point to the cooperation scenario, which builds on the tight economic relations between Turkey and the EU. The long joint history featuring flows of goods and services[6] together with finance[7] between Turkey and the EU has reached a stage of a positive-sum game where both parties win. Consequently, trade policy aims at raising the trading partners' income growth in both absolute and relative terms, encouraging adjustments in Turkey's productive structures that will speed up alignment in economic development levels. Most importantly, considering the long-term unobservable influence of institutions that mitigate economic relations, this will stimulate impact on consumer and producer preferences for European and Turkish products.[8] Financial flows can also be significantly affected by the tone of relations between the EU and Turkey. Especially when assuming that the EU stabilises itself in a world throughout which global liquidity evaporates, Turkish policy makers cannot afford the conflict scenario.[9] Even in a world of high global liquidity, the possibility of financial reversals causes substantial uncertainty and potentially high costs for Turkey. Thus, by simply focusing on the role

---

5 Berulava, George et al. Modes of Regional Cooperation and Their Political Economy. FEUTURE Online Paper No. 29, February 2019.
6 Mertzanis, Understanding the EU-Turkey Sectoral Trade Flows During 1990-2016.
7 Cömert, The Financial Flows and the Future of EU-Turkey Relations.
8 Mertzanis, Understanding the EU-Turkey Sectoral Trade Flows During 1990-2016.
9 Cömert, The Financial Flows and the Future of EU-Turkey Relations.

of financial flows, under normal conditions EU-Turkey relations are destined to evolve towards either convergence or cooperation.

At the same time, both sides have derived benefits from recent increase in knowledge flows.[10] Respective analysis demonstrates that Turkey has considerably enhanced its position in knowledge exchange, especially with regard to some of its developed regions, which can be seen as emergent knowledge hubs. These results indicate that Turkey's knowledge system is strongly tied to the European Research Area (ERA), thus reducing the probability of a conflict scenario.[11]

Hence, research on the economic dimension provides evidence for the cooperation scenario, even showing certain potential for tilting towards a convergence scenario. With accession talks effectively suspended, economic cooperationpresents itself as one of the few areas of dialogue between the EU and Turkey. On the one hand, Turkey is trying to reposition itself as a regional and global player weighing its options outside the EU in terms of economic cooperation. On the other hand, from a rational standpoint, both parties realise the need to upgrade the currently limited CU agreement. Additionally, the global trade regime is on the verge of major changes through mega trade agreements such as the Transatlantic Trade and Investment Partnership (TTIP). Although currently increasing trade wars seem to shadow the multilateral trade regime, big deals whether bilateral or otherwise will remain important drivers in global trade relations. More than the EU, Turkey will need to shape its trade policy not only to prevent being left out, but also to avoid potential losses.[12] Accordingly, together with evidence of political economy drivers, the most probable scenario at least in the medium term seems to be cooperation.

The remainder of this chapter is organised as follows. Section 2 identifies and discusses drivers in the three relevant flows. Section 3 summarises the economic drivers and their possible link to the three ideal-type scenarios within a detailed table to discuss the future of EU-Turkey relations from the perspective of their economic dimension.

---

10 Akçomak et al., Knowledge Cohesion in European Regions.
11 Ibid.
12 Berulava et al., Modes of Regional Cooperation and Their Political Economy.

2. How Do Flows of Finance, Goods and Services Together With Knowledge Affect EU-Turkey Relations?

2.1 Flows of Goods and Services

The EU is Turkey's most important trading partner.[13] These tight trade relations build on the 1995 Customs Union Agreement, whose effects have been extensively discussed in the literature. Mertzanis' study[14], for instance, focuses on the CU's impact in regard to industrial goods and processed agricultural goods. It evaluates these impacts in general and on a sectoral level, attempting to analyse the pattern of Turkey's sectoral trade flows with the EU based on OECD panel data between 1990 and 2016. This timeframe enables us to make comparisons regarding the pre- and post-CU agreement period, with respective analysis applying the trade gravity model to a new data set covering a 27-year period, while considering trade flows both in aggregate terms and by sector. Further, a different classification between intermediate goods, consumption goods, capital goods, mixed-end goods and miscellaneous goods is applied as well as a dynamic panel estimation methodology to produce unbiased estimates. These novelties in research contribute substantially to refining policy decisions and scenario analysis for the economic dimension of EU-Turkey relations.

Empirical analysis for the aggregate trade volume and sectoral composition underlines the following results:

- Methodological and empirical validity of results confirms that the standard gravity model is a fair predictor of bilateral trade volume between Turkey and its trading partners.
- There are few differences in trading patterns between the different sectors, with capital goods, mix-end and miscellaneous goods being highlighted as those where the potential impact of expanded trade may be relatively greater than those from other sectors.
- Among the gravity model trading variables, those that are robust include the level of income and the population-weighted distance between Turkey and its trading partners. However, the latter's effect is

---

13 The share of exports to EU-28 is 51.6% and the share of imports from EU28 is 33.3% by the end of 2019.
14 Mertzanis, Understanding the EU-Turkey Sectoral Trade Flows During 1990-2016.

very small and it would be expected that transport costs may inhibit trade opportunities.

- The level of economic development may or may not be a significant predictor of trade volume. This depends on the model used and the various controls included in the analysis. Furthermore, in the case of significant predictor, this concerns Turkey relatively more than its trading partners. Hence, it is implied that Turkey is facing a challenge in trying to catching up with the productive structures of its trading partners, which varies in dependence on the different sectors of trade activity considered.
- Non-economic factors, especially legal institutions, directly or indirectly affecting incentive and trade volume, may be significant predictors of trade flows between Turkey and its trading partners. Hence, they should be given due consideration.
- Collapse of the CU would seem to be more damaging for Turkey than the EU, while an upgraded CU would have potential benefits for both sides in the long run.[15]
- Trade agreements generally provide an upgrade in technological skill sets, as with the existing CU agreement, especially where asymmetries in skill sets are observed between partners. Moreover, this presents the opportunity for a competitive transformation of production structure in Turkey.
- EU trade seems to have a stabilising impact on the Turkish economy, both in terms of direct economic benefits and indirect institutional impacts.

Against this background, it can be seen that there are specific drivers that could affect the future of EU-Turkey economic relations:

- the upgrading or cancelling of the EU-Turkey CU,
- the EU reaching an agreement with the US on the Transatlantic Trade and Investment Partnership (TTIP),
- EU trade developing a stabilising impact,
- Turkey gradually increasing production (and export) of high-technology goods,
- increasing income levels and more equitable income distribution in Turkey,

---

15 Akgüç, Mehtap et al. Strengthening EU-Turkey economic relations. Can services revitalize the customs union. Istanbul Policy Center. Istanbul, March 2018.

- negative changes in Turkey's non-economic and institutional factors,
- the competitive transformation of Turkey's production structure.

Several dynamics in EU-Turkey relations can result from the interplay between different issues on this list of drivers. Firstly, the value of trade flows between Turkey and the EU appears to have evolved in a stable fashion, relative to trade between Turkey and the non-EU sample countries.[16] This implies that any factors which may disrupt the trade process, including political instability, are expected to weigh more on non-EU than EU trade in either direction. However, the fact that bilateral trade flows between the EU and Turkey have become increasingly volatile through time implies that factors linked to uncertainty, including political uncertainty, exert a persistent and transient influence on trade flows. This shows that the EU remains a more stabilising, albeit a less dynamic, factor for Turkish trade flows. Thus, given that EU-Turkish trade flows are already high, both partners would have a lot to lose were there to be any future decrease in those flows. Moreover, to the extent that Turkish trade policy is committed to maintaining stable and higher levels of foreign trade, a scenario of cooperation between the EU and Turkey is more likely to occur in the coming years.

Secondly, most of Turkey's trade volume concentrates on intermediate goods. However, given not only that the share in Turkey's trade with non-EU countries exceeds trade with EU countries, but also that semi-processed materials are increasingly obtained from non-EU countries, non-EU countries have a significant cost advantage. Additionally, the share of consumption and capital goods in Turkey-non-EU trade is lower than that with Turkey's EU partners. Hence, consumer preferences in Turkey seem to favour European quality goods and businesses seem to meet their capital needs with European technological products. To the extent that Turkish trade flows are driven mainly by cost/price factors, a diversion of trade away from the EU may be expected, which would make a scenario of potential conflict more likely. This is so because EU exporters, facing potential business losses, would tend to support stricter EU membership policy towards Turkey. However, if Turkish consumers and businesses remain strong supporters of European quality consumer and capital goods, a scenario of overall cooperation may actually prevail.

Thirdly, it appears that the value of EU-Turkey trade will benefit rising income levels more in Turkey than in the EU. The implementation of pol-

---

16 These non-EU countries are USA, China, Japan, Russia and Iran.

icies to push technological progress in Turkey will facilitate adjustment in the composition of overall demand and help further align institutional. Furthermore, legal infrastructure relevant to trade will have the same effect. To the extent that domestic Turkish policy is committed to raising income levels and establishing a more equitable income distribution in Turkey, a scenario of cooperation is more likely to occur as Turkish consumers and businesses will have a better financial capacity to meet their preferences for European quality goods.

In conclusion, the assessment of the flows of goods and services points to a high probability for the EU-Turkey cooperation scenario. However, the gravity model's predictions are conditional upon the significant mitigating role of institutional factors within both the EU and Turkey. In general, it should be expected that the role of non-economic and other institutional factors would be more pronounced over the coming years. Their overall impact on trade flows in general and between the EU and Turkey in particular, will be determined by their specific effect on consumer and producer preferences and the overall composition of domestic demand for financial flows, notwithstanding that potential political and institutional instability could increase the probability of conflict.

Research findings on the political economy[17] suggest that the economic relationship between the two longstanding partners is actually a strategic partnership that spans more than sixty years. Indeed, trade relations exceed the scope of the CU. However, as things stand the CU and therefore evolution of the trade relationship between the EU and Turkey remain the backbone of dialogue whilst accession talks are at an impasse due to the volatile nature of the EU-Turkey political relationship. As highlighted above, the CU has greatly benefitted Turkey over the years, reflected not only in trade expansion due to reduced tariffs, but also increased Foreign Direct Investments (FDI) along with accompanying positive externalities. In general, Turkey has enjoyed increased productivity and further integration into global value chains. Finally, the importance of governance within the trade relationship is fundamentally important for Turkey, signifying its most viable option in seeking to be part of mega trade deals at a global level.[18] It seems that CU modernisation with the TTIP in sight forms the most beneficial outcome economically, politically and strategically for both sides, which inevitably facilitates and deepens the cooperation scenario in the

---

17 Berulava et al., Modes of Regional Cooperation and Their Political Economy.
18 Ibid, p. 21.

medium term. However, its likelihood is uncertain due to recent political developments.

2.2 Flows of Finance

Financial flows have become an important aspect of funding short- and long-term operations of the Turkish economy. Just looking at the FDI numbers, one can see that Turkey has invested about $20 Billion in EU countries during the 2002-2016 period, while EU countries have invested about $95 Billion in Turkey.[19] This is an important contribution to the Turkish economy, where savings are short and part of the investment is financed by financial flows.[20] Generally speaking, factors that affect EU-Turkey relations, both economic and political, are of utmost importance for the Turkish economy.

The list of key drivers of EU-Turkey relations in view of financial flows contains:

* high global liquidity with uncertainty about a financial reversal shock;
* adverse global liquidity conditions; financial instability in the EU and crises in Turkey;
* EU monetary policy affecting financial flows;
* political instability in Turkey resulting in capital outflow as well as decreased FDI from the EU;
* Turkish government forcing tight monetary controls governing international flows;
* Turkey's current account deficit continuing to be financed by short-term capital inflows.

Starting with collapse of the Bretton Woods system in the 1970s, the world economy has financialised.[21] Turkey has been among the frontrunners in this development. As a result of full financial liberalisation, by the end of the 1980s both Turkish citizens and foreigners were allowed to make financial transactions without any restrictions. Since then financial flows have become increasingly important for the Turkish economy due to their

---

19 Cömert, The Financial Flows and the Future of EU-Turkey Relations, p. 10.
20 Cömert, Hasan/ Düzçay, Guney. Understanding Developments in Current Accounts and Financial Flows in Light of Discussions on Global Imbalances and Recent Crises. In: Ekonomik Yaklasim, October 2015, Vol. 26, No. 96; Mehrling, Perry. The Inherent Hierarchy of Money. January 2012.
21 Epstein, Gerald A. Financialization and the World Economy. Cheltenham, 2006.

effects on macroeconomic variables, such as savings, investments and Gross Domestic Product (GDP). To the extent that the role of financial inflows has gradually increased in Turkey, the question of how they can drive EU-Turkey relations has become increasingly interesting to research. Thus, the analysis that this chapter draws from investigates which factors could affect the direction of flows by looking at respective trends between 1975 and 2016.[22]

Financial flows are composed of portfolio flows, FDI and other flows such as transactions of the central bank, government and other sectors in the form of loans, trade credits, currency and deposits. Analysing gross flows on assets and liabilities components in portfolio flows, other flows and FDI reported by the balance of payments statistics of the Central Bank of the Republic of Turkey (CBRT BOP Statistics) highlights an increase in financial inflows into Turkey. While financial outflows have been relatively shallow (only about 0.5% of the GDP between 2010-2016 and rather stable from the 1980s onward), financial inflows have gradually increased from less than $1 Billion representing 1.45% of GDP in the period of 1975-1989 to an average of $54 Billion and 5.25% of GDP in the period of 2010-2016. This means that Turkey in total attracted about $380 Billion worth of foreign capital in the form of borrowings, portfolio investments and FDI between 2010-2016.[23]

The difference between purchases and sales of domestic assets by foreigners is called net financial inflows, with one of the key characteristics of financial flows to the Turkish economy being their high volatility. It increased with the financial liberalisation process which started in the 1980s and was completed in 1989 with full capital account liberalisation. For instance, in 1994 net financial inflows to Turkey formed about 7% of GDP. However, in the very same year foreign reactions to Turkey's economic crises, namely selling Turkish assets, decreased the net financial inflows to minus 6% of GDP in 1995.[24] In the wake of the 1990s, net financial inflows have continued to be characterised by sharp volatility, indicating high uncertainty in the supply of foreign credits and foreign exchanges in developing countries, which can easily be translated into foreign exchange and/or financial crises. Net flows of other financial assets are most volatile components whereas FDI demonstrates relatively high stability. After 2010, the volatility of other investment inflows and direct investment in-

---

22 Cömert. The Financial Flows and the Future of EU-Turkey Relations.
23 Ibid, p. 4.
24 Ibid, Figure 1, p. 3.

flows relatively declined whereas portfolio inflows became much more unpredictable. The EU's opening of accession negotiations with Turkey in 2005 as well as Turkey being accepted as a fully functioning emerging market economy could have contributed to this development. Stable inflows are extremely important for countries such as Turkey whose debt is financed by such inflows.[25]

Financial flows can affect the economy through various channels. Besides the direct impact of FDI, the effects of financial flows under the general heading of credit and asset price channels are just as relevant.[26] The credit channel works through borrowings within the banking sector and other non-financial large firms from the rest of the world. In this way, major firms can have access to relatively cheap and abundant credit sources. Financial flows in the form of domestic banks' borrowings can increase banks' capacity to provide more credits to domestic consumers and firms. Those banks with access to cheap credits from the international financial markets can generate more credits domestically. Since 2010, Turkish private firms have obtained enormous amount of credits averaging $96.8 billion and banks have borrowed about $119.5 billion.[27] These borrowings were partially responsible for Turkey's massive credit expansion. High financial flows and high GDP growth can create a virtuous credit cycle and feed each other until an external or endogenous shock hits the economy. This high positive correlation also applies in the case of Turkey. A financial reversal shock in global liquidity, financial instability in the EU and changes in EU monetary policy are just a few examples of external shocks that can end the virtuous cycle.[28] What we observed in the Turkish economy, especially after the exchange rate shock of 2017, was more of an endogenous shock related to the country's continuous reliance on short-term inflows and political crises linked to the new system of executive presidency and the 2019 municipal elections.

A second channel works through the effect of financial flows on domestic asset prices. The post-2010 period witnessed foreigners' increased de-

---

25 Cömert/ Düzçay, Understanding Developments in Current Accounts and Financial Flows.

26 Ibid.

27 Cömert, The Financial Flows and the Future of EU-Turkey Relations, p. 5.

28 Cömert, Hasan/ Yeldan, Erinc. A Tale of Three Crises Made in Turkey. 1994, 2001 and 2008-09. In: Güngen, Ali R. (Eds.). The Political Economy of Financial Transformation in Turkey. London, 2015; Akyüz, Yilmaz/ Boratav, Korkut. The Making of the Turkish Financial Crisis. In: World Development, September 2003, Vol. 31, No. 9, p. 8.

mand for Turkish securities which reached $107.3 billion.[29] Consequently, interest rates on these assets declined so that government and other sectors were able to benefit from relatively cheap bond issuing which also had spill-over effects for all other borrowers. A high level of financial inflows can also cause nominal or real appreciation of the domestic currency which can improve the balance sheets of domestic players with large foreign liabilities. As in the case of many other developing countries, Turkish firms have benefited from a relatively appreciated value of the Turkish currency, especially after 2002, although this has been reversed dramatically during the last three years. Furthermore, portfolio flows to the Istanbul Stock Exchange have played an important role in affecting Turkish macroeconomic conditions. Indeed, Cömert demonstrates that the main macroeconomic variables, such as credit growth, exchange rates and inflation in Turkey have been very sensitive to developments in financial flows.[30] The exogenous factors mentioned in the paragraph above also affect the impact of flows on domestic asset prices.

Considering the relationship between the components of financial inflows and GDP growth, one has to distinguish between FDI and other flows. The link between FDI and GDP growth seems to be rather weak, while other flows show strong interrelations. Hence, investors considering FDI in Turkey are not significantly sensitive to the short-term fluctuations of GDP growth. Excluding foreigners' real estate investments, Turkey attracted in total about $69 billion worth of FDI between 2002 and 2009 and $71 billion from 2010 to 2016. In the former period about $50 billion of FDIs originated from EU countries and $45 billion in the latter period. From 2002 to 2016, among EU countries the Netherlands, Austria, UK, Luxemburg, Germany, Belgium, Spain, France and Greece respectively contributed most to the FDI.[31] Although the EU's share of total FDI into Turkey has gradually declined, on average it still makes up more than 65% of the total in the period of 2010-2016. However, there is a certain degree of increasing diversification in the source countries of FDI. While the EU's role is gradually declining (but still high), Asia's role is gradually increasing, reaching about 20% in 2016.

Even in the case of political instability in Turkey, we argue that EU-originating FDI is less likely to be affected. The recent case of potentially huge investment plans for Volkswagen in Turkey is a case in point. The only fac-

---

29 Cömert, The Financial Flows and the Future of EU-Turkey Relations, p. 12.
30 Ibid.
31 Ibid, p. 6.

tor that can affect FDI flows as well as other flows between the two sides is some degree of capital market controls which would reverse the effects of financial liberalisation. Yet, this is unlikely especially for a country that uses financial flows to pay back loans and continue to invest. The Turkish economy has managed to cover its chronic current account deficits, has avoided debt repayment problems and has now started to accumulate considerable amounts of foreign currency reserves because of substantial financial flows. However, whenever the Turkish economy has encountered a sudden halt in financial flows or financial reversals, it could not avoid significant declines in GDP growth.[32] The economic crises of 1994, 2001 and partially 2009 were directly or indirectly caused by reversal or stops of financial flows. Furthermore, the main macroeconomic variables have been very sensitive to the movements in financial flows which have been considerably affected by global cycles.

Given the global liquidity conditions, there is a two-way causality between financial flows and EU-Turkey relations. On the one hand, future developments in the relations may affect the direction and the magnitude of financial flows. These could include: deeper integration by re-negotiating the CU; political tension that may arise due to Turkey moving away from the EU's Copenhagen criteria; and the specific political factors mentioned above. On the other hand, financial flows can impact the possible path of EU-Turkey relations. Given Turkey's dependence on financial flows from the EU in form of investment and debt financing, Turkish policymakers cannot afford the conflict scenario. Consequently, EU-Turkey economic relations are expected to evolve towards a state of convergence or cooperation.

2.3 Flows of Knowledge

Flows and diffusion of knowledge are central for economic cohesion in Europe. For this reason, numerous studies have analysed the extent, determinants and consequences of knowledge diffusion across different European regions.[33]

---

32 Ibid.
33 See for instance: Asheim, Bjorn et al. Constructing Regional Advantage. Platform Policies Based on Related Variety and Differentiated Knowledge Bases. In: Regional Studies, March 2011, Vol. 45, No. 7; Fitjar, Rune D./ Rodríguez-Pose, Andrés. Firm collaboration and modes of innovation in Norway. In: Research Policy, July 2011, Vol. 42, No. 1; Tödtling Franz/ Trippl, Michaela. One size fits all.

Knowledge flows within the EU as well as between the EU and Turkey can be analysed using research collaborations data. As such, one can illustrate whether or not there are emerging knowledge hubs[34] (such as Turkey[35]) and how research collaborations help sustain the relations between Turkey and the EU. This section disentangles EU-Turkey relations, building on the collaboration-induced knowledge diffusion literature.[36] It develops the analysis of international collaboration in research activities across Europe using Framework Programme (FP) data to see how knowledge production and diffusion have changed in the past thirty years and investigate further the role of research collaborations in achieving "knowledge convergence." The principal finding indicates a positive correlation between convergence not only of European economies in terms of income,[37] but also European countries' knowledge bases. Knowledge convergence is defined as the accumulation and intensification of knowledge that is shared within the context of collaboration among given (European) partners. Thus, the development of such convergence between Turkey and the EU can have a determining impact on the future of EU-Turkey relations.

Towards a differentiated regional innovation policy approach. In: Research Policy, October 2005, Vol. 34, No. 8; Bottazzi, Laura/ Peri, Giovanni. Innovation and spillovers in regions. Evidence from European patent data. In: European Economic Review, June 2003, Vol. 47, No. 4, p. 687.

34 Knowledge hub means a region with an ensemble of knowledge-intensive organisations.

35 Akçomak et al. Knowledge Cohesion in European Regions.

36 See for example Rigby, David L./ Van der Wouden, Frank. Co-inventor Networks and Knowledge Production in Specialized and Diversified Cities. In: Papers in Regional Science, February 2019, Vol. 98, No. 4, pp. 1833-1853; Autant-Bernard, Corinne. The role of R&D collaboration networks on regional knowledge creation. Evidence from information and communication technologies. In: Papers in Regional Science, December 2016, Vol. 97, No. 3, pp. 549-567; Bergman, Edward M./ Maier, Gunther. Network central. Regional positioning for innovative advantage. In: Annals of Regional Science, September 2009, Vol. 43, No. 3, pp. 615-644; Jones, Benjamin F. et al. The Increasing Dominance of Teams in Production of Knowledge. In: Science, June 2007, Vol. 316, No. 5827, pp. 1036-1039.

37 See for example Fagerberg, Jan/ Verspagen, Bart. Heading for divergence? Regional growth in Europe reconsidered. In: Journal of Common Market Studies, September 1996, Vol. 34, No. 3, pp. 431-448; Armstrong, Harvey W. Convergence among regions of the European Union. 1950-1990. In: Papers in Regional Science, April 1995, Vol. 74, No. 2, pp. 143-152.

Respective drivers that could potentially affect EU-Turkey economic relations in this area can be summarised as:

- Turkey leaving the ERA;
- continuation of transnational cooperationand bilateral research agreements;
- Turkey's removal of legal barriers to the flow of foreign scientific personnel from the EU as well as deepening student and staff exchange programmes with the EU;
- the European Commission's increasing opportunities for non-member countries within ERA;
- structural reform in Turkey's Higher Education Law towards more decentralised decision making.

The convergence of knowledge bases is a focal aspect of the ERA conceptualised as the backbone of the EU's knowledge production and diffusion strategy. FPs are ERA's central policy tools, facilitating transnational cooperation and bilateral research agreements as well as providing opportunities for non-member countries in ERA. In doing so, the European Commission aims at reducing economic and social disparities in Europe, such as differences in knowledge stock and varying capabilities of peripheral regions to accumulate and share knowledge.

The use of FP data to analyse collaboration-induced knowledge diffusion helps us to see where knowledge is created and with whom. The emergence of new knowledge hubs in cities and regions across Central and Eastern Europe including Turkey is a sign of knowledge convergenceA recent study has investigated cross-country research networks in Europe, using the entire set of project data during FP6, FP7 and H2020, and shows that peripheral countries have become more integrated in the core.[38] It is significant to note that the Commission provides a definition of the opportunity set that enables research and innovation collaborations. Of course, the individual efforts of peripheral countries such as Turkey are key for accessing research networks via various means, such as research agreements, student and staff exchanges as well as even creating local programmes that complement EU schemes and policies. Thus, these attempts integrate Turkish researchers to the ERA.

---

38 Balland, Pierre-Alexander et al. Network dynamics in collaborative research in the EU. 2003-2017. In: Papers in Evolutionary Economic Geography, May 2019, Vol. 27, No. 9.

To investigate whether or not there is knowledge convergence within Europe and between Turkey and Europe, research that this section draws from has used the EU's FP data from the first round (FP1, 1984-1987) until the last round (H2020, 2013-2020).[39] Using this data offers several advantages, in that the data is rich, enables comparison over the years and covers a wide range of scientific areas. The resulting analyis is based on 80,000 research and innovation projects as well as about two million links between the partners of these projects in about 340 NUTS2 regions[40] located in more than thirty countries.

The increasing number of nodes and links in the EU research network demonstrates that European regions display a growing tendency to cooperate and share knowledge. At the same time, acting in line with preferential attachment, new participants join the research network by linking to the already active partners' (thus, regions) successful performance. While this process increases the existing structure's sustainability (i.e., persistence of knowledge hubs in the ERA), diversification of the linked nodes demonstrates that there is at least a minimum level of knowledge convergenceAnother important finding illustrates that it is relatively likely and easy for two regions with no former links to cooperate towards knowledge creation in the future. As the number of nodes and density increases, such regions can form ties over a third region that connects these regions. This demonstrates that the structure is evolving into a direction that supports knowledge convergence Balland et al. validate this finding at the country level.[41]

Such a network analysis can be complemented by an econometric analysis. At regional level there are emerging signs of European knowledge convergencewith those regions that are less well-endowed in terms of knowledge tending to develop capabilities which promise to advance European integration. Yet, due to the persistence of top performers over the years, convergence is much stronger among the less developed regions. This analysis also demonstrates that there are emerging knowledge hubs in Europe, that may play a central role in regional as well as Europe-wide knowledge flows in the future. Thus, it can be concluded that European regions and countries have so far benefited from the financial and non-financial opportunities created by the EU for research collaboration (i.e., transnational co-

---

39 Akçomak et al. Knowledge Cohesion in European Regions.
40 NUTS stands for Nomenclature of Territorial Units for Statistics. For each EU member country, a hierarchy of three NUTS levels is established by Eurostat. For adetailed information, see Eurostat. NUTS. Nomenclature of Territorial Units for Statistics. 2020, https://ec.europa.eu/eurostat/web/nuts/background [31.08.20].
41 Balland et al. Network dynamics in collaborative research in the EU.

operation bilateral research agreements, student- and staff-exchange schemes).

Focussing on Turkey, the key question is whether or to what extent it belongs to these beneficiaries. In terms of knowledge convergence the EU and Turkey come close to a convergence scenario given the long history of EU-Turkey cooperation in knowledge which has been extended over the years. For instance, it is now easier for researchers from abroad to work in Turkey – TUBİTAK for instance offers various programmes that offers financial support for student and staff exchange between Turkey and European countries as well as application to FP projects themselves. These individual efforts by Turkish authorities and actors have been ongoing for over two decades, supported by new tools that facilitate collaboration with European research bodies. Nevertheless, a lot remains to be done in terms of supporting Turkish universities with respect to both their infrastructure and knowledge base. In particular, the reputable public universities could benefit from a more decentralised decision-making structure so as to be able to make autonomous decisions regarding matters such as research personnel and budget.

At regional level, Turkey has developed many partnerships with European regions (287 different regions during FP5, FP6 and FP7). However, analysis of these regions' performance reveals that the number of regions with which Turkey established links has increased from 171 in FP5, to 266 in FP6, and to 276 in FP7. At the same time, while the total number of links established in FP5 was 834, this figure increased to 7,104 in FP6 and 13,561 in FP7.[42] The growing number and depth of EU-Turkey links seems to have boosted mutual trust and facilitated tacit knowledge exchange, as such already establishing the roots of knowledge convergence

The numerous individual, institutional and national advantages of knowledge cooperation, especially for Turkey, prevent the Turkish side from triggering any conflictual actions that would put such benefits at risk (i.e., Turkey leaving the ERA). Given the political economy dimension that highlights modernisation of the CU along with the TTIP,[43] it is also unlikely that such an interruption would originate from the European side. The modernised CU covering services would require a programme of liberalisation in Turkey, particularly regarding professional services, which would in turn serve as a new source of productivity gain for the whole

---

42 Akçomak et al., Knowledge Cohesion in European Regions.
43 Berulava et al. Modes of Regional Cooperation and Their Political Economy.

Turkish economy. Inevitably, this would create further opportunities involving the creation and exchange of knowledge.

2.4 The Political Economy Dimension

The political economy dimension complements quantitative analysis dealing with the flows of goods, services, finance and knowledge offered above, comprising factors impacting the suggested drivers for each flow. Four different scenarios for the future of EU-Turkey trade relations are considered relevant in this context,[44] ranging from closest cooperation to conflict: (a) the modernisation of the EU-Turkey CU agreement, (b) Turkey's membership in the European Economic Area (EEA), (c) the completion of Deep and Comprehensive Free Trade Agreements (EFTA) with Turkey, (d) Transatlantic Trade and Investment Partnership (TTIP) with Turkey, and (e) Turkey's potential participation in the Shanghai Cooperation Organization (SCO).

It should be noted that ties between the EU and Turkey evolve within a political economy context where areas of conflict could make cooperation and convergence scenarios potentially difficult. The EU-Turkey relationship has recently been severely strained and an official end to membership negotiations would consequently be the most conflictual scenario. However, its realisation would be unlikely unless the EU and Turkey agreed on an alternative scenario that would replace the negotiations and put in place a new institutional framework governing their relations (for instance, Turkey abandoning the CU and joining EFTA).[45]

Several developments have proven pivotal for the EU-Turkey relationship. The 2010 Eurozone crisis paved the way for strengthening Eurosceptic political forces across the member states. The resulting political environment has made bilateral relations between the respective member states and Turkey more difficult. Furthermore, at EU level Turkey's adherence to the Copenhagen political criteria has faced problems, particularly with regard to erosion in the quality of Turkey's democratic institutions and fundamental freedoms. Apart from these political issues, a transactional, inter-

---

44 See Berulava et al. Modes of Regional Cooperation and Their Political Economy; Mertzanis. Understanding the EU-Turkey Sectoral Trade Flows During 1990-2016.
45 Saatçioğlu, Beken et al. The Future of EU-Turkey Relations. A Dynamic Association Framework amidst Conflictual Cooperation. FEUTURE Synthesis Paper, March 2019.

est-based approach shaped the EU's handling of the 2015/2016 Syrian refugee crisis. As the Syrian war continues, with an international resolution yet to be negotiated, Turkey and the EU will remain obliged to continue cooperationon issues regarding refugees and terrorism. This wider context reflects a knife-edge equilibrium where both parties strategically cling to their own positions, while keeping the ongoing economic and political relations intact. More significantly for the EU-Turkey relationship, it sets the ground for discussing the four scenarios mentioned above.

In an impact assessment study, the European Commission[46] sets two areas of operational objectives, namely, modernisation of the Bilateral Preferential Trade Frame (BPTF) addressing the deficiencies and modernisation of the CU. In the BPTF context operational objectives are to address problems related to the difficulties in achieving a parallel conclusion of FTAs by the EU and Turkey. Additionally, they should address Turkey's challenges in meeting its obligation on legislative alignment to EU law (concerning both EU commercial policy and EU technical regulations). Finally, an effective dispute settlement mechanism should be introduced.

For the second set of objectives, the CU modernisation process should address problems related to achieving the FTAs's parallel completion by both the EU and Turkey. Moreover, both sides would need to aim at improving market access for trade in services through the elimination, reduction or prevention of unnecessary barriers. Additionally, the parties would need to improve access to each other's public procurement market (in practice, this means that Turkey would have to open up its public procurement to the EU since the EU market is already open to Turkish bidders). Finally, both sides would have to agree on a wide range of rules that enable a more stable and predictable environment for bilateral trade and investment (e.g., trade and sustainable development, energy/raw materials, Small and Medium sized Enterprises (SMEs), transparency).[47]

Modernisation of the CU along with the TTIP seems to be a better and probable option for Turkey and is also compatible with Tocci's "functional cooperation" scenario.[48] Modernisation entails expansion into services – in particular, professional services – which would then be liberalised, result-

---

46 European Commission. Commission Staff Working Document accompanying the document Recommendation for a Council Decision authorising the opening of negotiations with Turkey on an Agreement on the extension of the scope of the bilateral preferential trade relationship and on the modernisation of the Customs Union. SWD(2016) 475 final, Brussels, 2016.

47 Ibid, p. 30.

48 Tocci, Turkey and the European Union, p. 12.

ing in productivity gains for the Turkish economy as well as increased FDI flows to Turkey.[49] This option is also politically feasible as it keeps the EU membership issue on the table. Berulava, Manoli and Selçuki take a clear stance in supporting this option: "Strategically, it prepares Turkey for "docking-in" to a potential TTIP agreement between the EU and the US in the future. This is crucial for Turkey. Unlike other third parties that signed FTAs with the EU, Turkey would have a difficult time negotiating a FTA with the US and if unprepared both in terms of sectors and regulations it would be harmed."[50]

The Deep and Comprehensive Free Trade Agreement (DCFTA) option provides a higher degree of integration towards cooperation, but it would also mean ending the CU. Considering that EFTA is a tool for non-EU countries and CU was a milestone for Turkey's path towards accession, it is highly unlikely that this option would be chosen, as it would imply a non-membership scenario for Turkey. Furthermore, it would be improbable given Turkey's economic and political situation since it would harm the AKP's political power. Moreover, according to this option, both parties would have net welfare losses from the combination of tariff reductions and the 'switchover' to an FTA relationship from the existing CU arrangement, which implies a 'rules of origin shock', in other words a 2% increase in trade costs, while they make welfare gains from the other elements of the DCFTA. In terms of new welfare gains, this option does not seem to be a better alternative compared to BPTF.[51] In the context of the BPTF option, for Turkey the challenge seems to lie in not only achieving liberalisation of agriculture, services, government procurement and investment between the EU and Turkey, but also to observe the EU rules on dispute settlement and trade in relation to sustainable development, labour and the environment. Yet, for the EU this is an opportunity to harness the economic and political potential of deeper integration with Turkey, through further liberalisation of trade in goods, services, agriculture and public procurement. Furthermore, this presents a chance to encourage investment and sustainable development, complemented with appropriate dispute settlement mechanisms.

Turkey's relations with organisations other than the EU may also emerge as key political economy drivers. In fact, Turkey has diversified its

---

49 Cömert, The Financial Flows and the Future of EU-Turkey Relations.
50 Berulava et al., Modes of Regional Cooperation and Their Political Economy, p. 23.
51 European Commission, Commission Staff Working Document, p. 31.

export destinations over the last 15 years[52] and has been actively working towards assuming a more pivotal regional and global role. Turkey's attempt to consider other regional cooperation organisations such as the SCO has political as well as economic implications. However, SCO is as yet far from what the EU has achieved to date and what it can offer Turkey. Thus, it is unlikely that Turkey would move towards other regional cooperation arrangements, as the EU still represents its primary anchor both politically and economically.

3. Conclusion: What Future For EU-Turkey Relations?

The basic premise of this chapter is to provide evidence-based drivers impacting the future of EU-Turkey economic relations. In doing so, we have built upon FEUTURE research into the flows of goods and services,[53] finance[54] and knowledge [55] as well as the political economy dimension of EU-Turkey relations, which has generated specific drivers (mentioned above) for each of these areas.[56] These drivers are presented in Table 1.

The long history in regard to flows of goods, services, finance and even, knowledge between Turkey and the EU has reached a stage of positive-sum game where both parties win. This is evident from Table 1 as 16 out of 24 identified drivers are associated with cooperation. The other categories of drivers' relevance for both the EU and Turkey as well as impact on EU-Turkey relations are also conducive to the cooperation scenario. Recent increases in knowledge flows benefited both parties. As shown in Table 1, the drivers linked with the flows of knowledge facilitate cooperation, or even convergence, especially considering that Turkey is a member of the ERA.[57] Based on these economic drivers and their respective relevance, timeframe, impact and likelihood, it is apparent that cooperation is the most likely scenario.

---

52 Mertzanis, Understanding the EU-Turkey Sectoral Trade Flows During 1990-2016.
53 Ibid.
54 Cömert, The Financial Flows and the Future of EU-Turkey Relations.
55 Akçomak et al., Knowledge Cohesion in European Regions.
56 Berulava et al., Modes of Regional Cooperation and Their Political Economy.
57 European Commission, ERA progress report 2018. COM(2019) 83, Brussels, 2019.

Table 1: Economic Drivers of EU-Turkey relations

Economic drivers	Cross-cutting drivers	Relevance for Turkey	Relevance for the EU	Timeframe	Likelihood	Impact	Scenarios
Flow of goods and service							
Turkey's Customs Union with the EU ceases	political	3	2	medium	uncertain	high	conflict
EU-Turkey Customs Union is upgraded	political	3	2	medium	uncertain	high	cooperation
The EU and US set a Transatlantic Trade and Investment Partnership (TTIP)	political & security	3	2	medium	wild card	medium	cooperation
Turkey gradually increases production (and export) of high-technology goods	-	2	1	long	projection	medium	cooperation
Stabilising impact of EU trade	political	2	1	medium	projection	medium	cooperation
Increasing income levels and more equitable income distribution in Turkey	-	3	1	medium	projection	low	cooperation
Negative changes in Turkey's non-economic and institutional factors	political & security	3	1	long	uncertain	medium	conflict
Competitive transformation of Turkey's production structure	-	3	1	long	projection	medium	cooperation
Flow of finance							
High global liquidity with uncertainty about a financial reversal shock	political	3	1	short	projection	medium	cooperation
Adverse global liquidity conditions	political	3	2	medium	uncertain	medium	cooperation
Financial instability in the EU and crises in Turkey	political	3	1	medium	projection	high	cooperation
EU monetary policy affects financial flows	political	3	1	short	uncertain	high	cooperation
Political instability in Turkey results in capital outflow as well as decreased FDI from the EU	-	3	2	medium	uncertain	high	cooperation
Turkish government forces tight monetary controls on international flows	political	2	1	medium	highly unlikely	low	conflict
Turkey's account deficit continues to be financed by short-term capital inflows	-	3	1	short	projection	medium	Cooperation

Economic drivers	Cross-cutting drivers	Relevance for Turkey	Relevance for the EU	Timeframe	Likelihood	Impact	Scenarios
Flow of knowledge							
Turkey leaves the European Research Area (ERA)	political	3	1	long	highly unlikely	low	conflict
Transnational cooperation and bilateral research agreements continue	political	3	1	short	projection	medium	convergence
Turkey removes legal barriers to the flow of foreign scientific personnel from the EU	migration	3	1	medium	projection	medium	convergence
Student and staff exchange programmes with the EU deepen	migration	3	2	medium	uncertain	medium	cooperation
The European Commission increases opportunities for non-member countries within ERA	political	3	1	long	uncertain	medium	cooperation
Structural reform in Turkey's Higher Education Law in Turkey towards more decentralised decision making	-	3	1	medium	projection	low	cooperation
Political Economy							
Turkey initiates a free trade agreement with Eurasian Customs Union	political	3	2	medium	wild card	high	conflict
Modernisation of the EU-Turkey Customs Union	political	3	3	medium	projection	high	Cooperation

Note: Cross cutting drivers relate to the other thematic dimensions of EU-Turkey relations: politics, security, energy, migration and identity. Relevance scores in the second and third column are 3: Relevant 2: Uncertain and 1: Irrelevant. The time-frame ranges from "long" and "medium" to "short" term. Likelihood categories are projections, which are very likely, uncertain and wild cards which are highly unlikely events that would have a high impact on the relationship. Impact column assesses the impact on overall bilateral relations ranging from low and medium to high.

Source: Own compilation.

Thus, on the economic side this chapter provides evidence for the cooperation scenario which can be labelled as "functional cooperation" as noted by Tocci.[58] Economic analysis covering the flows of goods and services, finance and knowledge shows that Turkey's economic engagement with the EU has grown and persisted even at times of political tension with the EU. Thus, functional cooperation understood as engagement without accession seems a plausible scenario in capturing EU-Turkey economic relations.

Concerning the flow of goods and services, most of the drivers point towards cooperation. This is particularly so because this economic activity relies heavily on trade, which is an area where both parties have expressed their intent to continue cooperation. Further, there is already a CU in place which governs this relationship with room to grow. The EU's prominence as a trading partner is unlikely to change for Turkey, notwithstanding the country's diversification of its export destinations. The CU's deepening along with potential impacts for a future TTIP between the EU and the US, increase cooperation across many sector-related issues. In such a scenario, Turkish exports in mid-high technology level to the EU would grow and the stabilising impact of EU trade would be felt through increased income and better distribution. As stressed above in section 2.4, modernisation of the CU with the TTIP is a more desirable option for both sides, which is also compatible with "functional cooperation". However, emerging barriers threaten its likelihood, such as recent changes in Syria, Cyprus issues, halted negotiations of TTIP and the like.

The unlikely event of ending the CU (i.e., Turkey switching towards establishing an FTA with the EU instead) is considered to be the main conflict scenario. Ongoing Brexit negotiations concerning trade could potentially provide a model applicable to EU-Turkey trade relations outside of a CU. However, this would represent a historic scaling back of the existing EU-Turkey trade relationship, affecting not only the flows of goods, services and finance but also knowledge. Hence, we consider this option unlikely in the foreseeable future.

In regard to the flow of finance, the drivers evaluated seem to be more critical for Turkey than the EU. This is because Turkey is heavily dependent on flows from the EU both in terms of credit and FDI. However, a reversal of this trend potentially implies conflict scenarios. Following the failed coup attempt of July 15, 2016, which was a major cause for risk per-

---

58 Tocci, Turkey and the European Union; see also Tekin, Funda. The future of EU-Turkey relations. In this volume, pp. 11-28.

ception due to political instability, Turkey was facing declining FDI figures from the EU. At its peak, the EU accounted for more than 70% of the inward FDI in Turkey. As discussed, EU-originating FDI contributes to the Turkish economy through several channels and is therefore essential for economic development.

Turkey's deviation from free market economy principles would additionally produce conflict between Turkey and the EU. If the Turkish government were to introduce monetary controls for international flows, this would scare away not only EU investment but also foreign capital. Such capital controls would have far-reaching negative consequences for EU-Turkey economic relations. Needless to say, this would also violate the principles laid out in Chapter 17 of EU-Turkey membership negotiations concerning monetary policy. Given the EU's strong economic performance and recovery from the Eurozone crisis, the EU remains Turkey's most reliable partner in terms of financial flows. Turkey's dependence on short- as well as long-term capital flows for financing its current account deficit amplify the importance of this partnership.

The flows of knowledge, while less important than flows of goods, services and finance, are also crucial for sustainable economic growth. They not only generate and help diffuse knowledge but also create and/or enhance human capital. The analysis in Section 2.3 and Table 1 clearly shows that EU-Turkey interactions regarding the flows of knowledge have proven mutually beneficial. We expect such relations of knowledge sharing and generation to continue and even deepen, which also supports the functional cooperation scenario

In sum, the analysis of economic drivers shows that from an economic standpoint, cooperation is the likely scenario for the future of EU-Turkey relations. Deepening trade and economic integration backed by knowledge convergence promises positive social welfare impacts for both sides. Ultimately, Ankara's self-declared goal of making Turkey one of the top ten economies of the world by 2023 (the centenary of the declaration of the Turkish Republic) inevitably also hinges on maintaining solid economic relations with the EU, culminating in deepened cooperation but not necessarily convergence.

So Near and Yet So Far: Conflictual Cooperation for EU-Turkey Energy Relations

Lorenzo Colantoni

1. Introduction

Energy is at the very core of EU-Turkey relations. This is so for a number of reasons: the structure of energy mixes, geographical issues and future energy trends for both the EU and Turkey. All combine to constitute a mutual relevance, which could easily lead to a naturally converging relationship. In spite of that, though, the potential for conflict remains high, which could cause the separation not only of energy policies, but also EU-Turkey economic and political relations in more general terms. Future developments will, therefore, depend on a number of key drivers: the energy sector's current rapid technological evolution; changing geopolitics in the area; together with regional and global trends. These are dominated by the expanding global fight against climate change, the spread of renewables and the energy transition. Alignment of energy and climate visions, as well as a number of other factors, will ultimately define whether or not the energy dimension will offer a chance for further cooperation or cause disagreement in EU-Turkey relations.

Our analysis of energy in this chapter will consider issues of climate policy whenever these influence energy transition and global diplomacy. This has become increasingly relevant in the aftermath of the United Nations Climate Change Conference (COP21) held in Paris at the end of 2015.

Many elements contribute to the closeness of European and Turkish energy sectors, such as their high dependence on Russian gas. The EU engages Turkey specifically in light of its geographical position, which makes the country an ideal partner for Middle East and Caspian oil and gas resources, at the core of the European energy diversification attempts over the past decade. Turkey is interested in Europe due to both its market size and extensive expertise in the regulatory sector, as well as development in the field of renewables. Beyond this, opportunities for cooperation also exist in sectors which are less prominent in the EU-Turkey energy debate, such as nuclear energy and climate cooperation.

Yet, there are also various issues limiting EU-Turkey energy relations. Geopolitical tensions in the area form the most prominent obstacle, particularly since Turkey has increased its conflictual attitude towards Cyprus in the past two years, blocking Cypriot gas exploration in favour of promoting its own investigations in waters claimed by a neighbour (as detailed in Section 3.4). This decision has also triggered a strong EU response, with the Union itself defining Turkish activities as illegal according to international law.[1] Other limiting factors relate to differences in the European and Turkish energy sectors. While European demand is flat, that of Turkey is growing, thereby pushing the country towards short-term generation capacity enhancement. This could lead to an increase in the use of coal, as Turkey owns domestic reserves which are often considered as the more easily available resource. Cooperation with the EU, which is among the world's climate leaders, could be significantly undermined by such a focus on solid fuels. This is exacerbated by Turkey's uncertain position vis-à-vis renewables and the Paris Climate Agreement. Furthermore, while the EU is indeed the greatest market for gas passing through Turkey, there is only limited potential for expansion due to the flat demand in Europe. This reduces the economic convenience and appeal of future energy infrastructures from Turkey to the EU (primarily gas pipelines and development of the Southern Corridor). Finally, fundamental differences in their respective energy narratives also limit EU-Turkey energy relations. The EU sees Turkey as an energy bridge, with a focus on its role as a transit country, while Turkey promotes the narrative of a regional energy hub, prioritising its role as a trading centre with the ability for price determination.[2] The latter constitutes a much wider ambition that could shift Turkish focus towards its eastern neighbours.

In short, the potential for EU-Turkey energy cooperation is significant given the joint development of renewables and gas plants. However, a realignment of policy trajectories would still be required, possibly starting in sectors where cooperation is relatively easy, particularly the electricity trade, and facilitated by supporting global trends as well as platforms such as energy transition or the G20's expanding role in the climate domain.

This chapter analyses such external and internal drivers by presenting: an overview of the Turkish and European energy sectors (Section 3.1); an

---

1 European External Action Service. Turkey. Statement by the Spokesperson on the announcement of a new drilling operation. Brussels, January 2020.
2 Schröder, Mirja et al. Turkey as an Energy Hub. Contributions on Turkey's Role. Baden-Baden, 1st ed., 2017.

analysis of the Moscow-Ankara-Brussels energy triangle (Section 3.2); an evaluation of global energy and climate trends' impact (Section 3.3); an in-depth discussion of EU-Turkey energy relations in the Caspian and the Middle East (Section 3.4); and an assessment of gas exploration efforts' impact in the Eastern Mediterranean on mutual relations (Section 3.5). The chapter will close with a delineation of the most likely future scenario for EU-Turkey energy relations, which we contend corresponds to "conflictual cooperation" (Section 4). Hence, despite substantial mutual interests suggesting converging trends, different political developments and a general uncertainty in the regional and global energy sector prevent Turkey and Europe from taking a smooth path towards convergence.

2. Methodology

This chapter is based on five research papers, produced within the framework of the Horizon 2020 research project "The Future of EU-Turkey Relations: Mapping Dynamics and Testing Scenarios" (FEUTURE).[3] It discusses and extrapolates the most relevant drivers defined as *the material/ ideational and structural/agency-related elements that determine a story's outcome*, namely the most relevant elements, either internal or external to EU-Turkey energy relations, influencing the most likely scenario that could range between the ideal-type scenarios of conflict, cooperation and convergence.[4]

Each section starts with a brief description of the issues at stake and proceeds with a discussion and assessment of the drivers. This analysis is considering

---

3 See Ala'Aldeen, Dlawer et al. EU and Turkish Energy Interests in the Caspian and Middle East Region. FEUTURE Online Paper No. 13, February 2018; Han, Ahmet K. et al. Gas Developments in the Eastern Mediterranean: Trigger or Obstacle for EU-Turkey Cooperation. FEUTURE Online Paper No. 22, May 2018; Colantoni, Lorenzo et al. Energy and Climate, Strategies, Interests and Priorities of the EU and Turkey. FEUTURE Online Paper No. 2, March 2017; Colantoni, Lorenzo et al. Energy and Climate Security Priorities and Challenges in the Changing Global Energy Order. FEUTURE Online Paper No. 6, September 2017; Mikhelidze, Nona et al. The Moscow-Ankara Energy Axis and the Future of EU-Turkey Relations. FEUTURE Online Paper No. 5, September 2017.

4 For detailed definition of these three ideal-type scenarios see Tekin, Funda. The future of EU-Turkey relations. In this volume, pp. 11-28 and Tocci, Nathalie. Turkey and the European Union: Scenarios for 2023. FEUTURE Background Paper, September 2016.

- the relevance of drivers for both the EU and Turkey as well as bilateral energy policies (ranging between low, medium and high);
- the time perspective in which the drivers will have a relevant effect (short term: 2-3 years from 2020, medium term: 2023-2028 and long term: beyond 2028);
- the drivers' likelihood (wild card, uncertainty and projection, ranging between minimum and maximum certainty; projections are considered as *known* drivers, uncertainties as *known unknowns* and wild cards as *unknown unknowns*);
- along with the scenario they are expected to result in (conflict, cooperation or convergence) and how great this impact will be on the overall EU-Turkey relationship (low, medium, high).

A table summarising this evaluation is provided at the end of each section, together with brief information regarding the components of each driver.

3. Discussion of the Drivers

3.1 The EU's and Turkey's Energy and Climate Strategies, Interests and Priorities

The European and Turkish energy sectors share a strong mutual relevance, due most importantly to Turkey's geographical position, the size of the European market, the importance of gas for both Turkey and the EU as well as the potential for cooperation in regard to renewable energies. A mutual importance is also reflected in institutional terms through the recently established EU-Turkey High Level Energy Dialogues and in the EU's Energy Union Strategy.[5]

Yet, several uncertainties hamper the development of energy cooperation between Turkey and the EU. The most important concerns the two sides' policy trajectories, looking at Turkey in particular. While the EU seems committed to a role as leader in energy transition through its promotion of renewables, along with general efficiency and the phasing out of coal, Turkey's future energy mix is relatively unclear as it includes nuclear, coal and renewables along with a mixed attitude towards decarbonisation.

---

5 Albayrak, Berat/ Cañete, Miguel Arias. Turkey-EU High Level Energy Dialogue. Istanbul, January 2016; European Commission. A Framework Strategy for a Resilient Energy Union with a Forward-Looking Climate Change Policy. COM/ 2015/080 final, Brussels, 2015.

Beyond specific energy-related issues, as the two parties engage in general energy-focussed talks aimed at seeking cooperation, dialogue is further complicated by conflictual positions in both political and security dimensions, especially in view of Turkey's rule of law issues and its approach to the tensions in Syria.[6]

A number of drivers are projected to produce some impact on the future of EU-Turkey energy relations, potentially boosting or reducing cooperation in this area, yet thankfully falling short of relaunching at one extreme and a full stop at the other. Future trends in energy demand (Driver 3.1.1), Turkey's concrete support for renewable energy penetration (Driver 3.1.2) and a process of liberalisation in the respective gas markets – more advanced in the EU (Driver 3.1.3) while still embryonic in Turkey – could trigger some level of cooperation between Ankara and Brussels.

European and Turkish energy demands are on significantly different paths, the former destined to remain stable or decrease, the latter growing faster than the respective resource development, thus increasing external dependency.[7] This dependency can potentially induce at least medium-term cooperation, if rising energy demand in Turkey[8] motivates Ankara to install new electricity generation and turn to Brussels for establishing a more effective and reliable energy market (i.e., Renewable Energy Services (RES) integration in the grid). At the same time, this could increase the partial misalignment between Turkish and European policies, hence mutual conflict potential in the case of coal – which is still a key option for Turkey, but being phased out by the EU.

In the field of renewables, while the EU is already a global leader, a more clearly defined strategy demonstrating Turkey's support under the 2023 goals framework, as presented by the then Prime Minister Recep Tayyip Erdoğan in 2010, would increase the chances for cooperation with Brussels. This could happen through collaboration between Turkish and European companies in developing joint projects as well as national or EU-level bilateral initiatives in the fields of knowledge exchange and capacity building under the High-Level

---

6 Şahin, Ümit. Türkiye'nin İklim Hedefi Ne Olmalı. Resmi INDC'nin Değerlendirilmesi. In: Yesilgazete.org, 19 October 2015, https://yesilgazete.org/blog/2015/10/19/turkiyenin-iklim-hedefi-ne-olmali-2-resmi-indcnin-degerlendirilmesi/ [11.09.20].

7 Turkish Petroleum. 2015 Ham Petrol ve Doğal Gaz Sektör Raporu. Çankaya, May 2015.

8 Even though many analysts believe official Turkish forecasts are overestimating its expected growth rate, see ibid.

Energy Dialogues umbrella or the European Network of Transmission System Operator for Electricity (ENTSO-E).

Enhanced energy trade between the EU and Turkey can boost cooperation in regard to gas and thus requires a compatible regulatory framework. The EU's third package of energy legislation and liberalisation of the energy sector – gas in particular – constitute such a structure and Turkey's greater involvement in this would favourably affect energy cooperation overall. Considering effects in the electricity sector during the past decade, liberalisation of the Turkish gas market, although still in its early stages,[9] coupled with completion of the EU's energy market liberalisation, would produce a medium level of impact on the EU-Turkey energy partnership, facilitating cooperation and potentially enhancing energy trade.

In contrast, phasing out coal (Driver 3.1.4), which is projected to advance in the EU but not in Turkey, may lead to conflictual outcomes in energy relations. It represents a top priority on the EU's decarbonisation agenda, an aim shared by several member states (e.g., Italy and Germany). In the medium term, Turkey's renewed focus on the exploitation of domestic solid fuel resources thus represents a major obstacle against energy cooperation with Europe. This not only puts the two on different policy trajectories, but also undermines the development of renewable energy generation, with Turkey installing coal generation capacity instead of solar and wind, thus significantly undermining its genuine commitment to the Paris Agreement targets, the EU's preferred priority.

Drivers with a higher degree of uncertainty such as the realisation of the Akkuyu nuclear plant and the acceleration of the Turkish nuclear programme (Driver 3.1.5) on the one hand, and Turkey's participation in the European Network of Transmission System Operators for Gas (ENTSO-G, Driver 3.1.6) on the other, could give rise to very different outcomes. Conflictual cooperation could result from the first case, due to Russia's role in Turkey's nuclear sector, set against (conflict) Turkish willingness to engage European companies in this domain (cooperation). However, potential convergence is demonstrated in the second case, with Turkey showing genuine interest in aligning itself with EU practices in the gas sector.

Nuclear power has been part of Turkey's energy strategy for years. Yet, construction of the first nuclear plant (Akkuyu power station) started only in April 2019 and has encountered numerous safety problems since then. The EU's strategy, in turn, is ambiguous regarding nuclear energy, with some member states still developing this resource while others have begun

---

9   Soysal, Cengiz et al. Doğal Gaz Sektör Araştirmas. Ankara, July 2012, p. 24.

to close their nuclear energy sector (e.g., Germany). Additionally, Turkey is building the Akkuyu power station in cooperation with Russia, which further limits cooperation with the EU.

Similarly, to what happened with ENTSO-E, Turkey's participation ENTSO-G as a member with observer status would provide some chances for convergence through the alignment of Turkish gas trading policies with the European energy single market. In the medium term, this would provide support for still timid liberalisation efforts in the Turkish gas market and boost energy trade through a common technical/regulatory convergence of EU-Turkey gas systems.

In general terms these factors would not be able to shape the energy and climate relationship between Brussels and Ankara dramatically. However, the case is different when it comes to opening the Energy Chapter (Chapter 15) in Turkey's EU accession negotiations (Driver 3.1.7) and Turkey's membership of the Energy Community (Driver 3.1.8). These two drivers can be considered 'wild cards', with long-standing deadlock making a positive outcome to negotiations highly improbable. Nevertheless, albeit a remote prospect, realisation would produce an exceptionally positive impact on the EU-Turkey energy partnership. This would lead the two sides towards a greater degree of convergence, bring about a radical change in the very structure of energy cooperation and thereby provide a legislative platform for the mutual alignment of their respective energy policies. Specifically, the energy chapter could finally be opened only if Turkey restored democratic rule, thereby fulfilling the EU's prerequisite for opening chapters with Turkey in general, and Cyprus removed its veto on the energy chapter. Furthermore, if Turkey proved politically willing to align with the energy *acquis*, the framework for convergence of European and Turkish energy policies would be optimal, in providing full alignment on key issues, such as regulatory and market designs. Thus, in a medium-term perspective the energy chapter could have significant, positive implications for both Brussels and Ankara as well as relations in general terms. Turkey's decision to enter the Energy Community – the organisation which aims at expanding the EU's energy rules and market to south-eastern neighbours – would in the medium term represent the second-best option for providing common policy trajectories and legislative ground for EU-Turkey energy cooperation as well as Turkeys compliance with the EU's energy *acquis*. Yet, Turkey's historic unwillingness to join the respective treaty (based on fears that it may slow down or even replace its EU accession negotiations) combined with the resistance of countries which are already part of the Energy Community to promote its expansion, restrict this option's realisability.

Table 1: Evaluation of drivers for energy and climate strategies, interests and priorities

Drivers	Relevance for Turkey	Relevance for the EU	Relevance for bilateral energy policies	Time perspective	Probability	Scenario	Impact on overall EU-Turkey relations
D3.1.1 Energy consumption increases due to sustained economic growth[10]	high	medium	medium	mid-term	projection	conflict/cooperation	medium to low
D3.1.2 Increasing support to renewable energy penetration	high	high	medium	mid-term	projection	cooperation	medium
D3.1.3 Further liberalisation and integration of the gas markets	medium	high	medium	mid-term	projection	cooperation	medium
D3.1.4 Pushing for phasing out of coal	low	high	low	mid-term	projection	conflict	low
D3.1.5 Accelerated realisation of the Akkuyu plant and the Turkish nuclear programme	high	medium	medium	mid-term	uncertainty	conflict/cooperation	low
D3.1.6 Turkey becoming an observer in ENTSO-G	medium	high	medium	mid-term	uncertainty	convergence	low
D3.1.7 Opening of the energy chapter in the accession negotiations	high	high	high	mid-term	wild card	convergence	high
D3.1.8 Turkey entering the Energy Community	medium	high	high	mid-term	wild card	convergence	medium to high

Source: Own compilation.

---

10 "D.3.1.1" stands for "Driver 1 of Subsection 1 of Section 3 of the paper".

3.2 The Brussels-Ankara-Moscow Energy Triangle

Russia is currently the key energy partner of both the EU and Turkey. The EU imports around one third of its external supplies of oil and natural gas from its eastern neighbour, whilst for Turkey dependence in the gas sector is much higher (above 50%) than in the oil sector (only 13%).[11] At the same time, both are key destination markets for Russian hydrocarbon exports, with Moscow largely depending on oil and gas revenues (36% of the country's federal budget in 2016, according to the OECD)[12] to keep its finances in order. Thus, energy interdependence is at the core of the Brussels-Ankara-Moscow triangle, that significantly affects EU-Turkey relations in a mixed conflict-cooperation scenario. In this context, it is likely that political factors – not directly related to energy and climate drivers – will contribute to swaying the balance from one extreme to the other. As tensions arise in the Eastern Mediterranean over Turkish and Cypriot drillings (see Section 3.5), conflict in the triangular relationship as well as EU-Turkey relations is likely to increase. Russia generally sides with Turkey, whilst America supports the EU including Cyprus, which contributes to further polarisation and hence destabilisation.

The growing energy dependence on Russia of both the EU and Turkey (Driver 3.2.1) is projected to influence their energy policies heavily in the short term with mixed outcomes.[13] On the one hand, it could encourage Brussels and Ankara to strengthen cooperative policies by way of reinforcing diversification in gas sources. On the other hand, given growing energy demands particularly from the Turkish side, competition over new supplies cannot be fully discarded as this could overlap with EU attempts to diversify its supplies from new Eastern Mediterranean resources or gas from the Black Sea.

Drivers with a higher degree of uncertainty, such as realising the second string of TurkStream connecting Russia to south-eastern Europe (Driver 3.2.2), Moscow's failure in interfering with implementation of the Southern Gas Corridor (Driver 3.2.3) and the related Turkish gas market liberalisation (Driver 3.2.4), could all pave the way for significant positive cooper-

---

11 Eurostat. Energy Database. 2020, https://ec.europa.eu/eurostat/web/energy/data/database [11.09.20].

12 OECD. Fossil Fuel Support Country Note. Paris, April 2019, http://stats.oecd.org/wbos/fileview2.aspx?IDFile=09aac246-c7ef-4159-898e-2a287deb3341 [11.09.20].

13 Eurostat. Energy Database; Shaffer, Brenda. Turkey's westward energy shift. January 2020, https://www.mei.edu/publications/turkeys-westward-energy-shift [11.09.20].

ation-convergence trajectories in EU-Turkey energy relations. Without Russian interference, full implementation of the Southern Gas Corridor (and potential expansion of capacity beyond the current 16/10 Bcm) could shift EU-Turkey cooperation in the direction of attracting new gas sources originating from the neighbouring regions.

Additionally, the direct and indirect advantages in becoming a gas bridge through development of the Corridor, could encourage Turkey to proceed with liberalisation of its gas market in order to become a true hub and beneficially integrate with the European system. In the medium term, convergence with the EU in this domain would offer Turkey a more competitive internal market (with cheaper prices for companies and households) and bring greater investments along with trade turnover financial flows into the country.

Realisation of TurkStream delivering gas to Europe could also positively contribute to bilateral cooperation between Brussels and Ankara, by reinforcing Turkey's role as a key gas hub for the EU. However, by taking advantage of its energy transit status, Turkey's temptation to exert stronger political influence over the EU, for instance by pushing for more freedom of action in the Middle East or less interference in its domestic politics, cannot be discarded and would lead to conflictual outcomes in its relations with the EU.

In regard to the halting of Nord Stream 2 (Driver 3.2.5), this has lost importance and is now highly unlikely due to the already significant progress in finalising construction.[14] Nonetheless, if it did materialise Russia would be forced to find alternative routes to reach EU markets without passing through Ukraine. In this case, the second string of TurkStream would be the perfect infrastructure to accommodate increasing volumes of gas destined for European consumers and Turkey would further strengthen its role as a transit country with huge implications for its energy partnership with the EU. However, Turkey could also take advantage of its energy transit status to exert stronger political influence over the EU.

---

14 Knolle, Kirsti. Nord Stream 2 pipeline can still be built on schedule: OMV. 29.08.2019, https://www.reuters.com/article/us-gazprom-nord-stream-2-omv/nord-stream-2-pipeline-can-still-be-built-on-schedule-omv-idUSKCN1VJ0PD [13.09.19].

Table 2: Evaluation of drivers related to the Moscow-Ankara-Brussels Energy Axis

Drivers	Relevance for Turkey	Relevance for the EU	Relevance for bilateral energy policies	Time perspective	Probability	Scenario	Impact on overall EU-Turkey relations
D3.2.1 Increasing gas dependence from Russia	high	high	high	short-term	projection	conflict/ cooperation	high
D3.2.2 Realising the second string of TurkStream	high	high	high	mid-term	uncertainty	conflict/ cooperation	high
D3.2.3 Progress on realisation of the Southern Gas Corridor without Russian interferences	high	high	high	mid-term	uncertainty	cooperation	high
D3.2.4 Realisation of the Southern Gas corridor encouraging Turkey to liberalise its gas system and integrating it with the European one to become a hub.	medium	medium	high	mid-term	uncertainty	convergence	high
D3.2.5 Blockage of Nord Stream 2	medium	high	high	mid-term	wild card	conflict/ cooperation	high

Source: Own compilation.

3.3 Energy and Climate Security Priorities and Challenges in the Changing Global Energy Order

EU-Turkey relations are unfolding in a global energy context marked by historic changes, the most important being: the Paris Agreement and its impact on the energy transition; the falling cost of renewables; fossil fuels' instability; along with the rise of new institutions on the global energy and climate scene. Yet, these changes are still affected by a significant degree of uncertainty due to their relative novelty. Generally speaking, they have a two-fold influence on Turkey and the EU. On the one hand, energy transition and hence the dramatic fall in the cost of renewables are pushing for a major shift in the global energy mix and a greater penetration of solar and wind energy. This promotes convergence of European and Turkish energy and largely climate policies, as the EU is leader in this sector and Turkey could benefit from greater European support in its development of renewables. On the other hand, Turkey's fluctuating attitude towards energy transition is far from the European policy trajectory and would thus reduce the opportunities for cooperation. Indeed, this could eventually cause conflict, as has happened in the case of confrontation in international platforms such as the COPs. Yet, this could be changed by a further development in renewables and greater global support for the Paris Agreement. Additional elements, such as the future role of gas and the instability of oil prices could increase the demand for diversification by both the EU and Turkey, further aligning their energy needs.

The only projected driver that can significantly promote cooperation between Turkey and the EU is the falling costs of the renewables (D.3.3.1). Between 2010 and 2015, costs of solar energy dropped by 80% and onshore winds by 40%/60%[15]. This can explain the major expansion of renewables over the past five years. If such cost decreases continue at the current or a higher rate, in the medium term it will be more cost effective for Turkey to expand its renewable capacity instead of promoting coal, thus leading to cooperation with the EU and its increasingly ambitious policies in this domain. Such cooperation could be reduced only if Turkey found greater advantage in expanding its renewable capacity through other, non-EU partners – in particular, Asian countries or the US – which, considering General Electric's recent involvement in the country, is a likely option.[16]

Less expected but still probable is the expansion of gas and particularly LNG trade at global level (D.3.3.2). In the framework of ongoing energy transition, gas is a resource at a crossroads in its development. Since it is likely to play a core role in the shift towards a low carbon energy mix, for instance by offering a solution to renewables' intermittence and a baseload alternative to coal, the impact on both the EU's and Turkey's energy policies can be significant. However, a coherent inclusion of gas in Ankara's energy transition plans is hampered by the political use of this resource by Turkey. This is so, for instance, with obstruction in the exploration of Eastern Mediterranean gas resources, where conflict with the EU is put ahead of an agreement to promote exploitation. Global growth in the use of methane for energy generation and also for industrial uses could bolster

---

15 IRENA. Renewable Power Generation Costs in 2018. Abu Dhabi, 2019, p. 20.
16 Daily Sabah. GE to supply equipment for 158 MW wind farms in Turkey. In: Dailysabah.com, 19 July 2019, https://www.dailysabah.com/energy/2019/07/19/ge-to-supply-equipment-for-158-mw-wind-farms-in-turkey [13.09.2019].

Turkish interests in this regard and thus promote cooperation between Ankara and Brussels in formulating a joint strategy.

Other drivers studied are clearly uncertain. This is the case with implementation of the Paris Agreement (D.3.3.3), which provided the fundamental political framework for energy transition, adding to an already strong economic and industrial growth trend. Increased support for the Paris Agreement by its Parties will present some incentive for Turkey to reinforce its commitment to the treaty, thus promoting cooperation with strong pro-climate European policies. Despite America's declaration to exit the Agreement, ratification has proceeded steadily and by March 2020 only eight countries from the 175 signatories had failed to do so. Turkey is amongst those that have yet to ratify due to its ongoing debates about the possibility of accessing climate finance under more favourable conditions.[17]

Although still very difficult to predict due to various uncertain factors, including unconventional production, geopolitics of oil supply, in the medium term oil prices' volatility (D.3.3.4) can be considered as determining driver for cooperation between Turkey and the EU. As low oil prices can result in the resource's reduced availability due to decreased investments within the sector and geopolitical instability in *rentier* countries,[18] diversification of supply and reduction of consumption is likely to be boosted in such a scenario for both the EU and Turkey. This would bring the two parties closer together in terms not only of promoting energy efficiency (an EU priority), but also opening up new supply routes, with impacts on both the energy and climate sectors leading to cooperation.

Finally, transformation of the G20 into an institutional reference for climate change policies (D.3.3.5) could have a positive effect on EU-Turkey energy and climate cooperation. Greater emphasis placed on climate change and energy security in the latest G20 summits attest to the growing importance of these themes on the global stage and the increased role the institution can play as a framework for negotiations in the energy and climate sectors.[19] Although its success in channelling international debate towards climate issues is still uncertain, the G20 could become a positive platform for global cooperation. However, the emphasis attached by

---

17 Apparicio, Siola/ Sauer, Natalie. Which countries have not ratified the Paris climate agreement. In: climatechangenews.com, 13 August 2020, https://www.clima techangenews.com/2020/03/01/countries-yet-ratify-paris-agreement/ [11.09.20].

18 A rentier country is a state deriving all or the majority of its income from the exploitation of a single resource.

19 European Council. G20 Osaka Leaders' Declaration. Brussels, June 2019.

Turkey and the EU to its role is likely to be different due to the availability of alternative platforms for the latter and the low involvement of Ankara in the UN COPs. This will generate a limit on overall EU-Turkey cooperation in the climate domain.

Table 3: Evaluation of drivers related to the changing global energy and climate order

Driver	Relevance for Turkey	Relevance for the EU	Relevance for bilateral energy policies	Time perspective	Probability	Scenario	Impact on overall EU-Turkey relations
D.3.3.1 Falling costs of renewables encouraging quicker and deeper penetration	medium	medium	low	mid-term	uncertainty	cooperation	low
D.3.3.2 Global expansion of gas and LNG trade	high	high	medium	mid-term	probability	cooperation	medium
D.3.3.3 Turkey's ratification of the Paris Agreement	high	high	low	mid-term	uncertainty	cooperation	low
D.3.3.4 Oil prices remain highly volatile	low	low	low	mid-term	uncertainty	cooperation	low
D.3.3.5 G20 becomes one of the world institutional references for climate change policies	low	medium	low	mid-term	uncertainty	cooperation	low

Source: Own compilation.

3.4 Energy Interests of the EU and Turkey in the Caspian and the Middle East

Turkey is geographically located between European markets and the rich hydrocarbon resources available in its eastern neighbourhood, the Caspian, Middle East, the Gulf. Consequently, Ankara has sought the strategic role of an energy bridge in order to consolidate its political relationship with the EU. Turkey has been able to link energy cooperation initiatives with the EU accession negotiation process, because the region constituted an important element in the EU's strategy to diversify its energy supplies and reduce dependence on Russia. The Southern Gas Corridor initiative is an attempt by Brussels and Ankara to develop an energy partnership, strengthening mutual energy security and bringing the EU and Turkey politically closer.

However, for a number of different political, economic and industry-related reasons, the expected gains from the Southern Gas Corridor failed to materialise. In particular, the EU's gas demand has been significantly lower than expectations as political relations between Europe and Turkey have been much more problematic than they were in the previous decade.[20] Today, the initiative looks much less ambitious than when it was launched. At the same time, there is still a significant level of uncertainty over key energy developments in the region, which might open the door to unexpected cooperative scenarios.

At present, the most likely driver is Russia's projected capacity to oppose regional cooperative initiatives enabling the successful exploitation and commercialisation of gas resources available in the Caspian/Central Asia (D.3.4.1). So far, Moscow has blocked resolution of the still undefined status of the Caspian Sea, *de facto* restricting the Southern Gas Corridor's access to Azerbaijani gas and hence, the possibility of both Turkey and the EU gaining access to new gas resources.[21] In the medium term, failure to extend the Corridor towards gas-rich countries such as Turkmenistan, Uzbekistan and Kazakhstan could limit the scope of EU-Turkey regional energy cooperation.

Drivers with a higher degree of uncertainty, such as the future of the Kurdistan Regional Government (KRG) both in terms of political/security instability (D.3.4.2) and growing Russian influence in the area (D.3.4.3), can lead to mixed conflict-cooperation outcomes. Northern Iraq is among the potential suppliers of gas to both Turkey and the EU through the Southern Gas Corridor. However, the fragile security situation in the region slows down the process of gas resources exploitation as well as plans to interconnect this region with the Corridor network. Development of the Corridor and EU-Turkey energy cooperation in general, would be jeopardised if the region continues to be characterised by enduring insecurity

---

20 Koranyi, David/ Sartori, Nicolò. EU-Turkish Energy Relations in the Context of EU Accession Negotiations. Focus on Natural Gas. Global Turkey in Europe No. 5, Rome, December 2013.

21 Nanay, Julia/ Stegen, Smith K. Russia and the Caspian region. Challenges for transatlantic energy security. In: Journal of Transatlantic Studies, December 2012, Vol. 10, No. 4, pp. 343-357.

and instability. Failure to connect the KRG gas resources to the Southern Gas Corridor could thus limit the extent of this project itself and consequently energy cooperation between Ankara and Brussels in general terms. Furthermore, the increasing presence and influence of Russia in the KRG energy sector, could in the medium term limit the extent to which local authorities would be attracted to deeper engagement with Turkey and the EU in the gas sector, with consequential implications for diversification policies.[22] Yet, Moscow's growing energy presence in the area could be perceived by both Turkey and the EU as a common threat to their diversification policies, as such triggering deeper EU-Turkey bilateral cooperation to balance Russian regional influence.

Against this backdrop, regional wild cards could significantly improve the prospect of mutually beneficial EU-Turkey cooperation. These include the possibility of Azerbaijan making new relevant gas discoveries (D.3.4.4), the Iran pipeline gas export strategy towards the EU (D.3.4.5) and Turkmenistan's connection to the Corridor (D.3.4.6). The limited amount of gas resources available in Azerbaijan is one of the key limits to development of the Southern Gas Corridor. New relevant discoveries in that country, the geological potential of which is as yet questionable,[23] would allow consolidation and expansion of the Corridor initiative, with positive implications for both the EU and Turkey. In the medium term, this would further strengthen the ties between Brussels and Ankara, driving them towards greater energy cooperation at regional level. Iran is the world's richest country in terms of natural gas reserves and its return to the international arena following the Joint Comprehensive Plan of Action (JCPOA) could boost the country's domestic natural gas production and related exports. In the long term, should the Iranian leadership decide to focus its exports strategy on a mix between LNG-based trade and pipeline-based supplies, part of Tehran's resources could be destined for Turkish and European markets, thus revitalising the Southern Gas Corridor initiative with positive impact on EU-Turkey energy policies and cooperation.

---

22 Katona, Viktor. Russia's Kurdish Pipeline Gamble. September 2017, https://oilpri ce.com/Geopolitics/International/Russias-Kurdish-Pipeline-Gamble.html [13.09.19].

23 Today in Energy. Oil and natural gas production is growing in Caspian Sea region. September 2013, https://www.eia.gov/todayinenergy/detail.php?id=12911 [13.09.19].

Table 4: Evaluation of drivers related to energy interests in the Caspian and Middle East Region

Drivers	Relevance for Turkey	Relevance for the EU	Relevance for bilateral energy policies	Time perspective	Probability	Scenario	Impact on overall EU-Turkey relations
D.3.4.1 Russia successfully blocks cooperative initiatives in the Caspian energy sector	high	high	medium	mid-term	projection	conflict	medium
D.3.4.2 Instability in the Kurdistan Region hinders gas production and exports	high	high	high	short-term	uncertainty	conflict	medium
D.3.4.3 Russia strengthens its influence within the KRG energy sector	high	high	medium	mid-term	uncertainty	cooperation	medium
D.3.4.4 Azerbaijan finds new gas resources in the Caspian	high	high	high	mid-term	wild card	cooperation	high
D.3.4.5 Iran increases its focus on energy trade with Europe and Turkey	high	high	high	long-term	wild card	cooperation	high
D.3.4.6 Turkmenistan joins the Southern Gas Corridor Initiative	high	high	high	medium-term	wild card	cooperation	medium

Source: Own compilation.

As third largest country in the world in terms of natural gas reserves, Turkmenistan's[24] potential participation in the Southern Gas Corridor could significantly affect EU-Turkey energy cooperation strategies, since it would provide access to new, abundant gas resources in the medium term, which would in turn prove instrumental in enabling effective diversification pol-

---

24 Nanay/ Stegen, Russia and the Caspian region.

icies. However, due to both Russian obstructionism in the region and tense bilateral relations between Turkmenistan and Azerbaijan – the only possible route for Turkmen gas to flow westward – this outcome is currently highly unlikely. Hence, new relevant discoveries in Azerbaijan,[25] as well as the possibility of transporting relevant volumes of gas from Iran and/or Turkmenistan, would allow consolidation and expansion of the Corridor initiative, with positive implications for both the EU and Turkey. In the medium term, this would further strengthen ties between Brussels and Ankara, driving them towards greater energy cooperation at regional level.

3.5 Gas developments in the Eastern Mediterranean: Trigger or Obstacle For EU-Turkey Cooperation?

If in the next few years significant gas resources are found in the Eastern Mediterranean region (Driver 3.5.1), as has been the case with recent discoveries in Egypt,[26] export options to the EU excluding transit from Turkey could be economically/commercially sustainable, hence obviating the need for ensuring Ankara's collaboration. Either an LNG terminal in Cyprus/Israel or a pipeline directly connecting the fields in the area to the European market could be realised in the case of reserve discoveries in Cyprus/Israel waters, as such excluding Turkey from the regional game and risking heightened tensions between the parties.

The Eastern Mediterranean region hosts rich hydrocarbon resources, specifically in the Israeli, Egyptian and Cypriot territorial waters. Following a number of discoveries initiated in 2010 with the Leviathan field in Israel and culminated in the giant gas field of Zohr off the Egyptian coasts, the area has attracted various regional and international actors' attention, including the EU and Turkey. Since Cyprus is an EU member state, resources located in its offshore would be considered as 'domestic' European resources, consequently reducing the bloc's external dependence in the natural gas sector. At the same time, though, Turkey claims its direct and indirect rights to be involved in the regional energy game. This is a situation that raises concerns about the already fragile situation around Cyprus

25 Jafarova, Aynur. Shah Deniz reserves may rise by a quarter. In: Azernews.az, 08.05.2013, https://www.azernews.az/oil_and_gas/53553.html [13.09.19].

26 Offshore Energy Today. Eni makes new gas discovery offshore Egypt. 14.05.2019, https://www.offshoreenergytoday.com/eni-makes-new-gas-discovery-offshore-egyp t/ [13.09.19].

and risks jeopardising efforts to maintain and deepen EU-Turkey energy cooperation. Indeed, tensions have escalated in the area after Turkey's seizing of Eni's SAIPEM 1200 in February 2018 and the start of Turkish drilling activities during the Summer of 2019 in areas considered by the Republic of Cyprus to be part of its Exclusive Economic Zone (Driver 3.5.2). These developments triggered a strong reaction by Cyprus which recently received both Greek and European support on this issue. Similarly, the EU condemned Turkish drilling through the Council, freezing several initiatives of cooperation with Ankara and seeking to limit future European Investment Bank (EIB) lending to the country.[27] This situation would almost certainly lead in the medium term to a progressive drift between Ankara and Brussels. Bilateral energy cooperation would head towards a non-return point, as the Republic of Cyprus is now going ahead with its exploration and production activities, having the full support of the EU and against the wishes of Turkey and Northern Cyprus's desiderata.[28]

In addition, Turkey is well aware not only of its importance as a transit country for gas extracted in the Eastern Mediterranean, but also of the risk of its being marginalised, either by the use of Egypt-based LNG facilities or a new pipeline from Greece to Italy. Turkey's concern with being sidelined might have been one of the root causes for Ankara's actions that increased tensions in the area. However, nowadays the development of infrastructure for gas export from the Eastern Mediterranean region is additionally hindered by low global gas prices (Driver 3.5.3), which would lower cost-effectiveness and reduce the likelihood of such a project. In the medium term, low prices could force different regional stakeholders to seek cheap and more flexible options (such as LNG). As Turkey would be excluded from these developments, this could in turn motivate Ankara to increase bilateral efforts with the EU to sustain the development of transit infrastructure, which it cannot finance using domestic resources alone.

Regional cooperation in this domain is further constrained by the strategic interests and priorities of different players involved in the energy game, such as Egypt which aims to exploit its Zohr resources to become the Eastern Mediterranean gas hub and Israel which is maintaining focus on security linked to its development of national energy resources. This situation has led to a slowdown with the development of energy resources in the

---

27 Council of the European Union. Turkey's illegal drilling activities in the Eastern Mediterranean Council adopts framework for sanctions. Brussels, November 2019.

28 Ibid.

area and a lose-lose outcome for all the parties involved. These include not only the producers, such as Cyprus and Israel, but also potential markets of destination/consumers, such as the entire EU territory and Turkey. While the situation has improved in recent years, particularly regarding Egypt-Israel relations, Turkey's isolation in relation to its potential Eastern Mediterranean partners is still the major impediment in attempting to develop a solid export strategy, which would necessarily have to involve all key area actors in gathering the required amount of investments and securing the shortest and safest routes.[29]

Table 5: Evaluation of the drivers related to gas developments in the Eastern Mediterranean

Drivers	Relevance for Turkey	Relevance for the EU	Relevance for bilateral energy policies	Time perspective	Probability	Scenario	Impact on overall EU-Turkey relations
D.3.5.1 Relevant gas resources are found in the East Med offshore	high	high	high	short-term	uncertainty	conflict	high
D.3.5.2 Tensions regarding the Cyprus issue increase	high	high	high	mid-term	projection	conflict	high
D.3.5.3 Global LNG prices remain low	high	high	medium	mid-term	projection	cooperation	high
D.3.5.4 Turkey-Israel relations improve, leading to closer energy cooperation	high	high	high	mid-term	uncertainty	cooperation	medium
D.3.5.5 Cyprus-Israel-Egypt energy cooperation improves	high	high	high	mid-term	projection	conflict	high

Source: Own compilation.

---

29 Ibid.

Yet, if a softer approach to gas exploitation in the Eastern Mediterranean were to be chosen, the way for stronger energy ties between Brussels and Ankara would be paved. Such a development could also be eased by an improvement in Israel-Turkey relations (Driver 3.5.4). An improved political atmosphere between Turkey and Israel could potentially allow Turkey to direct offshore gas under Israeli sovereignty to Turkey through a newly constructed pipeline. In a medium-term perspective, this outcome would dent the feasibility of a trilateral Israel-Egypt-Cyprus partnership (Driver 3.5.5), bringing the Turkish option for transit of Eastern Mediterranean resources back to the table for consideration by relevant regional actors and the EU. The strengthening of this trilateral partnership to enable the exploitation and export of regional resources, either by using the Egypt-based LNG facilities or building a new pipeline to Greece to export gas from the Eastern Mediterranean fields to EU markets would further marginalise Turkey. Consequently, in the medium term, Ankara could not only slow down bilateral energy cooperation with the EU but also seek to undermine or challenge any initiative seeking to bypass the Turkish territory for exports to Europe (i.e., the Southern Corridor).

4. Conclusion: Future Energy and Climate Scenarios

Our assessment of drivers in the area of energy presented here suggests that in the foreseeable future relations between Brussels and Ankara will evolve towards a scenario of conflictual cooperation.

This means that, despite clear interests and priorities that can push the parties towards greater cooperation in the energy domain, the EU-Turkey energy dialogue can turn increasingly conflictual. Above all, this is closely linked to tensions over drilling in the Eastern Mediterranean as well as relations with Russia, together with domestic political developments in Turkey and the EU. Indeed, Ankara's manifest opposition to further exploration and production activities off the coast of Cyprus as well as the potential competition between Ankara and Brussels to reduce the growing dependence on Russian gas, are key drivers inducing a drift that can be mitigated by the mutual need to strengthen gas diversification strategies. Other elements add to this twofold scenario. In the case of nuclear energy, for instance, potential cooperation with EU member states is hindered by significant Russian involvement, which is marked by political rather than economic interests.

This evaluation is confirmed even if we consider other factors and trends which, despite their positive outlook, suffer from an uncertainty mostly due to Turkey's unclear positions or political influence over key decisions. For instance, a certain degree of cooperation can result from mutual attempts to strengthen the Southern Gas Corridor initiative, despite potential interferences from Moscow and possible enduring instability in the Middle East (KRG in particular). However, this driver can easily turn into a cause for bilateral tension if not addressed by Ankara and Brussels through a positive and/or constructive approach. The more we explore medium-term prospects, the more this trend is confirmed, but at the same time uncertainty increases. This is so, for instance, with the role of coal in Turkey's energy mix along with uncertainties surrounding ratification of the Paris Agreement. It is possible to assume that one of the causes for this uncertainty is a wait-and-see attitude being adopted by both the EU and Turkey, due to the impossibility of defining the future of key energy trends for both. European and Turkish gas demands could be different than expected in the years to come, which could result from an uncertain recovery on the EU's side and perhaps an overestimation of its own capacity by Turkey. This is seen when considering the role of renewables resulting from, inter alia, the lack of an adequate policy support in Turkey and troubles with integrating higher shares of RES in Europe.

Globally speaking, the evaluation of energy and climate drivers is positive, in that their general trends and specific bilateral conditions are likely to align the EU's and Turkey's interests further, but due to the absence of political will to exploit and develop such an alignment, the projected scenario is conflictual cooperation. This scenario could also result from either a marked change in EU-Turkey overall relations or a decisive turn of already existing energy and climate trends, albeit their evolution is uncertain. However, this change is unlikely to materialise in the foreseeable future and would be achieved only by firstly resolving the Eastern Mediterranean drilling controversy and in turn the Cyprus question, thereby reducing Turkey's foreign policy isolation in relation to other countries in the area (Israel and Egypt in particular) and secondly easing the political tensions between Brussels and Ankara.

EU-Turkey Relations on Migration: Transactional Partnership

Angeliki Dimitriadi, Ayhan Kaya

1. Introduction

In view of EU-Turkey relations, both regular and irregular migration as well as asylum are determined by domestic events in Turkey and the EU along with external developments in the EU's neighbourhood and beyond. Push factors for migration vary. Prominent examples are crises together with political, economic and environmental factors as well as poverty and insecurity (e.g., threat of terrorism). Additionally, increased development can in the short and medium term generate migration, since it provides those aspiring migrants with the financial means to undertake the journey abroad. In recent years, irregular migration and asylum in particular have received new impetus. By the end of 2015, 65.3 million people were displaced around the globe, of whom 21.3 million were recognised as refugees.[1]

The large-scale movement of persons in turn impacts the countries of origin, transit and destination, forming an intrinsic connection between the three. In other words, it is a rarity for these countries to remain unaffected, especially when situated in the geographical proximity of emerging crises. At present, this is particularly so for the EU and Turkey with the Mediterranean and Aegean Seas, as well as the Middle East, Afghanistan and Iran generating mixed migratory flows comprised of economic migrants, asylum seekers and forced migrants. Acknowledging the significance of migration, research conducted for this chapter sought to unpack the EU-Turkey relationship in the area of migration from 1999 until early 2020. The aim was to identify and analyse actors as well as events driving relations across four dimensions: the EU, Turkey, their neighbourhood and the global scene.

Two elements largely determined this chapter's research focus. The first is the occurrence of large, mixed migratory flows in 2015 and 2016, which placed the discussion of migration, especially irregular migration and asylum, at the centre of EU-Turkey relations. The second is the European

---

1 UNHCR. Global trends. Forced displacement in 2015. Geneva, June 2016.

Agenda on Migration of May 2015, which outlined the EU's priority for five years (until 2020),[2] focusing not only on irregular migration, asylum and responsibility-sharing, but also the attraction of highly skilled, legal migrants to the EU; this topic also ranked high on Turkey's agenda. Thus, three focal issues guide our research: irregular migration, asylum and highly skilled labour mobility. They were selected due to their prominence and potential impact on the EU-Turkey relationship.

Our research into highly skilled migration as the first focal issue focused on the bidirectional movement of Turkish and EU citizens, with analysis demonstrating that highly skilled migration has not been a central issue in the EU-Turkey relationship during the period studied. This is a crucial finding, considering that legal migration in general, with highly skilled migration in particular, was a central topic in the "Europe 2020 Strategy" and the European Agenda on Migration as well as the 10th Development Plan of Turkey. Our study of irregular migration, the second focal issue, focused on the movement of persons in transit from Turkey to the EU, that is irregular transitory movement from Turkey to the external borders of the Union, with an emphasis on the Greek-Turkish maritime borders. This key issue was chosen since irregular transitory movement became a priority for the EU as it began to focus attention on Turkey in the period after 2010. Finally, asylum, the third focal issue, is linked to irregular migration particularly when determining who is responsible for its processing in the EU. The EU-Turkey Statement of 18 March 2016 (henceforth the Statement) was largely made possible due to Turkey's asylum reforms, thus highlighting its importance in the EU-Turkey relationship.

Research across our three focal issues looked at the period between 1999 and early 2020 to retrace the relationship's progression. This was done by looking at the drivers that determined the management of highly skilled migration, irregular migration and asylum between Turkey and the EU throughout this period. In regard to migration, several drivers have shaped the EU-Turkey relationship, producing periods of convergence, conflict and cooperation.[3] Some are weighted equally by Turkey and the EU whereas others lead to different emphasis for each player. Examples of identified drivers include: irregular transitory movement from Turkey to the EU generated by events in the immediate and wider neighbourhoods

---

2 The Pact on Migration and Asylum will be the new framework on migration; however, at the time of writing it had yet to be released by the European Commission.
3 For a definition of drivers as well as the scenarios of convergence, cooperation and conflict, see Tekin, Funda. The future of EU-Turkey relations. In this volume, pp. 11-28.

(Syria and Afghanistan); the volume of arrivals, which is of significance to the EU; Turkey's prospect of EU accession and the Europeanisation of Turkish migration policy; security, including the militarisation of migration management and Turkey's migration diplomacy; as well as identity in light of rising populism in the EU and Turkey along with neo-Ottomanism. All these elements horizontally impact our three focal issues.

Data for this research was collected through interviews with relevant officials[4] and migration experts in Ankara, Istanbul, Amsterdam, Athens, Berlin, Brussels and in the Western Balkans along with material from secondary sources. Our analysis of each focal issue sought to generate an historical insight into the relationship while identifying the drivers influencing its current state, thereby not only advancing our understanding of the relationship to date, but also developing scenarios for the future in regard to migration. When considering the issue of migration for the EU and Turkey, we suggest how different conditions may drive a variety of scenarios, namely: conflict, cooperation and convergence or any combination thereof. In our research across the three focal issues, we have defined convergence as full membership, cooperation as the current status of mid-level (and occasionally high-level) collaboration and conflict as a rift, with Turkey and the EU adopting different and often conflicting migration policies.

This chapter discusses the key drivers within these three focal issues, in other words the elements that influence highly skilled labour mobility, irregular migration and asylum. Drivers are clustered as migration-related as well as political, security, economic and identity-oriented factors. Political and security drivers have been found to be the most influential, with the former often generating a conflictual relationship between the EU and Turkey, as opposed to the security drivers that bring the actors closer to cooperation within the realm of migration. By discussing the respective influence of these drivers, a clearer picture emerges of a possible future EU-Turkey relationship. The chapter concludes by briefly outlining the three scenarios and suggesting that the most likely scenario for the future is co-

---

4 The institutional affiliations of the interviewees were the European Commission (Migration and Home Affairs, Neighbourhood and Enlargement Negotiations), the European Parliament, the European External Action Service (Turkey Division), FRONTEX staff in Athens and Poland, the Ministry of Security and Justice, the Immigration and Naturalisation Service of the Netherlands, bureaucrats in Brussels, the Netherlands and Germany, and, finally, migration experts based in Europe from European and Turkish think tanks as well as NGOs in Greece and the Western Balkans.

operation, albeit heavily diluted by conflictual elements, something which is evident in the present context.

2. Numbers in Transit

EU migration policies are linked to the domestic needs and agendas of EU member states, which in turn has created different levels of interest in the subject over time. When numbers of irregular arrivals and asylum seekers appear high, interest peaks. In other words, volume is the *key policy determinant*. This is illustrated by developments in the periods before 2011 and after 2015. Prior to 2011, countries at the EU's external borders largely addressed migratory pressures on their own, through bilateral partnerships (e.g., Italian-Libyan Treaty of Friendship in 2008 or Spanish Moroccan readmission agreement in 1992). In the years thereafter, a gradual shift has become apparent in line with other member states' growing concerns about controlling migratory inflows from the EU's external borders. This has largely resulted from the 2011 Arab Spring which brought about significant arrivals in Italy, thus alerting member states to the porous nature of external borders as well as the transitory movement of arrivals within the Schengen area.

From 2014 onwards, the issue of irregular movement gained in significance for the EU due to the gradual increase of arrivals through the southeastern migratory corridor (Turkey-Greece) and "their secondary movement to other EU member states. Border management relied mostly on the bilateral cooperation between Greece and Turkey, which had not proved to be particularly successful in the period until 2014".[5] Although cooperation temporarily improved in 2015 and 2016, it has since deteriorated. Indicative of this is Turkey's unilateral suspension of its Readmission Agreement[6] with Greece in 2018, after which the latter decided not to extradite Turkish citizens who were claimed to have been involved in Turkey's 2016

---

5 Dimitriadi, Angeliki et al. EU-Turkey Relations and Irregular Migration. Transactional Cooperation in the Making. FEUTURE Online Paper No. 16, March 2018, p. 6.
6 The Readmission Agreement is a technical document for the return of citizens apprehended for irregular entry and/or stay in the territory of the signatory parties. It also includes a 'third country nationals' clause, which allows for EU member states to return irregular migrants to the country of transit from which they have entered the EU. The EURA effectively transfers the responsibility for the return of third country nationals to Turkey.

failed coup attempt. More recently, the relationship has become even worse with the early 2020 events in Evros, which witnessed thousands of asylum seekers trying to reach the land border with Greece.[7] This move was perceived not only as a reminder of Turkey's ability to instrumentalise migration, but also its way of exerting pressure on the European Commission in light of a new round of negotiations for renewal of the Statement.

In 2015 and 2016, at the height of the mass movement of refugees coming to Europe, the transit corridor extended from Turkey and Greece to northern Europe through the Western Balkan route.[8] Approximately 850,000 people entered via the Greek maritime border,[9] most of them Syrians, Afghanis, Somalis, Iraqis and nationals from sub-Saharan African countries.[10] The humanitarian crisis unfolding in the Aegean Sea and the Western Balkan route quickly evolved into a political crisis that continues to this day. The gradual reintroduction of border controls by member states concerned with various issues such as the lack of registration in Greece, the Hungarian fences,[11] the November 2015 terrorist attacks in Paris and the New Years' events in Cologne, shifted the narrative from one of hospitality to the deterrence of movement and protection of the Schengen area.[12] Notwithstanding deep political divisions, member states remained united in their determination to protect the Schengen area, which was perceived to be threatened by a secondary movement of arriving migrants to the external borders. Thus, it was the size and transitory nature of movement to and within the EU that triggered the Joint Action Plan with Turkey on 29 November 2015. The resultant November 2015 Statement is indicative of the EU's approach to the refugee 'crisis' since cooperation

---

7 Chebil, Mehdi. Evros river crossing. Turkey sends migrants there at night, Greece pushes them back at dawn. In: Infomigrant.net, 09 March 2020, https://www.info migrants.net/en/post/23304/evros-river-crossing-turkey-sends-migrants-there-at-nig ht-greece-pushes-them-back-at-dawn [09.03.20].

8 Dimitriadi, Angeliki. Irregular Afghan Migration to Europe. At the Margins. Looking in. 1st ed., London, 2018; Squire, Vicki et al. Crossing the Mediterranean Sea by boat. Mapping and documenting migratory journeys and experiences. Coventry, 2017.

9 UNHCR. Operation Portal. Refugee Situations. 2020, https://data2.unhcr.org/en/s ituations/mediterranean/location/5179 [06.11.2019].

10 FRONTEX. Annual Risk Analysis. Warsaw, March 2016.

11 In July 2015, Hungary began building a barrier along the border with Serbia (completed in September that year). This was soon followed by the building of a fence along the border with Croatia and closure of the border in October 2015.

12 Dimitriadi, Angeliki/ Malamidis, Haris. What role for values in EU migration policy. Essen, 2019.

with Turkey "is primarily aimed at reducing the number of asylum seekers and migrants reaching the EU".[13]

Similarly, for Turkey the number of Syrian refugees, aggravated by the persistent Syrian conflict, provided a strong motivation for cooperation with the EU. Turkey's geographical position allowed it to function not only as a transit country for irregular migrants and asylum seekers moving from the east and the south to the west, but also a destination in its own right.[14] In the 1990s, urban centres such as Istanbul emerged as critical hubs for both legal and irregular migration. In the early days of the Syrian conflict, Turkey did not seek assistance from its neighbouring countries, assuming that the crisis would soon de-escalate and the Syrians would return home. According to Kale *et al.*, "Turkish former experiences in mass influx situations were misleading, because in the Iraqi case, hundreds of thousands of Iraqi Kurdish refugees were able to return back to their home country after the establishment of a no-fly zone".[15] Escalation of the Syrian conflict raised complicated political, social and security-related challenges for Turkey.[16] In addition to these challenges, the financial costs of hosting refugees were also mounting.[17] Thus, by 2015 the high number of people entering the EU, particularly Syrian refugees, had also become a driver for Turkey, with the latter encouraging a regional and/or global solution to the growing crisis in its neighbourhood.

In contrast to the EU, transit has proven beneficial for Turkey. In the period since 2009, Turkey has facilitated its visa regime for arrivals, particularly from Africa and the Middle East, as part of its foreign policy that was adopted under the direction of former Minister of Foreign Affairs, Ahmet Davutoğlu. Turkey's new approach combined foreign policy activism, trade, humanitarian aid and soft power capabilities.[18] The country also extended the no-visa requirement to Albania, Libya, Morocco, Lebanon, Jor-

---

13 Roman, Emanuela et al. Analysis Why Turkey is Not a "Safe Country". State-watch Analysis. London, February 2016, p. 9.

14 İçduygu, Ahmet. International Migration and Human Development in Turkey. In: Human Development Research Paper, October 2009, No. 52, p. 52.

15 Kale, Başak et al. Asylum Policy and the Future of Turkey-EU Relations. Between Cooperation and Conflict. FEUTURE Online Paper No. 18, April 2018, p. 14.

16 Ibid.

17 Between 2011 and August 2015, the Turkish government had spent roughly $5.6 to $6.0 billion on the assistance and protection of refugees. International assistance amounted to less than $400 million; Kirişci, Kemal/ Ferris, Elizabeth. Not Likely to Go Home. Syrian Refugees and the Challenges to Turkey and the International Community. In: Turkey Project Policy Paper N0 7, September 2015.

18 Kale et al., Asylum Policy and the Future of Turkey-EU Relations, p. 10.

dan and Ukraine, alongside Syria and Saudi Arabia. For the EU, visa-free travel is an important 'pull' factor for irregular migrants and asylum seekers that can opt for a safe and quick journey to a neighbouring transit country before continuing their onward journey to the EU. By transforming itself into an attractive transit destination, Turkey instrumentalised its position and increased its leverage with the EU. This was implicitly acknowledged by the European Commission's February 2016 report on Turkey's progress in implementing the Joint Action Plan. The report noted that Turkey needed to take urgent action in aligning its visa policy with that of the EU, particularly prioritising the source countries of irregular migration to the EU.[19] Despite de-alignment of the visa regime, cooperation between the EU and Turkey was not hindered in addressing the refugee 'crisis'. Nonetheless, the issue remains as an important driver for the EU in particular.

3. Security

Irregular migration is heavily influenced by security drivers, which in turn are a direct result of events in neighbouring countries and beyond. Overall, such drivers have served to facilitate cooperation between the EU and Turkey, particularly through institutions with a security-oriented mandate. A security perspective has been integrated into the EU's management of migration since the 1990s. The establishment of a common external border for the Schengen area enabling the free internal movement of citizens necessitated stronger border controls to prevent irregular arrivals and unauthorised stays in the Union. This security dimension is also relevant for Turkey since it directly impacts its relationship with the EU. Due to Turkey's official EU candidacy status and the European Commission's limited interest in the south-eastern corridor,[20] the security dimension of migration was initially addressed at institutional level through FRONTEX and pilot projects providing training to Turkish coast and border guards, as well as improvements in technical capabilities. Reliance on FRONTEX was not particularly welcomed by Turkey, an outsider to the agency's decision-making mechanisms, due to concerns that the agency contributed to the development of asymmetrical power relations in the Aegean.

---

19 European Commission. Turkey 2016 Report. SWD(2016) 366 final, Brussels, 2016.
20 Dimitriadi et al., EU-Turkey Relations and Irregular Migration.

Evolution of the institutional relationship between FRONTEX and Turkey is indicative of a broader pattern observed in the area of migration. Until 2012, the agency was negotiating a working agreement document that was eventually relegated to a Memorandum of Understanding allowing for the exchange of data and risk analysis, as well as occasional working group meetings. Similarly to negotiations on the EU-Turkey Readmission Agreement (EURA), the question was how Turkey would benefit from offering more concessions due to the absence of burden and responsibility-sharing mechanisms established with the EU in the light of little progress on the country's EU accession. Nonetheless, interviews with FRONTEX and Greek Law Enforcement Agency staff (LEA),[21] have highlighted how important it is for the agency to establish dialogue and cooperation at a technical level, something that has persisted despite fluctuating political developments. When interviewed, FRONTEX staff reported[22] that institutional cooperation was also benefitting Turkey, since they informed EU policy makers about Turkey's border management practices as well as its challenges and needs. The October 2015 EU-Turkey Joint Action Plan built on the pre-existing institutional dimension, by including an exchange of liaison officers between FRONTEX and Turkey. It is clear that cooperation is focused on the technical level, which has allowed it to remain largely unaffected by political developments.

Within this framework, NATO was a recent addition. Initiated by Germany and Turkey, deployment of NATO forces in the Aegean Sea began on 11 February 2016. Under German leadership, NATO now operates in both the international waters and in the territorial waters of Greece and Turkey, providing data to the Hellenic and Turkish coastguards as well as FRONTEX. From the outset, Turkey sought to limit the operational area so as to extend no further than the islands of Lesvos and Chios.[23] Furthermore, after the July 2016 attempted coup in Turkey,[24] NATO's presence became particularly controversial. NATO forces' engagement attests to the growing militarisation of migration management on the EU's part, which stands in sharp contrast to Turkey's civilian policy. Yet, these differences do not seem to have negatively affected the relationship between institu-

---

21 Ibid. p. 11.
22 Ibid, p. 9.
23 Athanasopoulos, Angelos. Fortress Europe. The Aegean Sea Frontier and the Strengthening of EU's External Borders. In: International Reports of the Konrad-Adenauer-Stiftung, April 2017, p. 18.
24 Parkes, Roderick. Nobody Move. Myths of the EU Migration Crisis. In: Chaillot Paper No. 143, December 2017.

tional actors and their representatives, or the day-to-day operational partnership in place between the EU and Turkey.

4. Political Drivers

Political drivers heavily influence relations regarding migration. The key determinant has been Turkey's *accession* process to the EU that underscores most elements of the partnership, from the EU-Turkey Readmission Agreement to visa liberalisation and the growing visibility of high-skilled migration.

4.1 Europeanisation of Turkey's Asylum Policy

Turkey's Europeanisation process along with subsequent reforms of its migration and asylum procedures have created positive conditions for cooperation with the EU, although their impact varies across the different focal issues. Overall, what emerges is a direct link between accession and migration cooperation not only due to the nature of accession itself,[25] but also because the accession process and its trade-offs have functioned as an incentive to achieve migration cooperation. However, Turkey's failed coup attempt in July 2016 and its aftermath raised a unique challenge to further positive steps in this direction. It effectively put an end to the aspired revitalisation of accession negotiations and negatively interfered with cooperation on the EU-Turkey Statement, visa liberalisation for Turkish citizens, as well as Turkey's bilateral relations with its immediate neighbour and 'partner in implementation', Greece.

Turkey's reforms in the areas of migration and asylum were driven by multiple factors such as the country's domestic needs and political changes in and around its neighbourhood as well as globalisation, which have necessitated the establishment of a migration management system somewhat compatible with the existing European models.[26] Despite some steps undertaken prior to 2006, Turkey generally delayed major reforms until 2013

---

25 In theory, the final goal is membership in a group with common rules and procedures on migration management.

26 Kale et al. Asylum Policy and the Future of Turkey-EU Relations.

due to burden-sharing concerns.[27] It was clear that by fully aligning its asylum system to the European framework, signing a Readmission Agreement (EURA) and undertaking the external border controls required, Turkey would end up with significant numbers of irregular migrants from Africa and Asia. Nonetheless, the Europeanisation process yielded significant reforms in Turkey's legal framework. In 2014, the Europeanisation of Turkish asylum policy culminated in adoption of the Law on Foreigners and International Protection (LFIP, Law No. 6458) that "was developed under the influence of the EU accession process with a surprisingly open-minded and liberal approach since 2008".[28] The LFIP established the main pillars of Turkey's national asylum system and shifted responsibility for all proceedings of foreigners in Turkey to the Directorate General of Migration Management (DGMM).

The impact of this Europeanisation process is also evident in the Temporary Protection Regulation that Turkey adopted on 22 October 2014. This sets out the rights, obligations and procedures for individuals who are granted temporary protection, a status resembling the subsidiary protection status that exists in the EU. Beneficiaries are offered the right to stay in Turkey. However, based on vulnerabilities and other criteria, Syrians may also be directed to resettlement in a third country (either through the UNHCR-led global resettlement programme or the resettlement programme offered by the EU via the 2016 EU-Turkey Statement). Yet, they are also protected from *refoulement* and can access a range of rights, services and assistance. The Temporary Protection Regulation proved instrumental for facilitating the 2016 EU-Turkey Statement. By guaranteeing protection from *refoulement* and the right of stay, returns from the EU to Turkey could take place in line with the 1951 Convention provisions.

4.2 EU-Turkey Readmission Agreement (EURA)

In contrast to asylum, the impact of Europeanisation on irregular migration can at best be described as 'partial' and is mostly evident in the signing of the EURA and the alignment of Turkey's visa regime. For the EU, Turkey serves as a buffer zone to its external borders by virtue of its geo-

---

27 İçduygu, Ahmet et al. Migration Profile Turkey. The Demographic-Economic Framework of Migration. The Legal Framework of Migration. The Socio-Political Framework of Migration. Florence, June 2013.

28 Kale et al., Asylum Policy and the Future of Turkey-EU Relations, p. 13.

graphical position and non-membership to the EU. For Turkey, this position has proven useful for seeking concessions over issues beyond migration management (e.g., visa liberalisation). Since irregular migration does not entail asylum's normative aspects nor international legal obligations, it constitutes an area where Europeanisation is less visible.

Turkey and the EU signed the EURA on 16 December 2013 following an intense negotiation process. For the EU, this is an important driver in facilitating further cooperation, primarily due to its technical nature.[29] Turkey agreed to proceed with the agreement only following the EU's announcement that a visa liberalisation process would be launched, thus laying the foundation for a transactional EU-Turkey partnership that would later materialise with the Statement. Of concern for Turkey was the absence of burden-sharing, which was partly responsible for Turkey's delay in signing the agreement.[30] The EURA had also been instrumentalised by Turkey which has used it as a bargaining chip during times of crises with the EU. The latest crisis between the two sides emerged during Turkey's gas drilling operations in Cypriot waters during the second half of 2019, which resulted in EU sanctions concerning, inter alia, its financial assistance to Turkey. Turkey reacted by announcing that it would suspend the Readmission Agreement which had been effective since March 2016.[31] However, under the 2016 EU-Turkey Statement, returns of irregular migrants can still take place from Greece to Turkey. Consequently, despite conflict that has been on the rise, migration cooperation has prevailed. The early 2020 events in Evros effectively ended the cooperative framework between Greece and Turkey.

---

29 The Readmission Agreement is a technical document for the return of citizens apprehended for irregular entry and/or stay in the territory of the signatory parties. It also includes a 'third country nationals' clause, which allows for EU member states to return irregular migrants to the country of transit from which they have entered the EU. The EURA effectively transfers the responsibility for the return of third country nationals to Turkey.

30 Dimitriadi et al. EU-Turkey Relations and Irregular Migration; Kale et al. Asylum Policy and the Future of Turkey-EU Relations.

31 For more information on the suspension of the Readmission Agreement by Turkey, see Eck, Daniel. Turkey suspends deal with the EU on migrant readmission. In: Euractive.com, 24 July 2019, https://www.euractiv.com/section/global-eu rope/news/turkey-suspends-deal-with-the-eu-on-migrant-readmission/ [11.09.20].

4.3 Highly Skilled Migration

High-skilled labour mobility, partially impacted by Europeanisation, is an additional identified driver which has yielded mixed results. Although it appears to be an official priority for the EU, research[32] suggests that the reality is quite different. High-skilled labour mobility has been affected by the 2010 Eurozone crisis which has generated internal movement, rising populism in both the EU and Turkey and EU-Turkey differentiation on whom to attract. For the EU, high-skilled labour mobility remains heavily regulated by member states' domestic labour markets, while for Turkey a shift towards attracting returnees or EU citizens of Turkish origin seems to be taking place.[33]

The financial crisis that has severely affected some member states also impacted the EU as a whole, creating an increase in intra-EU and intra-Eurozone migration, originating particularly from the southern member states.[34] While some members in the southern periphery witnessed an unprecedented 'brain drain' (e.g., Greece), others experienced a 'brain gain' (e.g., Germany). Although not unprecedented, the difference between the 2010-2019 period and earlier waves of intra-EU mobility is that the migrants, particularly those from Europe's southern periphery, are university graduates a significant percentage of whom are highly skilled.[35] As they move from the periphery to the core, it is likely that they will trigger demographic changes and raise the demand for specific labour sectors. In the short term, this also poses a challenge for highly skilled non-EU migrants who not only need to seek employment opportunities and secure some form of entry visa, either via the Blue Card Scheme or the Single Permit, but also 'compete' with the rising tide of highly skilled intra-EU migrants.

Specifically in relation to highly skilled Turkish migrants, research has shown that "there is a limited number of countries where they can access with relative ease the labour market, namely Germany and the Netherlands".[36] This is conditioned by the available labour opportunities and the stable financial conditions along with the Turkish diaspora in those coun-

---

32 Sánchez-Montijano, Elena et al. Highly Skilled Migration between EU and Turkey. Drivers and Scenarios. FEUTURE Online Paper No. 21, April 2018.

33 Ibid.

34 Ibid.

35 Bräuninger, Dieter. The dynamics of migration in the euro area. Deutsche Bank Research. Frankfurt am Main, July 2014.

36 Sánchez-Montijano et al. Highly Skilled Migration between EU and Turkey, p. 21.

tries. Turkey signed Labour Recruitment Agreements with Germany as early as 1961 and the Netherlands in 1964. Although the legal framework has since changed considerably, the initial establishment of labour recruitment schemes has enabled the gradual settlement and integration of Turkish citizens in Germany and the Netherlands, as well as the eventual growth of a significant Turkish diaspora representing a 'pull' factor for aspiring migrants.

When it comes to the EU citizens, research has shown that they had two principal motivations for seeking to move to Turkey: the country's booming economy in the 2000s and the EU accession process.[37] Turkey's post-2014 legal reforms were clearly influenced by its Europeanisation undertaken for accession.[38] At the same time, the EU anchor was not enough to trigger EU citizens' preferential treatment by Turkey. Furthermore, legal reforms have also been undercut by Turkey's political developments since 2017. Qualified EU citizens are expected to follow the same track as other third country nationals. However, they remain privileged in regard to the probability of their applications' acceptance[39] and evaluation for the extension of their stay in Turkey.

In general, there is an imbalance between receiving and sending skilled migrants, which is also made evident by the higher education sector, including both students and academics. Statistics show that between 2004 and 2016, Turkey's total number of incoming Erasmus students amounted to 38,552 while the number of outgoing Erasmus students was 116,143. As far as academic staff mobility is concerned, in the same period the total number of outgoing staff was 22,219 while the number of incoming staff was only 13,717.[40] According to European Commission statistics, Turkey is second to Poland in sending the highest number of academics to European countries for exchange.[41] In the final analysis, it could be argued that

---

37 Ibid, p. 25.
38 State actors prepared a new Law on International Work Force (Law No. 6735), which came into force on 13 August 2016. Among other changes, the law introduced a new type of work permit, the 'Turquoise Card' to attract a qualified international work force, also easing the conditions of stay and work for spouses and relatives. Skilled migrants can apply to the Ministry of Family, Labour and Social Services for recruitment opportunities. Provisions are included to facilitate family integration and are available for the spouse and/or dependent children of a Turquoise Card holder. See ibid.
39 Ibid.
40 European Commission. Education and Training Depository. January 2020, https://ec.europa.eu/programmes/erasmus-plus/about/statistics_en [15.05.20].
41 Ibid.

Turkey's accession process has temporarily resulted in cooperation between the EU and Turkey, with the possibility for convergence in the distant future. However, Turkey's post-2016 political developments alongside the EU's changing political landscape have generated a de facto freeze of Turkey's long-standing membership talks. In turn, this has strengthened the transactional features of the EU-Turkey relationship, particularly with respect to the management of migratory flows. Currently, the latter largely depends on the continuation of EU financial assistance to Turkey, which is necessary in implementing the 2016 EU-Turkey Statement.

5. The EU-Turkey Statement of March 2016

The most significant development for migration from a political perspective has been the announcement of the EU-Turkey Statement in March 2016. The Statement established a model of cooperation between the EU and Turkey and represents a significant driver in the relationship. The agreement was forged in the context of the ripple effects from the Syrian civil war, which were not contained at the EU's external borders and quickly shifted to Europe and the Schengen area. Triggered by the EU's 'political crisis' in managing refugee flows, the Statement was facilitated by recent reforms in the Turkish and Greek asylum systems as well as Turkey's successful instrumentalisation of its position as a transit country.[42]

Alongside the EURA, the Statement is another concrete example of the EU seeking to establish transactional migration cooperation with Turkey. Accordingly, the prospect of visa liberalisation, financial support and the opening of several accession negotiation chapters were all offered to Turkey in an attempt to enhance this functional cooperation.[43] Initially, the EU committed 3 billion euros under the Facility for Refugees in Turkey. This sum comprised 1 billion euros from the EU's budget and 2 billion euros from member states' contributions.[44] An additional 3 billion

---

42 Saatcioğlu, Beken. The European Union's Refugee Crisis and Rising Functionalism in EU-Turkey Relations. In: Turkish Studies, March 2019, Vol. 21, pp. 169-187.

43 Ibid.; Kale et al. Asylum Policy and the Future of Turkey-EU Relations, p. 19.

44 European Commission. EU Facility for Refugees in Turkey. The Commission proposes to mobilise additional funds for Syrian refugees. Brussels, March 2018, https://ec.europa.eu/neighbourhood-enlargement/news_corner/migration_en [11.09.20].

euros has been agreed for release both for continuing support of 3.5 million Syrians registered in Turkey during 2015-2016 and also maintenance of the EU-Turkey Statement. In itself, financial assistance is evidence of burden-sharing and EU acknowledgement that management of the Syrian refugee crisis is not solely Turkey's responsibility. However, as noted by Kale *et al.*, "EU funding aiming to support services for refugee protection, if not implemented effectively, can create tensions with the partner countries and the actors involved in implementing these policies".[45] For example, in regard to the Western Balkans, EU financial support was used to strengthen border controls rather than improve facilities for refugees. In Turkey, EU-imposed restrictions on how the funds would be used was a point of contention along with the EU's delays in submitting the promised sums. Furthermore, the Statement did not serve to enhance future refugee protection. Rather, it revealed the short-term effects and long-term uncertainty of externalisation efforts practised by the EU. For Turkey, the Statement's financial benefits are a welcome reprieve but not a long-term solution. Many middle-class and highly educated Syrians already crossed into Europe during 2015 and 2016.[46] This means that relatively speaking, the majority of Syrians left behind are either low-skilled or not as highly skilled, which in turn poses an integration challenge for Turkey's local communities. They are reportedly discontent with hosting large numbers of Syrians for extended periods of time, prompting debate as to when the Syrians will return home.[47]

As far as the other incentives promised by the Statement are concerned, visa liberalisation has yet to be delivered for Turkish citizens. Our research has demonstrated that this would be beneficial for the EU since it would facilitate the flow of Turkish students, academics and entrepreneurs who bring with them not only economic but also social and cultural benefits.[48] In contrast, failure to deliver on visa liberalisation endangers the EURA

---

45 Kale et al. Asylum Policy and the Future of Turkey-EU Relations, p. 21.

46 A UNHCR Survey conducted between April and September 2015 showed that 16 per cent of participants indicated they had been studying before they fled, followed by: merchants - nine per cent; carpenters, electricians, plumbers - seven per cent; engineers, architects - five per cent; doctors, pharmacists - four per cent. UNHCR determined that the overall profile of arrivals during 2015 was that of a highly-skilled migrant population. UNHCR. Statistical Yearbook 2014. Geneva, December 2015.

47 Khattab, Asser. Syrian refugees under pressure as neighbours' goodwill runs out. In: Financial Times, 05.032018, https://www.ft.com/content/bf696a82-1d47-11e8-956a-43db76e69936 [10.09.20].

48 Sánchez-Montijano et al. Highly Skilled Migration between EU and Turkey.

and has to date been perceived by the Turkish government as a signal that European counterparts are not committed to their promises. It is worth noting that since the EU-Turkey Statement was signed, the Turkish government has consistently stressed that unless the European counterparts offered what was agreed upon, Turkey would unilaterally suspend the Statement. In practice, the Statement has not been implemented as designed. From March 2016 until February 2020, Greece has returned 2,117 persons to Turkey in the framework of the Statement, with the majority (35%) from Pakistan and only 19% Syrians.[49] Turkey's move to 'open the border' allowing approximately 35,000 migrants and asylum seekers to gather on the Greek side of Evros, not only escalated tensions between the two countries but also between Turkey and the EU. However, instrumentalisation of migration to achieve political gains is neither a new nor an unexpected move from Turkey. As present research has shown, migration has consistently been utilised to drive the relationship forward or backwards, depending on Turkey's domestic needs. This means that a future renegotiation of the Statement is likely to include both financial assistance to Turkey for: the safe zone it is establishing in Syria; the refugees in Turkey; as well as a visa-free regime for Turkish citizens.

6. Populism and Neo-Ottomanism

Identity drivers horizontally impact migration and the focal issues of our analysis. Our research has identified two critical drivers: populist discourse in both the EU and Turkey; and neo-Ottomanism in Turkey.[50] Running in parallel is rising xenophobia and Islamophobia in the EU. The Turkish government and right-wing mainstream as well as populist political parties in the EU member states are inclined to exploit identity-based narratives[51] by way of appealing to their respective audiences and have invoked integration issues for Muslim migrants in the EU, whom the EU has portrayed as a security issue with Turkey responsible for providing protection.

---

49 UNHCR. Returns from Greece to Turkey. Geneva, March 2020.
50 For more information on the main tenets of the 'Brand Turkey' imbued with Islamic and neo-Ottoman characteristics, see Secretariat General for European Union Affairs. Turkey's European Union Communication Strategy (EUCS). Ankara, January 2010.
51 Özbey, Ebru Ece et.al. Narratives of a contested relationship. In this volume, pp. 31-56.

Identity-based elements can be traced in Turkey's 'open door' policy for the Syrians, that has in turn impacted both the EU and EU-Turkey relations on migration. Turkey adopted this policy during the early days of the crisis, due in part to its assumptions that the conflict would de-escalate and the Syrians would return home. Based on normative principles and values, echoing to some extent those promoted by the EU, this new foreign policy sought to make Turkey a global player and predominantly the protector of Muslim communities. Hospitality, burden-sharing and asylum were concepts associated with a religious and historical responsibility to provide refuge to the Syrians. Yet, the Syrian refugees in Turkey are not officially recognised as refugees by the Turkish state since official refugee status is granted only to foreigners entering the country through European borders.[52] From the Syrian civil war's outbreak in 2011, Turkey has regarded Syrian refugees fleeing the war as 'guests'. The guest status of Syrian refugees was also coupled with the political discourse of the '*Ansar* spirit', which President Erdoğan and the AKP leadership advocated. '*Ansar* spirit' is a metaphor that was used to qualify the role that the Turkish state and pious Muslim Turks should play for Syrians in Turkey. *Ansar* means 'helpers' in Arabic, literally referring to the people of Medina, who supported the Prophet Mohammad and Muslims in his company (*Muhajirun*, or 'migrants'), who migrated there from Mecca which was then under pagan control. This metaphor originally refers to a temporary situation, as Muslims later returned to Mecca following their forces' recapturing of the city from the pagans. Thus, the Turkish government has used Islamic symbolism to legitimise its resolutions regarding the Syrian refugee crisis. The government leaders have consistently compared Turkey's role in assisting the Syrian refugees to that of the *Ansar*. Furthermore, framing Syrian refugees within the discourse of *Ansar* and *Muhajirun* has elevated public and private efforts to accommodate Syrian refugees from a humanitarian responsibility to a religious and charity-based duty.[53]

The influence of identity-based factors can also be found in the case of highly skilled migration. Following the notion of 'European identity', Turkey's growing de-Europeanisation following the July 2016 failed coup

---

52 For the text of the Geneva Convention and Protocol Relating to the Status of Refugees, see UNHCR. Convention and Protocol Relating to the Status of Refugees. Geneva, 1950/1967, https://www.unhcr.org/protection/basic/3b66c2aa1 0/convention-protocol-relating-status-refugees.html [06.11.19].

53 Erdemir, Aykan. The Syrian Refugee Crisis. Can Turkey be an Effective Partner? March 2016, https://www.fdd.org/analysis/2016/03/07/eu-refugee-crisis-turkey-as-a n-effective-partner/ [06.11.19].

attempt functions as a negative driver for attracting skilled migrants from the EU. Democracy, free speech, human rights and the rule of law are critical elements in the construction of European identity and 'pull' factors for highly skilled migrants' destination choices. This poses a challenge for the attraction of skilled migration from the EU to Turkey. Additionally, Turkey has rather focused on attracting skilled labour from people of Turkish origin, either EU citizens or Turkish nationals. While Turkey offered 'pull' factors to highly skilled migrants, in the EU 'push' factors encouraged (re)migration to Turkey. Such 'push' factors included social discrimination, language barriers and the lack of language courses prior to arrival as well as discrimination based on nationality and religion faced by many Turks in countries with an already significant presence of Turkish diaspora (mainly in the Netherlands and Germany). Recently, this trend has deteriorated due to the escalation of political crises in Turkey. Should the populist rhetoric continue in Turkey, "Turkish-origin skilled and highly skilled individuals may still opt for migrating to Turkey, but the native EU citizens may not be risking their careers by coming to politically turbulent Turkey".[54] Similarly, should the populist rhetoric increase further in the EU, it is likely to become less of an attractive destination for highly skilled Turkish migrants. However, due to the escalation of political turbulence in Turkey following the attempted coup on 15 July 2016, there is a growing number of young and educated people migrating to EU member states, primarily Germany, for work and education as well as asylum purposes. For instance, between the attempted coup and 31 December 2019, some 36,303 Turkish citizens have reportedly applied for asylum in Germany.[55]

Rising populist discourse in the EU and Turkey has become a shared characteristic over recent years. Increasingly in the EU, Muslim faith-based populations are treated with caution and concern, their presence being tied not only to traditional security threats such as terrorism, but also societal insecurity linked to integration. The rise of populist parties in Europe has resulted in a 'value-based' discourse, portrayed as European and linked to the notion of European identity and posited in contrast to the identity of 'others', usually, Muslim faith-based states. The transactional character of the EU-Turkey relationship during the refugee crisis did not fundamen-

---

54 Sánchez-Montijano et al. Highly Skilled Migration between EU and Turkey, p. 26.

55 For more detail see: Duvar, English. 47.4 percent of Turkish asylum seekers granted protection in Germany in 2019. 11.01.2020, https://www.duvarenglish.com/human-rights/2020/01/11/47-4-percent-of-turkish-asylum-seekers-granted-protection-in-germany-in-2019/ [11.09.20].

tally alter the status quo, but rather offered a potentially different framework for cooperation and engagement between the two parties. In parallel, the rise of populism in Europe and the xenophobic discourse utilised by its proponents are also hampering Turkey's potential EU membership, a scenario that seems increasingly unlikely.

7. Conclusion

This chapter has evaluated the three ideal-type scenarios of convergence, cooperation and conflict in the area of migration for the future of EU-Turkey relations. In our research across three focal issues, convergence was approached as full membership, cooperation as the current status based on mid-level (and occasional high level) collaboration and conflict as a rift in the relationship, with Turkey and the EU undertaking different and often conflicting policies in the field of migration. Research has concluded that none of the three was deemed representative of a future relationship in the migration and asylum dimensions, with outward conflict and full-blown convergence considered the least likely.

Cooperation resulted in 2015, motivated by the Syrian refugee exodus. Yet, a mixed scenario with elements of conflict and cooperation seems to be most likely for the foreseeable future. This scenario has already been unfolding since 2018. The coexistence of conflict and cooperation is largely influenced by political and security drivers that currently shape the relationship on migration, with the former particularly introducing conflictual elements. Visa facilitation was offered in exchange for the EURA and the EU-Turkey Statement, yet at the time of writing, implementation of the former remains unlikely despite having been a critical incentive for Turkey to cooperate on migration. The attempted July 2016 coup and its aftermath caused friction between Ankara and various European capitals while the rise of populism affects how the EU and Turkey see each other. Although the political drivers are currently generating conflict, both the EU and Turkey share security concerns over irregular migration, potential links with terrorism and border security. In fact, the sides have established operational cooperation that has proven resilient even amidst conflictual elements. The EU-Turkey Statement remains in place despite suspension of the EURA and Greece-Turkey Readmission Agreements. On the one hand, Turkey is currently hosting roughly 4 million Syrians and an increasing number of other nationalities, including Afghans. On the other hand, the number of arrivals in Greece significantly increased in 2020, raising concern that Turkey is seeking additional incentives to strengthen patrol of its maritime borders. In 2018, 32,494 arrivals were recorded by sea and 18,014 by land. In 2019, the numbers increased to 59,726 sea arrivals and 14,887 via the land border. In parallel, more than 36,387 people remain stranded in hotspots across five Greek islands. Following events in Evros, a new round of negotiations have begun on the Statement, with the Greek side seeking to lift the geographical containment on the islands to allow for transfers from the mainland to Turkey, while Turkey appears to push for further financial assistance, support for the repatriation of Syrians in the 'safe zone' and visa free regime for Turkish citizens. It is also likely that a different format of cooperation will be identified, perhaps as part of a broader framework of transactional partnership with Turkey. For this scenario to unfold, though, and considering the previous conflictual relationship (2019-2020), the transactional element is key. In other words, Turkey is unlikely to sign off and/or implement an agreement that does not offer sufficient short and medium term incentives not only in the field of migration but also in relation to the economy and the geopolitical situation unfolding in the Mediterranean (i.e. Turkey's role in Libya as well as in the Eastern Mediterranean). Without this, despite the potential it is unlikely that the cooperation aspect will unfold fully.

In the face of demographic changes taking place due to declining birth rates in Europe, overpopulation in certain regions combined with large youth populations in search of better opportunities, climate change and continuous insecurity generated by conflicts in the neighbourhood and beyond, migration is rising in the political agendas of the EU and Turkey. Yet, it is unlikely to make or break the EU-Turkey relationship, irrespective of the 'weight' attributed to migration as a political issue, depending on changing dominant domestic and external drivers.

Under the right conditions (mutual interests, transactional elements) migration can be a driver for closer cooperation that could spill over to issues associated with migration, such as security, climate change and the economy. By contrast, as evident in 2020, such cooperation is highly susceptible to political influences, domestic pressures in Turkey as well as the incentives on offer. For transactional partnerships to be maintained, both sides need to deliver. To date, it seems that neither is fully willing or even able to do so.

Conclusions

EU-Turkey Relations: Towards a Transactional Future amid Conflictual Cooperation?

Beken Saatçioğlu

Relations between Turkey and the European Union (EU) have reached their lowest point in history. Following its receipt of EU candidacy status in December 1999, Turkey embarked on an EU harmonisation and reform agenda, which triggered the start of accession negotiations in 2005. Yet, since then, confrontational dynamics arising on multiple levels have increasingly strained the EU-Turkey relationship. Consequently, Turkey's EU accession process is practically deadlocked as Turkey has steadily moved away from the EU in normative and democratic terms. Furthermore, outside of accession, critical political, security and geopolitical challenges have impeded the full potential of the EU-Turkey partnership, lowering the scope of issue-based, transactional cooperation between Ankara and Brussels. Additionally, these developments have unfolded in an atmosphere of mistrust where neither side views the other as a reliable partner. Yet, despite all its difficulties, the EU-Turkey relationship has proven to be resilient. Realistically, neither the EU nor Turkey can afford to break their multifaceted relations and forego potentially beneficial mutual engagement, whatever its shape may be. Indeed, even under the direst circumstances where Turkey is perceived as undermining regional stability and security in the EU's neighbourhood (i.e. Eastern Mediterranean), EU foreign ministers have recognised that "the EU and Turkey have a strong interest in an improvement of their relations through a dialogue which is intended to create an environment of trust".[1]

The chapters in this volume have unpacked the persistent complexity of EU-Turkey relations in all their thematic dimensions while acknowledging that the future of the relationship represents a moving target. Furthermore, the chapter on the narratives has offered valuable insights into the history of the relationship, assessing how the sides have viewed each other

---

1 Council of the European Union. Statement of the EU Foreign Ministers on the situation in the Eastern Mediterranean. Press release, 15.05.2020, https://www.consili um.europa.eu/en/press/press-releases/2020/05/15/statement-of-the-eu-foreign-minist ers-on-the-situation-in-the-eastern-mediterranean/ [19.07.20].

and their relations in the context of critical events shaping the interactions since the 1950s.

Three principal aims have guided the volume. First, the contributions studying the themes of identity, politics, security, economy, energy and migration determined the drivers impacting EU-Turkey relations in these areas and, in particular, with respect to the focal issues within them, that have been identified as relevant. The drivers were studied on a multiplicity of levels, highlighting the causal factors operating in Turkey, the EU, the EU's neighbourhood and the global scene. Second, the chapters evaluated how the drivers influence the likelihood of the three ideal-type scenarios of convergence, cooperation and conflict.[2] The goal was to advance a future scenario for EU-Turkey relations in light of the relative significance and weight of the assessed drivers as well as focal issues bearing on the relationship in the different areas. Hence, each chapter put forward a relationship scenario in its respective area of study. Third, the volume synthesised the chapters' empirical findings in order to conceptualise a scenario for the future of EU-Turkey relations as a whole.

In realising these aims, the volume also promises an original contribution to the literature on EU-Turkey relations, where scenario-driven studies covering all the dimensions of the relationship have yet to be conducted. Hence, with its future-oriented approach, it complements existing works pursuing comprehensive thematic analysis of EU-Turkey ties without necessarily engaging in full-scale scenario analysis.[3]

This conclusion first summarises and synthesises the findings of the chapters in order to advance an overall scenario for the future of EU-Turkey relations, which is "conflictual cooperation".[4] It then elaborates on the scenario based on the drivers emanating from the chapters and the recent critical developments weighing on the relations. It concludes by reflecting on the future of the relations in light of their current transactional nature which has been growing since the 2015 Syrian refugee crisis.

---

2 For an explanation of the drivers and scenarios see Tekin, Funda. The future of EU-Turkey relations. In this volume, p. 11-28.

3 Aydın-Düzgit, Senem/ Tocci, Nathalie. Turkey and the European Union. London, 2015.

4 The scenario is also assessed in the FEUTURE project's final synthesis paper. See, Saatçioğlu, Beken/ Tekin, Funda/ Ekim, Sinan/ Tocci, Nathalie. The Future of EU-Turkey Relations: A Dynamic Association Framework amidst Conflictual Cooperation. March 2019.

1. Taking Stock of the Volume's Findings

Having studied EU-Turkey interactions in their respective areas, the chapters of the volume have concluded that a scenario of conflictual cooperation is likely to define the relations in the foreseeable future. This suggests that the EU-Turkey relationship exhibits cooperation mixed with conflict, with the degree of conflict being more or less intense in the various areas investigated. The mixed scenario is the direct result of the complex, multidimensional nature of EU-Turkey ties: While conflict dominates the relations in the identity realm and is also quite severe in the area of politics, a combination of cooperation and conflict shapes the engagements in security, migration and energy, which is also demonstrated by the narrative analysis. The economy is the most positive component of the relationship since functional cooperation coupled with minimal conflict shapes the economic interactions between the two sides.

Specifically, the deep divergences observed in politics and identity rule out both convergence - understood as Turkey's EU membership – and a scenario of pure cooperation. At the same time, given the mutual gains arising from functionally oriented cooperation in the areas of the economy, security, migration and energy, a wholesale conflict scenario is also not plausible. Hence, despite conflict permeating all areas, interactions remain within the confines of cooperation. Consequently, it would be fair to argue that the upper boundaries of the EU-Turkey relationship are set by conflictual politics and identity dynamics while the lower limits are drawn by mutual interests in the other thematic areas, which prevents the interactions from breaking or turning outright conflictual.[5] This conclusion is also confirmed by the history of EU-Turkey relations, which is characterised by "oscillations and coexistence between conflict and convergence".[6]

Politics is the principal source of conflict between the EU and Turkey. The chapter by Soler i Lecha, Sökmen and Tekin amply discussed the state of play in politics by studying the political drivers across the focal issues of political change, democracy and human rights, and public opinion. The analysis captured the political developments arising not only in Turkey but also the EU, and in the neighbourhood and global scenes. Hence, a rich cluster of factors was assessed in making sense of EU-Turkey relations in

---

5   Tocci, Nathalie. FEUTURE Voices. Beyond the Storm in EU-Turkey Relations. January 2018.
6   Ibid., p. 2.

this area. At the EU level, these principally include: (a) the EU's "Turkey fatigue" stemming from concerns about EU absorption capacity, and European political opposition to Turkey's membership; (b) the EU's deviations from credible membership conditionality vis-à-vis Turkey, which has in turn damaged Turkey's reform commitment during the course of accession negotiations; (c) the EU's post-2010 multiple crises that served to shift its focus away from widening towards integration while bringing to the fore differentiated integration. The combined effect of these factors was highlighted as increased politicisation and mistrust (which are also reflected in Turkish public opinion towards the EU) as far as accession-oriented EU-Turkey relations are concerned. Yet, from an objective standpoint, Turkey's persistent non-compliance with the Copenhagen political criteria, which has gained particular speed since 2013, was also pointed out as a pivotal driver capable of foreclosing on its own the option of membership for the country. This finding is supported by the European Commission's yearly Turkey reports which have raised growing concerns about Turkey's "serious backsliding" in democracy, rule of law and fundamental freedoms in recent years, and referred to Turkey more as a "key partner" than a viable EU membership candidate. It also emanates from the European Parliament (EP)'s even sharper criticisms which culminated in its March 2019 resolution calling for the formal suspension of Turkey's EU membership negotiations. In light of these worrisome developments, the authors conclude that all things being equal, the EU and Turkey are bound to diverging from one another in the political realm, which is more consistent with conflict than cooperation.

Identity follows politics as an area which has been loaded with conflictual dynamics since 2013. The chapter by Aydın-Düzgit and Rumelili demonstrates this finding in abundant detail by studying the discursive, mutual identity representations that are produced by Turkey and Europe in the course of their historical (1839-1999) and contemporary interactions (1999-present). The authors highlight the critical focal issues arising in the context of key historical events (i.e. political and cultural drivers) that have triggered identity debates in EU-Turkey relations. Specifically, nationalism, civilisation, status in international society and state-society relations are investigated as the issues "with respect to which Europe (or Turkey) constitutes its identity by comparing itself with and/or differentiating itself from its significant Other, that is Turkey (or Europe)".[7] Aydın-Düzgit and Rumelili argue that while all four have given way to mutually conflictual

---

7 Aydın-Düzgit, Senem/ Rumelili, Bahar. Contested identities. In this volume, p. 59.

identity depictions, civilisation and nationalism are likely to exercise relatively long-term impacts for keeping the relations in a conflictual state. This is because Turkish and European identities have historically been pitted against each other based on civilisational differences, which was also reflected in nationalist discourse and strategies. In the current context, the rise of right-wing populism and nationalism in both Turkey and Europe are fuelling conflict in the way the EU and Turkey see each other, and are likely to do so in the future. However, the authors do not view this as a steady future scenario since history (which is amply discussed in the chapter) has revealed that "conflict, convergence and/or cooperation constantly alternate in response to specific drivers over time".[8] Yet, it is unknown when the next shift towards a more positive scenario is bound to happen.

The economy is the area which is the least conflictual of all dimensions. In fact, all the components of EU-Turkey economic relations exhibit a high degree of cooperation and minimal conflict. The chapter by Erdil and Akçomak has conducted a thorough, data-based study of economic interactions by investigating the flows of goods and services, finance and knowledge connecting the two sides, along with the political economy variables impacting these exchanges. The authors argue that despite politically induced tension (e.g. political instability in Turkey) which has occasionally lowered the relations' economic potential, the persistent volume of flows attests to their mutually beneficial welfare and growth impacts. In 2019, the EU was by far Turkey's largest trading partner while Turkey was the EU's fifth largest partner. The Union also remains the biggest source of foreign direct investment in Turkey. This is coupled with EU-Turkey research collaboration within the context of activities such as Turkey's participation to Framework Programmes (FPs) and membership in the European Research Area (ERA). On the whole, the flows suggest significant economic integration between the EU and Turkey. Yet, what keeps them from culminating in convergence is the presence of factors stemming from the political economy dimension, that preclude, inter alia, the modernisation of the 1995 EU-Turkey Customs Union (CU) agreement which would maximise EU-Turkey trade and generate growth (especially for Turkey).

Migration is second to the economy in representing a key avenue of EU-Turkey cooperation despite a relatively high dose of simultaneous conflict. The chapter by Dimitriadi and Kaya has investigated the relations in this area by focusing on three focal issues: irregular migration, asylum and highly skilled labour mobility. The authors have unpacked the political, se-

---

8 Ibid., p. 76.

curity, economic as well as identity-oriented and migration-related drivers influencing these issues in the period between 1999 and early 2020. They reached two findings. First, highly skilled migration (understood as the bidirectional movement of Turkish and EU citizens) is not a key issue in EU-Turkey migration relations. Second, the twin issues of irregular migration and asylum, which have risen to the fore in the context of the 2015/2016 Syrian refugee crisis, have remained at the centre of EU-Turkey transactional interactions. Yet, due to the influence of political drivers, initial cooperation over these issues has been marred with conflict since early 2020, shifting the relations towards a future scenario of conflictual cooperation.

Security represents an area where conflict has gradually risen despite persistent, yet increasingly difficult, cooperation. Critical disagreements have recently heightened tension between the EU and Turkey, particularly in the context of developments in Syria, the Eastern Mediterranean and Libya. The chapter by Ergun and Ülgen takes stock of EU-Turkey security relations and the relevant drivers since 1999. The authors argue that the relations have shifted from a "cooperation bordering convergence" scenario to conflictual cooperation driven by the sides' increasingly divergent security and foreign policy interests, and priorities. They discuss how a widening gap has characterised the security relationship particularly since 2014. Notable sources of conflict are analysed in relation to: (a) the Syrian civil war, namely, Turkey's insistence on a military operation against Bashar el-Assad (which was met by the EU's refusal); security problems along the Turkish-Syrian border, jeopardising the fight against the Islamic State in Iraq and Syria (ISIS) until 2015/2016; disagreements regarding the Syrian Kurdish militia known as the YPG (People's Protection Units) which Turkey considers to be an affiliate of the Kurdish terror group PKK, culminating in its Operation Olive Branch (January-March 2018) that attracted the EU's criticism; (b) Turkey's cooperation with Russia (including its actions in Syria and purchase of S-400 missile defence system from Russia) coupled with its reluctance to support EU sanctions against Russia motivated by Russian actions in Crimea and the Ukraine. Nevertheless, the authors conclude that there is room for EU-Turkey security cooperation with respect to topics including, inter alia, the non-proliferation of Weapons of Mass Destruction (WMD), collaboration in the military industrial realm, the fight against ISIS (which has improved over time), intelligence sharing, border security to prevent transit migration from Turkey to Europe, and peace and reconstruction efforts in Syria.

In energy, the projected scenario is also conflictual cooperation. Colantoni's chapter reaches this conclusion based on a thorough investigation of the drivers that influence: (a) the EU's and Turkey's energy (and when relevant, climate) strategies, interests and priorities; (b) the Moscow-Ankara-Brussels energy triangle; (c) EU-Turkey engagement in relation to the changing global energy and climate order; (d) EU-Turkey energy relations in the Caspian and the Middle East; (e) gas exploration efforts in the Eastern Mediterranean. The author shows that despite the potential for EU-Turkey cooperation to reduce mutual dependence on Russian gas (e.g. via initiatives such as the Southern Gas Corridor) and explore opportunities in the nuclear energy and climate areas, conflict has gained prominence. He argues that this is especially due to the rising "drilling controversy" caused by Turkey's hydrocarbon exploration activities in the Eastern Mediterranean, which are considered as illegal (and against the sovereignty of the Republic of Cyprus) by the EU. The controversy is far-reaching and complex since it has its roots in an another longstanding conflict: the Cyprus question. Other discussed sources of conflict include, inter alia, Turkey's insufficient commitment to the development of renewable energy strategies, which has in turn precluded its phasing out of coal. Last but not least, the fact that the opening of the energy chapter (as part of EU-Turkey accession negotiations) remains under Cyprus' veto since 2009, has complicated Turkey's compliance with the EU's energy acquis, adding to the conflictual dynamics in this area.

To reflect the overall tone of the EU-Turkey relationship, the chapter on the narratives has analysed the relations by focusing on how Turkish and European actors have experienced and recounted the critical events that shaped the relationship in the period between 1958 and 2017. Departing from the assumption that Turkish and EU narratives on the relationship affect the evolution of EU-Turkey relations and vice versa, Özbey et al. conducted a rich, qualitative coding analysis of 282 official statements, speeches and documents drawn from both Turkish and European sources. In doing so, they highlighted the future narratives and related relationship scenarios involving the EU and Turkey. The study of the rich narratives defined as "interpretations by political actors of the nature, evolution, drivers and end-goals of EU-Turkey relations"[9] revealed two major findings. First, Turkish and EU narratives differ in terms of their portrayal of the EU-Turkey relationship. Although Turkish narratives invariably emphasise Turkey's EU membership as the desired *finalité* of the relationship, EU narratives vary in this respect while stressing Turkey's role as an important to the EU. Second, competing and even divergent narratives have increased

---

9 Özbey et al., in this volume, p. 34-35.

on both sides since the 1960s. This is directly reflective of the conflictual patterns and tension engulfing recent EU-Turkey ties. Since 2016 (i.e. following Turkey's 15 July 2016 coup attempt, and foreign policy actions diverging from the EU), the "Turkey as a strategic partner to the EU" narrative has increasingly been rivalled by "Turkey as a distant, or even hostile neighbour to the EU" rhetoric. The coexistence of these opposing narratives implies the presence of cooperation and conflict, which points towards a future conflictual cooperation scenario.

2. Looking Further Ahead: What to Expect from the EU-Turkey Relationship?

2.1 The Evolving Context of EU-Turkey Relations

The findings of the volume pinpoint conflictual cooperation as the most likely scenario for the future of EU-Turkey relations. Therefore, foreseeable relations fall much short of convergence. However, they are still to remain within the confines of transactional - yet increasingly difficult - cooperation owing to the mutual interests sustaining the interactions. In the current context, this is consistent with a relationship that effectively approximates what can be viewed as an uneasy strategic partnership.

There are three fundamental issues preventing the relationship from evolving towards convergence: (1) Turkey's post-2010 de-Europeanisation[10] and democratic backsliding amounting to competitive authoritarianism,[11] (2) the unresolved Cyprus dispute, (3) the EU's decreased appetite for enlargement in general, and skepticism towards integrating Turkey as a member,[12] in particular. By itself, the first factor has driven the member states to conclude that Turkey's accession process has come to a standstill. In June 2018, the EU Council stated:

> The Council is especially concerned about the continuing and deeply worrying backsliding on the rule of law and on fundamental rights in-

---

10 Saatçioğlu, Beken. De-Europeanisation in Turkey: The Case of the Rule of Law. In: South European Society and Politics, 2016, Vol. 21 (1), p. 133-146.

11 Esen, Berk/ Gümüşçü, Şebnem. Building a competitive authoritarian regime: state–business relations in the AKP's Turkey. In: Journal of Balkan and near Eastern Studies, 2018, Vol. 20 (4), p. 349–372.

12 Aydın-Düzgit, Senem/ Şenyuva, Özgehan. Turkey: A Vicious Cycle of Euroscepticism? In: Michael Kaeding, Johannes Pollak, Paul Schmidt (eds). Euroscepticism and the Future of Europe. Palgrave Macmillan, Cham. https://doi.org/10.1007/97 8-3-030-41272-2_38.

cluding the freedom of expression ... Turkey has been moving further away from the European Union. Turkey's accession negotiations have therefore effectively come to a standstill and no further chapters can be considered for opening or closing.[13]

Yet, without the resolution of the Cyprus dispute, membership would still be unlikely even if Turkey restored its democracy. This is because Cyprus has been cited as a separate membership criterion by the EU since 1997,[14] and its resolution is considered as a major step towards good neighbourly relations and normalisation of Turkey's relations with a member state (Republic of Cyprus). The deadlock over Cyprus also stands as one of the root causes of ongoing EU-Turkey tension over drilling in the Eastern Mediterranean. Turkey justifies its hydrocarbon exploration efforts by arguing: (a) the exploration area falls within its continental shelf, (b) it is exercising its legal status as the guarantor state for the Turkish Republic of Northern Cyprus (officially recognised only by Turkey) which is entitled to its share of the island's maritime natural resources. In contrast, the EU considers this as a violation of international law, and in particular, the sovereign rights of the Republic of Cyprus over the entire island, including its territorial waters and exclusive economic zone. Consequently, as discussed further below, EU sanctions have been imposed on Turkey, which represents the first instance where this has ever happened to an official EU candidate.

Membership being thus ruled out under the current circumstances, the most that the EU and Turkey can realistically establish is an improved transactional engagement. Yet, even here there are problems that are lowering the potential for smooth, conflict-free cooperation. As noted above, confrontational dynamics are currently prominent in the areas of energy and security. Notably, the EU has taken punitive measures against Turkey, in response to its "illegal" drilling activities in the Eastern Mediterranean. A series of sanctions was decided at consecutive European Council meetings held in July, October and November 2019. These respectively included, inter alia: (1) suspension of the negotiations on the Comprehensive Air Transport Agreement as well as the meetings of the EU-Turkey Association Council and High-Level Dialogues, reduction of pre-accession assistance to

---

13 Council of the European Union. Enlargement and Stabilisation and Association Process, Council Conclusions. 26.06.2018, pp. 12-13, https://www.consilium.euro pa.eu/media/35863/st10555-en18.pdf [02.08.20].

14 Council of the European Union. Luxembourg Council Presidency Conclusions. 12-13 December 1997, paragraph 35, http://aei.pitt.edu/43332/1/LUXEMBOURG_ EUROPEAN_COUNCIL.pdf [05.08.20].

Turkey for 2020;[15] (2) "a framework regime of restrictive measures targeting natural and legal persons responsible for or involved in the illegal drilling activity of hydrocarbons in the Eastern Mediterranean";[16] (3) follow-up measures that included "a travel ban to the EU and an asset freeze for persons, and an asset freeze for entities" involved in unauthorised drilling activities.[17] Further limited sanctions against individuals and companies involved in drilling were announced by the December 2020 European Council,[18] pursuant to the October 2020 European Council, which had foreseen restrictive measures "in case of [Turkey's] renewed unilateral actions or provocations in breach of international law" in the region, i.e. with respect to Greece and the Republic of Cyprus.[19] It was also decided that the situation would be reassessed at the latest by the March 2021 European Council, following a report by the EU High Representative for Foreign Affairs and Security Policy (HR/VP), and the Commission.[20]

In security, divergences over Syria have remained persistent. In October 2019, Turkey's military incursion in northeastern Syria ("Operation Peace Spring") received the EU's condemnation on the basis that it "seriously undermines the stability and the security of the whole region"[21], "threatens heavily European security"[22] by shifting the focus away from the fight against ISIS (towards YPG), and contradicts international humanitarian

---

15 Council of the European Union. Outcome of the Council Meeting. Foreign Affairs. 11269/19. 15.07.2019, p. 10, https://www.consilium.europa.eu/media/41183/st11260-en19.pdf [03.08.2020].

16 Council of the European Union. Outcome of the Council Meeting. Foreign Affairs. 13066/19. 14.10.2019, p. 5, https://www.consilium.europa.eu/media/41182/st13066-en19.pdf [03.08.2020].

17 Council of the European Union. Outcome of the Council Meeting. Foreign Affairs. 13976/19. 11-12 November 2019, p. 7. https://www.consilium.europa.eu/media/42006/st13976-en19-fv.pdf [03.08.20].

18 European Council. Conclusions. EUCO 22/20. 11 December 2020, p. 11. https://www.consilium.europa.eu/media/35863/st10555-en18.pdf [13.12.2020].

19 European Council. Conclusions. EUCO 13/20. 2 October 2020, p. 8. https://www.consilium.europa.eu/media/45910/021020-euco-final-conclusions.pdf [29.10.20].

20 Ibid., p. 12.

21 Council of the European Union. Outcome of the Council Meeting. Foreign Affairs. 13066/19. 14.10.2019, p. 4, https://www.consilium.europa.eu/media/41182/st13066-en19.pdf [03.08.20].

22 European Council. EUCO 23/19. 18.10.2019, p. 2, https://www.consilium.europa.eu/media/41123/17-18-euco-final-conclusions-en.pdf [03.08.20].

law.[23] Consequently, "member states have decided to halt their arms exports licensing to Turkey".[24]

Libya is another item that was recently added to the list of divergent foreign policy issues between the EU and Turkey. At the core of the controversy are the two deals signed in November 2019 by Turkey and Libya's internationally recognised Government of National Accord (GNA) concerning the delimitation of maritime boundaries, and subsequently, security and military cooperation. While Ankara argues that its maritime boundaries with Libya are consequently extended from Turkey's southwest coast to Libya's Derna-Tobruk coast (thereby claiming the right to engage in hydrocarbon drilling in this area), this is vehemently opposed by Greece and the Republic of Cyprus which find it against their geostrategic interests in the region. Furthermore, the EU has expressed solidarity with both member states.[25] Additionally, Turkey's military alliance with the GNA, which happened as a *quid pro quo* following the maritime deal favouring Turkish interests in the Eastern Mediterranean, was also opposed by the EU. In particular, France (which supports the rival Libyan faction led by General Haftar in the Libyan civil war, along with Russia, Egypt and the United Arab Emirates) criticised the initiative on the grounds that Turkey's military involvement in Libya violates the outcomes of the January 2020 Berlin international conference on Libya.

The critical tensions over Libya and the Eastern Mediterranean were discussed in detail at an EU debate on Turkey. The EU Foreign Affairs Council (FAC) met on 13 July 2020 and importantly declared:

> There was consensus among member states that EU-Turkey relations were currently under strain because of worrying developments affecting the EU's interests, in particular in the Eastern Mediterranean and Libya. Ministers agreed that several serious issues had to be addressed by Turkey in order to change the current confrontational dynamic, and create an environment of trust... [I]t was stressed that Turkey's unilateral actions – in particular in the Eastern Mediterranean, which run counter to EU interests, to the sovereign rights of EU member

23 Ibid., p. 2.
24 Ibid., p. 2.
25 Council of the European Union. Remarks by HR/VP Josep Borrell. Informal Meeting of EU Foreign Ministers (Gymnich). Press Conference. 28.08.2020, https://eeas.europa.eu/headquarters/headquarters-homepage/84516/informal-meeting-eu-foreign-ministers-gymnich-remarks-hrvp-josep-borrell-press-conference_en [06.09.20].

states and to international law – must come to an end ... Ministers also called on Turkey to contribute actively to a political solution in Libya and to respect the commitments it had made within the framework of the Berlin process, including the UN arms embargo.[26]

These developments have intensified conflict between the EU and Turkey in a growing atmosphere of mutual mistrust where constructive dialogue to address disagreements on a fair footing is currently missing. Rather than proving productive, EU sanctions on Turkey have pitted the two sides further against each other by effectively placing Turkey among the ranks of non-EU candidate countries like Russia and Iran that are normatively distanced from the EU and are also subject to EU sanctions. From the EU's standpoint, Turkey is perceived not only as an unreliable strategic partner and a "distant and problematic neighbour"[27] but also one that repeatedly violates international law (in Syria, Libya and the Eastern Mediterranean) along with EU democratic values. Besides complicating actual EU-Turkey cooperation, this situation may also carry repercussions on the identity front: Damage to Turkey's status in international society and civilisational standing (which are two of the important drivers emphasised by Aydın-Düzgit and Rumelili in this volume) may potentially foster mutually conflictual identity representations in Turkey and Europe.

Nevertheless, despite all the difficulties and mutual conflict perceptions straining the relationship, both the EU and Turkey realise the strategic significance of maintaining engagement in one form or another. As HR/VP Josep Borrell stated when summarising the FAC's Turkey debate on 13 July 2020: "Turkey is an important country for the EU with whom we would wish to see our relations strengthened and developing".[28] Similarly, referring to the conclusions of the informal meeting of EU Foreign Ministers in Gymnich on 28 August 2020, Borrell argued: "What we want is to find paths towards a healthier relationship".[29] More significantly, the October 2020 European Council promised a "positive political EU-Turkey agenda"

---

26 Council of the European Union. Outcome of the Council Meeting. Foreign Affairs. 9459/20. 13.07.2020, p. 4, https://www.consilium.europa.eu/media/45019/st0 9459-en20.pdf [04.08.20].

27 Wessels, Wolfgang. Narratives Matter: In Search of a Partnership Strategy. IPC-Mercator Policy Brief. Istanbul, April 2020.

28 Foreign Affairs Council. Main Results, 13.07.2020, https://www.consilium.europa .eu/en/meetings/fac/2020/07/13/ [06.08.20].

29 Council of the European Union. Remarks by HR/VP Josep Borrell.

contingent on Turkey's "constructive efforts to stop illegal activities vis-à-vis Greece and Cyprus".[30]

2.2 Towards a Transactional Future?

As the chapters have demonstrated, nowhere is transactionalism more evident than it is in migration. The refugee crisis of 2015/2016 has shown how much the EU and Turkey depend on each other, the former significantly more so than the latter. When the crisis hit in the spring of 2015, the EU sought to execute a common "European solution" which prioritised initiatives such as refugees' relocation and resettlement to Europe in line with the principles of "solidarity" and "fair sharing of responsibility" pertaining to EU migration management. Yet, over time, growing disagreements among the member states hijacked the implementation of a common European asylum policy in solving the crisis. Consequently, the management of the crisis was "externalised" to Turkey, with the March 2016 EU-Turkey refugee deal emerging as this policy's principal instrument.[31] In the following period, preserving the deal became the EU's utmost priority to stop the refugee flows to Europe and maintain the Schengen regime as a core pillar of European integration. Therefore, as long as the EU is unable and/or unwilling to commit to a common European asylum policy, dependence on Turkey as a key partner in migration management will keep Brussels on board for transactional cooperation in this area.

For Turkey as well, there are political benefits attached to continued migration cooperation with the EU. Principally, Turkey commands significant leverage over the EU as a result of the refugee deal. In fact, using this leverage and blackmailing tactics (e.g. using the refugees hosted in Turkey as a bargaining chip),[32] Ankara was able to extract concessions from the EU in the course of bargaining for the deal.[33] The terms of the March 2016

---

30 European Council. Conclusions. EUCO 13/20. 2.10.2020.

31 See also Reiners, Wulf/ Tekin, Funda. Taking Refuge in Leadership? Facilitators and Constraints of Germany's Influence in EU Migration Policy and EU-Turkey Affairs during the Refugee Crisis (2015–2016). In: German Politics, 2020, Vol. 29 (1), pp. 115-130.

32 Greenhill, Kelly M. Open Arms Behind Barred Doors: Fear, Hypocrisy and Policy Schizophrenia in the European Migration Crisis. In: European Law Journal, 2016, Vol. 22 (3), p. 317-332.

33 Saatçioğlu, Beken. The European Union's Refugee Crisis and Rising Functionalism in EU-Turkey Relations. In: Turkish Studies, 2020, Vol. 21 (2), p. 169-187, DOI: 10.1080/14683849.2019.1586542.

EU-Turkey Statement included increased financial aid to address refugees' needs in Turkey, a "re-energised" EU accession process, the promise – albeit conditional – to fasten visa liberalisation for Turkish citizens travelling to the Schengen area, and a reference to the prospective modernisation of the 1995 CU agreement.

Following the deal's finalisation, the Turkish government continued to instrumentalise it by threatening to send its refugees – among whom, suspected ISIS members - to Europe. This was done in an attempt to steer EU-Turkey foreign policy disagreements in Ankara's favour in places like Syria in October 2019 (e.g. the establishment of a safe zone in northern Syria, where Turkey could send some of its extensive refugee population) and the Eastern Mediterranean (November 2019) regarding Turkish drilling rights.[34] In addition, normatively speaking, Ankara extracts moral legitimacy from its migration cooperation with Brussels and has not shied away from using it to deflect the EU's criticism of its own democracy. As Turkish President Tayyip Erdoğan argued: "At a time when Turkey is hosting three million migrants, those who are unable to find space for a handful of refugees, who in the middle of Europe keep these innocents in shameful conditions, must first look at themselves".[35] Indeed, with 4 million refugees (3.6 million of which are Syrians) within its borders, Turkey is the world's top refugee-hosting country. At a time when it is globally perceived as a violator of international law, and core EU principles such as democracy and rule of law, this moral legitimacy represents a key normative asset which may potentially serve to counterbalance the country's negative image and enhance its status in international society.

In short, migration forms the core of EU-Turkey transactional cooperation, followed by trade and counterterrorism. However, this cooperation too could be deepened if the sides overcame the problem of mistrust. It could be argued that at the root of mistrust lie the sides' different expectations from the refugee deal, with each accusing the other of violating it. Turkey claims that Brussels has failed to offer in full the incentives it promised Ankara within the context of the deal, i.e. the agreed financial package for the refugees (6 billion euros), visa liberalisation and CU upgrade. In response, Brussels argues that the financial package is still in the process of being delivered under the Facility for Refugees, and the deal

---

34 Gall, Carlotta. Erdoğan Warns that Turkey Will Keep Deporting ISIS Detainees. In: The New York Times, 12.11.2019.
35 EU strikes deal to return new migrants to Turkey. In: The Washington Post, 18.03.2016.

made no direct promise regarding the visa and CU upgrade issues (since both are contingent on the fulfillment of separate conditions by Turkey). According to the EU, Ankara was also not justified in suspending the deal by opening its border with Greece to the refugee flows to Europe in late February 2020.

Whether these disagreements will trigger a new refugee deal is a complex question. On the one hand, the need to overhaul the deal so as to remove references to visa liberalisation and CU upgrade (on the grounds that Turkey has turned authoritarian since 2016) from the March 2016 Statement, was raised in European circles.[36] On the other, with the EU-Turkey positive agenda declared by the October 2020 European Council, the prospect of implementing the Statement with all its carrots (CU upgrade, trade facilitation, "people to people contacts", High Level dialogues)[37] has been brought back to the table by the EU. It remains to be seen whether the agenda is merely a tactical move to de-escalate tension in the Eastern Mediterranean or a genuine EU initiative which would be carried out as promised (i.e. if Turkey ameliorated its relations with Greece and Cyprus in the region).

While it is not possible to predict the precise developments that will shape each thematic area of EU-Turkey relations in the future, one thing is certain: The relations have turned increasingly transactional since the refugee crisis[38] and are likely to remain so, at least in the foreseeable future. This transactionalism is as much a result of actual cooperation on the ground as it is the direct consequence of the EU's common political approach to relations with Turkey. Since late 2015 when the EU first reached out to Ankara to secure migration cooperation, both general European narrative and EU official discourse labelling Turkey as a "key partner to the EU" have intensified.[39] References to Turkey as a strategic partner have surpassed those emphasising Turkey's official EU candidacy and accession prospects. Notwithstanding their political differences with respect to European integration and enlargement, EU officials and European politicians seem united in their conviction about the unlikelihood of Turkish accession along with the strategic need to maintain a *de facto* partnership with Turkey.

---

36 Fraser, Susan. Turkey calls on EU to be "honest" in dispute with members. In: The Washington Post, 06.07.2020.
37 European Council. Conclusions. EUCO 13/20. 2.10.2020, p. 8.
38 Saatçioğlu. The European Union's Refugee Crisis.
39 Wessels. Narratives Matter.

Transactionalism is also apparent in muted European criticism of Turkey's democracy and rule of law deficits. Since 2015, both the EU and European politicians have lowered their criticisms of Turkey due to strategic reasons related to migration cooperation[40] and the predominant belief that Turkey's accession process has already reached a dead end after 2016 (which obviates the need to pressure Ankara for further compliance with the Copenhagen political criteria). Although Turkey's democratic shortcomings are documented in detail in the Commission's yearly reports and - in even sharper terms - the EP's resolutions, regular and credible democratic pressure on Ankara has been in short supply in Brussels. Furthermore, these issues are no longer raised within the context of Turkey's EU accession where EU membership conditionality is still officially in existence given the country's EU candidacy status. Rather, they are occasionally brought up in relation to two separate issues that have no direct bearing on accession: (Schengen) visa liberalisation for Turkish citizens and the CU's modernisation. The former requires Ankara to meet two democratic benchmarks out of the six conditions yet to be fulfilled; namely, the revision of Turkey's Anti-Terror Law in line with the European Convention on Human Rights (ECHR) and the European Court of Human Rights (ECtHR) case law; and the amendment of the law on Personal Data Protection to ensure, inter alia, the independence of Turkey's data protection authority. The latter is more generally linked to the restoration of Turkish democracy, pursuant to the June 2018 EU Council decision: "The Council notes that Turkey has been moving further away from the European Union... no further work towards the modernisation of the EU-Turkey Customs Union is foreseen".[41]

What this transactionalism may evolve into from an institutional standpoint is the most complex question pertaining to the future of EU-Turkey relations. While both sides are aware that Turkey's EU membership is unlikely as long as the current circumstances prevail, neither is willing to terminate the country's official accession process and negotiate a new institutional arrangement for several reasons. First, both Brussels and Ankara seem content with the "transactional equilibrium" that has come to define their interactions in parallel to the deadlock in the accession negotiations. Both are willing to exploit this transactionalism to their best advantage when dealing with issues of mutual interest. What they disagree about is

---

40 Saatçioğlu. The European Union's Refugee Crisis.
41 Council of the European Union. Enlargement and Stabilisation and Association Process, p. 13.

the preferred method for managing it: While the Turkish government prefers a compartmentalised approach to tackling these issues with the EU, Brussels opts for a rather integrated holistic stance for addressing topics such as refugees, energy and the Eastern Mediterranean. Furthermore, the EU's asymmetric dependence on Turkey on the migration front makes it extra cautious about alienating Ankara via altering the status quo by formally ending the accession track. This hesitation is compounded by normative concerns in some European circles about the implications of ending the EU's remaining democratic leverage over Turkey, which would result from formally halting the accession negotiations. A related problem is the near-irreversibility of a formal EU decision to cut the membership talks with Ankara since their subsequent restart would require unanimity in the European Council.

Second, notwithstanding their strategic importance, future relations with Turkey – coupled with the twin question of what type of alternative institutional framework could guide them – are not debated within the EU. Neither the new EU leadership that took over in December 2019 nor the current German EU presidency has Turkey in their agenda. Clearly, the EU's priorities lie elsewhere, considering the growing need to manage both health and economic implications of the ongoing COVID-19 crisis along with issues such as digitalisation, the EU's green deal and debates about the future of Europe. Hence, no common EU strategy has yet been advanced with respect to relations with Turkey. On 20 June 2019, the European Council agreed on a new strategic agenda for 2019-2024, which does not even mention Turkey. While key European leaders such as German Chancellor Angela Merkel and French President Emmanuel Macron have referred to Turkey as an effective strategic partner with which the EU needs to be more "realistic", no EU-level initiative has been undertaken to conceptualise an alternative relationship model with Turkey (instead of accession). It would also be unrealistic to expect such an endeavour in the foreseeable future since the EU-Turkey partnership has reached its most difficult phase owing to the growing tension in the Eastern Mediterranean and Libya; and bilateral clashes between Turkey and Greece, Turkey and the Republic of Cyprus, and Turkey and France over a host of issues.[42]

Yet, the EU-Turkey relationship remains highly dynamic and resilient, and may very well move past the current deadlocks and points of contention. When that moment comes, the sides would have much to benefit

---

42 Kenyon, Peter/ Beardsley, Eleanor. France, Turkey and the Charlie Hebdo Cartoons: What's Behind the Dispute?. In: NPR, 28.10.2020.

from working towards a rules-based relationship that would be maintained not as a replacement to Turkey's EU membership but as a complementary framework to the country's – albeit stalled - formal accession track.[43] The prospect of a modernised CU still represents the principal arrangement that approximates this target.[44]

---

43 Saatçioğlu et al. The Future of EU-Turkey Relations.
44 Ülgen, Sinan. Trade as Turkey's EU Anchor. Carnegie Europe, 13.12.2017, https://carnegieeurope.eu/2017/12/13/trade-as-turkey-s-eu-anchor-pub-75002 [16.08.2020].

Acknowledgements

 This edited volume is one of the final outputs of the Research and Innovation Action "The Future of EU-Turkey Relations: Mapping Dynamics and Testing Scenarios" (FEUTURE), which presents, synthesises and expands upon its findings. The FEUTURE project has received funding from the *European Union's Horizon 2020 Research and Innovation Programme* under Grant Agreement No. 692976.

This publication solely reflects the views of its authors, and the European Commission cannot be held responsible for any use which may be made of the information contained therein.

About FEUTURE:

In the period between April 1, 2016 and March 31, 2019, FEUTURE explored fully different options for further EU-Turkey cooperation in the next decade.

To do so, FEUTURE applied a comprehensive research approach by:

1. Mapping the dynamics of the EU-Turkey relationship in terms of their underlying historical narratives and thematic key drivers.
2. Testing and substantiating the most likely scenario(s) for the future and assessing the implications (challenges and opportunities) these may have on the EU and Turkey, as well as the neighbourhood and the global scene.
3. Drawing policy recommendations for the EU and Turkey on the basis of a strong evidence-based foundation in the future trajectory of EU-Turkey relations.

FEUTURE was coordinated by Prof. Wolfgang Wessels, Director of the Centre for Turkey and European Union Studies (CETEUS) at the University of Cologne, and Dr. Nathalie Tocci, Director of Istituto Affari Internazionali, Rome. It was directed by Dr. Funda Tekin, Senior Researcher at CETEUS, University of Cologne.

The FEUTURE consortium consisted of 15 renowned universities and think tanks from the EU, Turkey and the neighbourhood.

For more information on FEUTURE, visit www.feuture.eu.

The finalisation of the present edited volume beyond the project's lifetime was supported by Institut für Europäische Politik, Berlin.

Notes on Contributors

İbrahim Semih Akçomak is Associate Professor and Director of the Research Center for Science and Technology Policy at Middle East Technical University, Ankara.

Lorenzo Colantoni is a researcher at the Energy, Climate and Resources Programme of the Rome based Istituto Affari Internazionali (IAI). Colantoni is specialised on the geopolitics of the energy transition, energy resources in Eastern Mediterranean and Sub Saharan Africa.

Angeliki Dimitriadi is Senior Research Fellow and Head of the Migration Programme at the Hellenic Foundation for European & Foreign Policy (ELIAMEP). Her work focuses on irregular migration and asylum as well as the interplay between migratory movement and policies of deterrence and protection.

Senem Aydın-Düzgit is Professor of International Relations at the Faculty of Arts and Social Sciences of Sabancı University and Senior Scholar and Research and Academic Affairs Coordinator at the Istanbul Policy Center. She is the co-author of Turkey and the European Union (Palgrave, 2015) and Constructions of European Identity (Palgrave, 2012). Her articles have been published in the Journal of Common Market Studies, West European Politics, Cooperation and Conflict, and Third World Quarterly among others.

Atila Eralp is a Mercator-IPC Senior Fellow at the Istanbul Policy Center, Sabancı University and Emeritus Professor of International Relations at the Middle East Technical University (METU), Ankara. He was awarded the Jean Monnet Chair in 2002 and served as the Director of the METU Center for European Studies from 1997 until 2017.

Erkan Erdil is Professor at the Department of Economics at Middle East Technical University, Ankara.

Doruk Ergun is an analyst on peace, conflict and security issues in Eurasia. Since 2018, he has worked as an individual consultant supporting the UNDP in various capacities on conflict prevention and peacebuilding issues. His contributions to this volume were provided under his previous capacity as a research fellow at the Centre for Economics and Foreign Policy Studies (EDAM), where he worked on the foreign policy, security, nuclear energy and cyber security portfolios.

Hanna-Lisa Hauge, M.A. is External Research Fellow at the Centre for Turkey and European Union Studies (CETEUS) at the University of Cologne.

Eduard Soler i Lecha, is Senior research fellow at CIDOB (Barcelona Centre for International Affairs). He holds a PhD in International Relations. He is also a part-time lecturer at the Autonomous University of Barcelona, IBEI and Ramon Llull University.

Ayhan Kaya is Professor of Political Science at the Department of International Relations at Istanbul Bilgi University, ERC Advanced Research Grantee, Jean Monnet Chair of European Politics of Interculturalism and holder of a Jean Monnet Centre of Excellence.

Ebru Ece Özbey is a doctoral student at the International Max Planck Research School on the Social and Political Constitution of the Economy (IMPRS-SPCE). Her research focuses on populism, Euroscepticism, European integration, electoral competition, and political communication.

Bahar Rumelili is Professor and Jean Monnet Chair in the Department of International Relations at Koc University, Istanbul.

Beken Saatcioğlu is an Associate Professor and Jean Monnet Chair (EU-TURDI: EU-Turkey Relations in an Era of Differentiated Integration) at the Department of Political Science and International Relations at MEF University, Istanbul. She is the co-author (with Funda Tekin, Sinan Ekim and Nathalie Tocci) of the FEUTURE final synthesis paper "The Future of EU-Turkey Relations: A Dynamic Association Framework amidst Conflictual Cooperation". Her articles on EU-Turkey relations, EU political conditionality and Europeanization have been published in South European Society and Politics, Turkish Studies, Democratisation, and Journal of Balkan and Near Eastern Studies, among others.

Melike Sökmen is a researcher previously associated with Barcelona Centre for International Affairs (CIDOB) and The Economic Research Forum (ERF). Her areas of interest include diaspora studies, migration, Turkish foreign policy and EU-Mediterranean relations.

Funda Tekin is Director at Institut für Europäische Politik in Berlin and Senior Research Fellow at the Centre for Turkey and European Union

Studies at the University of Cologne. She was Project Director of the H2020 Project "The Future of EU-Turkey Relations: Mapping Dynamics and Testing Scenarios" (FEUTURE), the Jean Monnet Network "Enhancing VIsibility of the Academic DialogUe on EU-Turkey CooperaTion" (VIADUCT) as well as the research project "TRIANGLE – Blickwechsel in EU/German-Turkish Relations Beyond Conflicts. Towards a Unique Partnership for a Contemporary Turkey?" funded by the Stiftung Mercator.

Sinan Ülgen is a former Turkish diplomat and the Chairman of Center for Economics and Foreign Policy Studies – EDAM. He is also a visiting scholar at Carnegie Europe in Brussels.

Wolfgang Wessels is Director of the Centre for Turkey and European Union Studies (CETEUS) and holder of an 'Ad Personam' Jean Monnet Chair at the University of Cologne and Academic Leader of the Master Degree Programme "European and international Affairs" of the Turkish-German University in Turkey.

Series Editors

Funda Tekin is one of the Directors at Institut für Europäische Politik (IEP) in Berlin and Senior Research Fellow at the Centre for Turkey and European Union Studies (CETEUS) at the University of Cologne, Germany.

Ebru Turhan is Assistant Professor at the Department of Political Science and International Relations at the Turkish-German University in Istanbul, Turkey and Senior Research Fellow at the Institute für Europäische Politik (IEP) in Berlin, Germany.

Wolfgang Wessels is Jean Monnet Professor ad personam and Director of the Centre for Turkey and European Union Studies (CETEUS) at the University of Cologne, Germany.

The Centre for Turkey and European Union Studies (CETEUS) was founded in 2016 at the University of Cologne. With its focus on research and teaching in EU and Turkey related affairs and on the institutional evolution of the EU, it continues the work of the Jean Monnet Chair for European Politics of Prof. Dr. Wolfgang Wessels.

CETEUS' research activities target the European integration process as well as EU-Turkey relations and links to contemporary Turkey studies. They are embedded in an EU-wide network founded on close relations to leading universities in the EU, Turkey and the neighbourhood. Within its research projects the centre engages in promoting academic exchange with young researchers from Germany, the EU and Turkey aiming at integrating them into the European Research Area.

www.ceteus.uni-koeln.de

https://www.facebook.com/JeanMonnetKoeln

Register

accession 15–18, 22, 36, 38–42, 46, 48, 51, 53–55, 70, 71, 75, 77, 79, 80, 84–86, 88, 90–93, 98–100, 104, 112, 121, 123, 127, 130, 139, 143, 151, 152, 158, 169, 174–176, 179, 180, 189, 192, 195–197, 202–206

accession track 89, 205

association 13, 51

asylum 21, 25, 167–173, 175, 176, 180, 182–185, 193, 201

capital flows 144

civilisation 59–63, 65, 66, 68, 71, 73, 192, 193, 200

clash of civilisations 65

Cold War 19, 24, 36, 42, 43, 47, 49, 51, 64, 65, 75, 103, 105, 109

conflictual partnership 110

Council of Europe 42, 43, 60, 62, 64, 65, 87

counter terrorism 106, 110

Countering America's Adversaries Through Sanctions Act (CAATSA) 111

coup attempt 13, 18, 36, 41, 53, 60, 62, 67, 71, 74, 79, 84, 86, 87, 98, 100, 110, 143, 171, 174, 175, 183, 185, 196

COVID-19 17, 80, 90, 92, 97, 205

Customs Union 13, 27, 36, 39–41, 49–51, 81, 95, 101, 121, 124, 141, 142, 193, 204

Cyprus 36, 41, 53, 65, 75, 79, 81, 88, 90, 92, 95, 97, 99

Cyprus dispute 103, 105, 107, 108, 118, 119, 146, 151, 153, 162, 164–166, 196, 197

de-Europeanisation 15, 183, 196

decarbonisation 148, 150

declining power 67

democratic backsliding 137, 196

Democratic Union Party (PYD) 109, 111, 114–116

differentiated integration 16, 39, 72, 94, 121, 133

distant neighbour 38, 41, 51, 53, 200

drivers 19, 20, 22–26, 35, 37, 39, 40, 49, 50, 53, 58, 59, 62, 64, 66–68, 70, 72, 74–76, 103–105, 112, 115, 117–119, 121–123, 125, 126, 128, 134, 137, 139–144, 190, 192, 194, 195, 200
- economic 49, 119, 122, 123, 140
- ernergy 145–159, 161–166
- identity 59, 76, 182
- migration 172, 177, 178, 180, 184, 186
- political 49, 57, 58, 72, 77, 82, 83, 88, 96, 100, 101, 175, 185
- security 96, 169, 173, 185

Eastern Mediterranean 11, 18, 24, 75, 79, 81, 87, 95, 97, 99, 100, 104, 105, 109, 118, 147, 153, 156, 162–166, 186, 189, 194, 195, 197, 199, 200, 202, 203, 205

economic crises 129, 132

energy acquis 151, 195

Energy Community 151, 152

energy dependence 153

enlargement fatigue 15, 27, 91

EU conditionality 91

EU-Turkey Association Council 13, 81, 197

EU-Turkey Readmission Agreement 174–177, 180, 181, 185